Oxford & Cherwell Valley College
Oxford Campus
Oxpens Road, Oxford OX1 1SA
LIBRARY
Books must be returned by the last date shown below

Books may be renewed by telephone or e-mail
Tel: 01865 551961 e-mail: library@ocvc.ac.uk

The Tortoise and the Hares

The Tortoise and the Hares

Attlee • Bevin • Cripps • Dalton • Morrison

Giles Radice

POLITICO'S

First published in Great Britain 2008 by
Politico's Publishing, an imprint of
Methuen Publishing Ltd
8 Artillery Row
London
SW1P 1RZ

10 9 8 7 6 5 4 3 2 1

Copyright © Giles Radice 2008

Giles Radice has asserted his right under the Copyright, Designs and Patents Act 1988 to be identified as the author of this work.

A CIP catalogue record for this book is available from the British Library.

ISBN 978-1-84275-223-4

Set in Baskerville by SX Composing DTP, Rayleigh, Essex
Printed and bound in Great Britain by Cromwell Press, Trowbridge, Wiltshire

Contents

To Lisanne (once again), Adele, Sophie,
Adam, Misia, Heti and Nikki

Acknowledgements

In one of my last conversations with Roy Jenkins, Clement Attlee's first biographer, he suggested that the time had come for a reappraisal of his premiership. Inspired by his advice, I decided that the best way forward would be a study of the relationship between Attlee and his four main cabinet ministers, Ernest Bevin, Stafford Cripps, Hugh Dalton and Herbert Morrison.

I would like to thank Andrew Blick, Brian Lapping, Roger Liddle, Lord Morgan and Lisanne Radice for commenting on drafts of the book.

I was fortunate enough to be able to interview Lord Croham, Lord Donoughue, Lord and Lady Healey, Professor Peter Hennessy, Dame Jennifer Jenkins, Professor David Marquand, Lord Rodgers, Robert Taylor and Baroness Williams.

I am grateful to Mark Barrington-Ward for allowing me to quote from the diaries of his father, R. M. Barrington-Ward.

Once again, thanks to Andrew Blick for his research in the National Archives and for his assistance in checking references.

The House of Lords library was as helpful as ever.

I would like to thank Alan Gordon Walker and Jonathan Wadman for their helpful editorial advice, Linda Silverman for her assistance with the photographs, and Sue Martin for her index.

I owe a debt of gratitude to Nikki Applewhite for making sense of my manuscript and for her enthusiasm for the project.

Finally, I take full responsibility for the opinions expressed in this book.

Introduction

'The tortoise' is the Labour Prime Minister from 1945 to 1951, Clement Attlee; 'the hares' are his leading Cabinet ministers, Ernest Bevin, Stafford Cripps, Hugh Dalton and Herbert Morrison. Two younger men, Aneurin Bevan and Hugh Gaitskell, prominent at the end of Labour's period in power and when the party went into opposition in 1951, also come into the story.

Attlee's standing as a Labour Prime Minister is as high today as it has ever been. Denis Healey, a former Labour Chancellor and deputy party leader, in his address at a memorial service in 2005 at Westminster Abbey for James Callaghan (a later Labour premier), said that Attlee was the benchmark. The experts agree with him. For Peter Hennessy, the notable contemporary historian, Attlee is, with Margaret Thatcher, in the 'very top flight',[1] while Ben Pimlott, the prince of political biographers, wrote: 'Clement Attlee – top deity in the modern Labour Party's pantheon.'[2]

Attlee's reputation rests mainly on the achievements of his governments. He presided over the administrations which created the welfare state and the National Health Service, nationalised the major utilities, gave independence to India, Pakistan and Ceylon (now Sri Lanka) and helped set up NATO and implement the Marshall plan. In a 2005 survey the members of the Political Studies Association voted Attlee's 1945 election victory the most decisive since the war because, even more than Thatcher's in 1979, it changed the political and social landscape.[3]

Attlee was renowned for his ability to manage his more charismatic colleagues. Harold Wilson, Labour Prime Minister in the 1960s and 1970s, said that Attlee was in complete charge of his Cabinet. He was also reputed to be a 'good butcher', saying to a departing minister, in one of his typical cricketing metaphors: 'Well, you've had a good innings; time to put your bat up in the pavilion.'[4] Above all, he was a wily politician who allowed the big beasts of his Cabinet to flourish but was adept at defending his own position when it came under attack.

Attlee was a most improbable premier. Hennessy, one of his greatest admirers, wrote that he had 'all the presence of a gerbil'.[5] Winston Churchill, in whose wartime coalition government Attlee served as deputy Prime Minister, is said to have described him as 'a modest man who has much to be modest about' and 'a sheep in sheep's clothing'. He was a pedestrian speaker, the monotony of his address mitigated only by its brevity. Attlee's terseness was legendary. In his autobiography, Healey recounted the quip of one of his colleagues at Labour Party headquarters: 'A conversation with Attlee was like throwing biscuits to a dog – all you could get out of him was yup, yup, yup.'[6] After spending a day with Attlee in the summer of 1965, I can confirm the difficulty of engaging the former Prime Minister in conversation. Only cricket engaged his full attention, though disdain for the newspapers also aroused his interest.

He became leader almost by accident, following the 1931 electoral disaster when all but three of Labour's ministers lost their seats. From his election in 1935 until the end of 1947, his leadership had a provisional flavour about it. Both in 1945 (see Prologue) and in 1947 (see Chapter 9) there were attempted coups launched against him. Even Bevin, the only one of his pre-eminent colleagues who always gave him loyal support, was sometimes exasperated by Attlee's failure to give a lead, particularly on economic issues (on which Wilson described him as 'tone deaf').[7] Indian independence and the Korean War were notable exceptions. A reassessment of his leadership, which this book aims to provide, must take account of the economic crises (especially those of 1947 and 1949) which rocked his administration, of the failure to avert Bevan's resignation in 1951, of Labour's subsequent election defeat and of Attlee's unhappy period in opposition from 1951 to 1955 as leader of a divided, rudderless and twice defeated party.

This book argues that, though Attlee was a first-rate chairman of Cabinet and manager of the government, he was largely dependent on the ideas, inspiration and drive of his more dynamic Cabinet ministers. When the energy and health of Bevin and Cripps and, later, of Morrison and Dalton too gave out, Attlee's government faltered. Politicians more gifted and charismatic than Attlee agreed to serve under him. He needed his colleagues just as much as they needed him – a judgement with which Attlee, who had little vanity in his make-up, would have agreed. An account of the Labour administration has to highlight not only the relationships between the Prime Minister and his brilliant colleagues but also theirs with one another.

Labour's second generation of leaders were a varied bunch, including the general secretary of the biggest trade union, London's local government supremo, a gifted Anglican lawyer and a Fabian academic. They were also exceptionally able. With justice if with typical immodesty, Bevin described himself as 'a turn-up in a million'. Born in rural poverty, he became Britain's most powerful trade unionist, an outstanding member of Churchill's War Cabinet and Attlee's Foreign Secretary, arguably the most creative holder of that office in the twentieth century. Bevin's rival, Morrison, was a brilliant political organiser who rose from being a Lambeth errand boy to become leader of London County Council, Churchill's Home Secretary in the wartime coalition and the man who steered Labour's legislation through parliament. Popular with the Tories, who saw him, with his quiff and sharp repartee, as a cockney 'cheeky chappie', Morrison's enemies on his own side included not just Bevin but also many on the left.

The third 'star' of Attlee's Cabinet was Cripps, about whom Churchill is said to have remarked: 'There but for the grace of God goes God.' A committed Christian, famously ascetic (though he smoked heavily) and with a razor-sharp lawyer's mind (he was the youngest king's counsel in the country), Cripps came from a rich and privileged background. After a turbulent period in the 1930s as the leader of the radical left, he was appointed during the Second World War Churchill's ambassador to Stalin and, for a time, a member of the War Cabinet. In 1947, Attlee made him Chancellor of the Exchequer and, until his health gave way in 1950, Cripps was, in tandem with Bevin, the government's dominant figure, setting the tone and style of the administration.

The fourth larger-than-life figure in Attlee's Cabinet was his first Chancellor of the Exchequer, Dalton. Tall with a large bald head and protuberant eyes, Dalton uttered indiscretions about his colleagues in a booming voice, which Attlee once described as a 'confidential whisper which echoed around the lobby'. Son of a canon of Windsor and educated at Eton and King's College, Cambridge, he expected to be made Foreign Secretary in 1945, but, at the last moment, Attlee switched him to the Treasury. For two heady years, Dalton's self-confidence and exuberance carried nearly all before him, until, in the crisis year of 1947, he was forced to resign, following a silly mistake (see page 166).

The last two years of Attlee's government were overshadowed by a struggle for dominance between two younger men, Bevan and Gaitskell, which led to Bevan's resignation. In opposition, this struggle plunged the party into fratricidal conflict which Attlee was unable to control. The two men had contrasting backgrounds and abilities. A Welsh mining MP, Bevan had made his parliamentary reputation as a silver-tongued rebel. Given his chance by Attlee, he revealed formidable creative powers, launching the National Health Service in 1948. Gaitskell was an economist who had been educated at Winchester and New College, Oxford and worked for Dalton during the war. His administrative ability was recognised by Attlee, who promoted him rapidly through the ministerial ranks. When Cripps resigned, Attlee appointed Gaitskell Chancellor of the Exchequer at the relatively youthful age of forty-four. The stage was set for a lengthy and costly battle between two heirs apparent.

The Tortoise and the Hares describes the protagonists' early lives in Victorian and Edwardian England and the impact on them of the First World War. It goes on to examine the inter-war period and the significance of the two minority Labour governments, especially the collapse of the second MacDonald administration, in the political development of the Labour's 'big five'. Without the 1931 *débâcle*, Attlee would not have become leader. The influence of the wartime coalition government on Attlee and his colleagues was just as great. In many ways, it helped set the scene for Labour's 1945 victory.

The second half of the book analyses the premiership of Clement Attlee and the relationships between Labour's 'big five'. It gives an account not only of the administration's record but also of how Attlee and his ministers responded to the many crises they had to face. It is partly a history of great achievements which helped shape post-war Britain. But it is also a story of how the Labour Party lost momentum, went down to defeat in 1951 and, instead of regrouping in opposition, wasted much of the 1950s in factional strife.

Prologue: A failed coup

On 26 July 1945, one of the strangest episodes in Labour's history occurred. Its leader, Clement Attlee, had to fight off an attempt to remove him at the very moment of, arguably, the party's greatest political triumph. The general election had taken place on 5 July but the announcement of the results was held back until the twenty-sixth, to allow for the collection of servicemen's votes from around the world and for separate ballots in Lancashire and Scottish towns affected by early July holidays. By lunchtime on Thursday 26 July it became clear that power was changing hands. The *Evening Standard* prepared for its front page a big picture of Attlee under the banner headline 'The New PM'. Labour had won the general election.

Most of the political class had been certain that the voters would reward Winston Churchill for leading the country to victory by giving the Tories a comfortable majority. On 25 July, he flew back from the Potsdam conference of the three victorious powers (the United States, the Soviet Union and the United Kingdom) to hear the election results. Both Truman and Stalin were convinced that he would soon be back, still as British Prime Minister. Arriving in London, he had a meeting at Buckingham Palace, during which he told the King that he expected a Conservative majority of between thirty and eighty.

Attlee, until two months previously deputy Prime Minister in the wartime coalition, had, at Churchill's invitation, accompanied the British negotiating team to Potsdam. He told the Soviet foreign minister, Vyacheslav Molotov, that the election would be close run. In a letter to Hugh Dalton on 13 July, Attlee wrote that he did not think that Labour would get an overall majority.[1] On the morning after his return from Potsdam, the Attlee family breakfasted together at their home in Stanmore (a north London suburb) before driving to Stepney for Attlee's count; they had no inkling that he was about to become Prime Minister.

Churchill had woken before dawn with the strong presentiment that he was going to be defeated. While in his bath, he was told that, according to the first election returns announced at ten o'clock, ten Conservative seats had already fallen to Labour. At twenty-five minutes past ten came the news that Harold Macmillan, a leading Tory minister and future premier, was out at Stockton-on-Tees. Thirty-two members of Churchill's caretaker administration subsequently lost their seats. Labour was winning not only big city seats but also suburban ones. Even voters in the countryside were turning to Labour. A political earthquake had taken place.

That afternoon, as the Labour Party stood on the brink of power, a dramatic meeting took place in Transport House, the building the Transport and General Workers' Union shared with Labour. The party's three most prominent leaders, Attlee, Ernest Bevin and Herbert Morrison (all of whom had conveniently won London seats), gathered, with the party's national secretary, Morgan Phillips, in Bevin's room to discuss the implications of Labour's victory.

The three leaders had played leading roles in Churchill's wartime coalition. Apart from Churchill, Bevin, his minister of labour, who had spent much of his life as a trade union leader, was acknowledged by most of his colleagues as the outstanding member of the War Cabinet. Morrison, who had been the first Labour leader of London County Council, was Churchill's Home Secretary, responsible for maintaining morale during the Blitz. He was also a lively campaigner for post-war reconstruction. By comparison with Bevin and Morrison, Attlee, despite holding the post of deputy Prime Minister, was less prominent. Though a highly competent committee chairman and excellent at running the Cabinet during Churchill's frequent absences abroad, Attlee had a retiring shy personality. R. M. Barrington-Ward, then editor of the *Times*, wrote of Attlee in his diary entry for 8 March 1942: 'He is worthy but limited – incredible that he should be where he is.'

Barrington-Ward's opinion of Attlee was shared by some in the Labour Party. The outgoing chairman, the fiery Ellen Wilkinson, and her successor, Professor Harold Laski of the London School of Economics, had both actively canvassed for a leadership change at the Blackpool party conference in May 1945. Immediately after the conference, Laski wrote to Attlee to tell him of the widespread feeling in the party 'that the continuance of your leadership . . . is a great handicap to our hopes of victory in the coming election'. Laski called upon him 'regretfully to draw the inference that your resignation of the leadership would now be a great service to the party'. Attlee's celebrated put-down was as follows: 'Dear Laski, Thank you for your letter, contents of which have been noted.'[2]

Morrison, who had unsuccessfully stood against Attlee in the 1935 leadership election, still thought that he would make the better leader. His ambitions had been rekindled by the central role he had played as chairman of the campaign committee in Labour's triumphant election campaign. In a letter which he wrote to Attlee at his home address on 24 July and which was awaiting the leader's return from Potsdam, Morrison said that he had been approached by a number of colleagues asking him to 'accept nomination for the leadership of the parliamentary party'; he argued that, whatever the result of the election, the new parliament was bound to include many new members, who should have 'the opportunity of deciding as to what type of leadership they want'. Morrison concluded by giving notice that, if elected to the new parliament, he intended to stand.[3]

Attlee had two extremely powerful cards in his hand. The first was a message which he had just received from Churchill and which he read out to his colleagues. Churchill conceded defeat and congratulated Attlee on his victory, adding that he was going to the palace at 7 p.m. to tender his resignation and would advise the King to send for Attlee to ask him to form a government.

Morrison interrupted to say that Attlee had no right to accept the King's invitation to form a government until the new parliamentary party had elected its leader. He also expressed reluctance to serve under Attlee. Morrison based his case for a fresh leadership election on a dubious reading of rules drawn up by the Labour Party after the 1931 MacDonald disaster (see page 82). These stated that there should be a party meeting to decide whether or not to form a government, but they nowhere mentioned the need for a fresh leadership election.

Attlee and Bevin firmly refuted Morrison's arguments on the grounds that it was constitutionally and politically out of the question for the leader of a party who had just won a general election to have then to submit to a party leadership election. Attlee was clear: 'If you're invited by the King to form a government you don't say you can't reply for forty-eight hours. You accept the commission and you either bring it off or you don't and if you don't you go back and say you can't and advise the King to send for someone else.'[4] The political point was that the voters had supported the Labour Party in the belief that, if Labour won, Attlee would be Prime Minister. To change leaders now would give the impression of an indecisive and divided party, incapable of running the country.

During the meeting, Morrison was called away to answer a telephone call from Stafford Cripps, who had also been in Churchill's War Cabinet and Lord Privy Seal. Cripps, who had been expelled from the party in the 1930s and had only recently returned to it, was then not so powerful a figure as he became later. Morrison claimed that Cripps agreed with him that there should be a new leadership election. Both expected Churchill to wait for the meeting of the new parliament before resigning, thus allowing time for a Labour leadership election.[5]

However, while Morrison was out of the room, a crucial conversation took place which brought Attlee's second card into play. First, Bevin asked Morgan Phillips: 'If I stood against Clem, should I win?'

Phillips replied: 'On a split vote, I think you would.'

Then Bevin, as if reassured as to the importance of his own position, turned to Attlee and said: 'Clem, you go to the palace straightaway.'[6]

There could hardly have been a greater contrast than between Attlee and Bevin: Attlee was laconic, dry and undemonstrative; Bevin was temperamental, passionate and exceptionally egocentric. If Attlee was a sober, pipe-smoking, cricket-loving member of the Edwardian professional classes (albeit one much affected by his experiences as a voluntary worker in the poverty-stricken East End of London), Bevin was the embodiment of the working man, a force of nature, heavyweight in personality as well as physique. However, during the war, Bevin had learnt to trust 'little Clem', as he called him, seeing him as Labour's Campbell-Bannerman, the unassuming Prime Minister who had managed to keep the highly talented reforming Liberal administration together at the beginning of the twentieth century.

Bevin had no leadership ambitions. He had spent most of his life as a trade union leader, and found the Parliamentary Labour Party and indeed Parliament itself difficult to handle. He preferred to serve under a self-effacing leader whom he could trust and who would give him his head, rather than under a strong charismatic leader in the Churchill mould. He would not serve under Morrison, whom he loathed. Morrison had more than proved himself in the wartime coalition. But Bevin thought him devious and distrusted his leadership ambitions. A few weeks later, Bevin sent for Francis Williams, Attlee's newly appointed adviser on public relations, and growled: 'Let me know if he [Morrison] gets up to any of his tricks. I wouldn't trust the little bugger any further than I could throw him.'[7]

The meeting at Transport House broke up inconclusively. Attlee took a late tea with his family at the Great Western Hotel, Paddington, in a room reserved for him by the owner, his friend Lord Portal, and was then driven to Buckingham Palace by his wife in their modest pre-war Hillman to keep his 7.30 p.m. appointment with the King. Ignoring Morrison's manoeuvres, Attlee immediately accepted the King's commission to form a government.

From the palace, Attlee and his wife went to a victory rally at Central Hall Westminster. Morrison had arrived earlier and, beaming with delight, had joined in the singing of 'John Brown's Body' and 'Three Blind Mice'. Behind the scenes, he and his friends were urging Labour MPs to support a fresh vote on the leadership. He said to John Parker, MP for Dagenham, as they entered the gentlemen's lavatory together: 'We cannot have this man as our leader.'[8] But Parker, like many others, felt it was too late to change.

The slight figure of Attlee appeared on the platform to ringing cheers. The cheers became deafening when Attlee announced that he had been to the palace and had accepted the King's invitation to form a government. Morrison's coup had failed.

Even so, Morrison persisted in his campaign. On the afternoon of 27 July, Attlee called a meeting of the former administrative committee of the PLP, which consisted of the party officers and the elected members of the Parliamentary Executive Committee. After Attlee had made an opening statement in which he stressed the need to establish a skeleton government while he was away at the Potsdam conference, Morrison intervened to raise again the leadership issue. He repeated the argument he had made at the

Transport House meeting the previous day: according to the 1933 Labour Party rules, there had to be a fresh leadership election before the party could accept the King's commission to form a government. However, while agreeing that the rules required that the party should be consulted before the formation of a government, this meeting concluded that they said nothing about the election of a new leader. The committee also took the view that, in calling the meeting, Attlee was in fact consulting them. They authorised him to go ahead and form a government. The meeting was over in thirty minutes, with Morrison completely isolated.

That morning Morrison had been to see Attlee and the chief whip, William Whiteley, to discuss his position in the Labour Cabinet. He asked for the Foreign Office. Morrison knew that Bevin was interested in taking over the Treasury, and thought he was entitled to be considered for the other big job. Attlee resisted Morrison's claim but offered him leadership on the home front as Lord President of the Council and leader of the House of Commons. Morrison at first refused, suspecting that he was being bought off with a grand-sounding but less important position. However, the persuasive powers of the chief whip, as well as Attlee's additional offer of the *de facto* recognition of Morrison as number two in the government, made him change his mind.

The appointment of Morrison as overlord on the home front had a knock-on effect on other Cabinet positions. Attlee had been undecided about whom to appoint to the Foreign Office. One candidate was Bevin, another was the old Etonian socialist Hugh Dalton, who had been president of the Board of Trade in the wartime coalition and was recognised as the party's foreign affairs specialist. At the Transport House meeting on 26 July, Bevin had taken Attlee aside and said that he would like to be Chancellor. When Attlee asked whom he would make Foreign Secretary, Bevin said: 'Hugh Dalton.' Attlee did not reply.

At the palace meeting on the evening of 26 July, the King had asked Attlee whom he was going to appoint to the Foreign Office. Attlee replied that he had been thinking of Dalton. The King urged him to consider his decision carefully and suggested that Bevin would be a better choice. However, when Attlee saw Dalton, who had come down from the north on the night train, shortly before lunch on 27 July, he told him that he would almost certainly be Foreign Secretary and advised him to pack his bag for Potsdam, saying that he would confirm the appointment later in the afternoon. Dalton, who had voted for Morrison in 1935, also made clear to Attlee that, as leader of the winning party, he had been right to accept the King's commission to form a government. He added that the fresh leadership election for which Morrison argued would have been appropriate if the party had been defeated.

When Dalton saw Attlee at 4 p.m., Attlee said: 'I think it had better be the Exchequer.' During the afternoon, Attlee had changed his mind and decided that Bevin would be the better choice at the Foreign Office and that Dalton, the trained economist, should become Chancellor. Significantly, Attlee mentioned Morrison's home front appointment and the need to keep Morrison and Bevin apart. 'If they were both on the home front they would quarrel all the time.'[9] Certainly, Bevin was furious that Morrison should be pressing for a fresh leadership election, while simultaneously asking Attlee to make him Foreign Secretary. According to Dalton, Bevin rang up Morrison and told him: 'If you go on mucking about like this, you won't be in the bloody government at all.'[10]

There was a second reason why Attlee saw Bevin as the better choice for Foreign Secretary. He wrote later: 'I thought foreign affairs were going to be pretty difficult and a heavy tank was what was going to be required rather than a sniper.'[11] An additional factor could also have been that, having resisted Morrison's claims to the Foreign Office, putting the other major Cabinet heavyweight in the post effectively blocked off any further designs Morrison may have had on the position.

On the next day, 28 July, Attlee announced his first appointments, including Bevin as Foreign Secretary, Dalton as Chancellor of the Exchequer, Morrison as Lord President of the Council, and Stafford Cripps as president of the Board of Trade. When the first group of ministers arrived at the palace to kiss hands and receive the seals of office, Bevin did not hide his disappointment. Pointing to Dalton, he said: 'I wanted the job he's got.'[12] Dalton had told Attlee the previous day that he was much less confident that he could do a good job at the Treasury than at the Foreign Office. Attlee replied: 'Of course you will and we will all help you.' It remained to be seen whether the last-minute switch of jobs between Bevin and Dalton, in part influenced by the Morrison problem, would prove a wise decision in the long term.

From the palace, the new Labour Cabinet ministers drove to Beaver Hall in the City, where a jubilant meeting of nearly 400 Labour MPs had gathered to greet them. The chief whip immediately called on Bevin, who, in an impromptu speech, moved a vote of confidence in the new Prime Minister. It was seconded by the new Lord Privy Seal, Arthur Greenwood, and supported by George Isaacs, chairman of the TUC. As Attlee rose to reply, the meeting gave him a standing ovation which lasted two minutes. This was the spontaneous answer to the efforts of Morrison and his allies to oust Attlee – although even at Beaver Hall, Ellen Wilkinson approached Edith Summerskill, MP for Fulham West, in the ladies' lavatory to try to gain her support for Morrison. Attlee spoke characteristically briefly, promising that he would proceed immediately to implement Labour's election manifesto. He then left with the new Foreign Secretary to fly to Potsdam, handing the meeting over to Morrison. Attlee's action established Morrison publicly as deputy leader but also underlined that he, and not Morrison, was in command.

Attlee had shown skill and determination in facing down Morrison, while at the same time putting together an impressive Cabinet. Morrison had seriously miscalculated both the timing of his attempted coup and the extent of his support. However, there were – and would continue to be – critics in the party who were unhappy with Attlee's understated style of leadership. By the same token, Attlee would need the energy and drive of heavyweights in Cabinet, especially Bevin, if his government was to be a success. The history of Labour's years in power was in part to be shaped by the relationship between Attlee and his senior ministers, between the tortoise and the hares.

1

The tortoise: Clement Attlee

The story begins in the reign of Queen Victoria. The leaders of the 1945 Labour government were all children of this era. Clement Attlee and Ernest Bevin were born at the beginning of the 1880s, while Herbert Morrison, Hugh Dalton and Stafford Cripps were born at the end of that decade.

Inevitably those growing up in the last quarter of Victoria's reign were brought up to believe that Britain's position as the world's greatest power was normal. In 1860, the British already had the world's largest empire, with India the 'jewel in the crown'. However, it was the 'scramble for Africa' of the big European powers which in the twenty years after 1880 turned Britain into the first global superpower. By the end of the nineteenth century, the British Empire covered a quarter of the world's surface and controlled about the same proportion of its population.[1] Maps alone did not convey the extent of British influence. London was the world banker. World trade was mostly financed by British money and carried in British ships, while the Queen's navy policed international shipping lanes. In 1897, the year of Queen Victoria's diamond jubilee, which the fourteen-year-old Clement Attlee celebrated by putting out a flag on the porch of his father's Putney home, the British Empire was the most extensive in world history, though there were already those who, like the bard of empire, Rudyard Kipling, in his poem 'Recessional', warned of the dangers of imperial hubris.

Within Victorian Britain, the disparities of wealth, class and social habit were glaring. One obvious difference was in dress. When Attlee's father, a successful solicitor, left Putney to go to his office in the City, he wore a top hat and a frock coat. Industrial labourers went to work in fustian or corduroy cloth, hobnail boots and flat caps.

The middle classes increasingly lived in quiet and leafy suburbs outside the big city centres and sent their children to the fee-paying 'public schools'.

Attlee went to Haileybury, Dalton to Eton and Cripps to Winchester, before all going on to university. The urban working classes were herded together in sordid tenement blocks and mean terraced houses inside the city. Poverty was widespread. Unemployment was endemic, while those in employment were often in insecure jobs. In his survey of York, the social investigator Seebohm Rowntree found that 43 per cent of wage earners received an income below the level of minimum needs. Educational opportunities open to working-class children were severely limited. The Education Act of 1870 had introduced state primary education but it did not become free until 1891 and then only to the age of twelve. Ernest Bevin left his Devonshire school at eleven, while Herbert Morrison was fortunate to stay on at St Andrew's Church of England School, Brixton until his fourteenth birthday.

The enfranchisement of working-class men by the Reform Acts of 1867 and 1884 had led to fierce competition between the Conservative and Liberal parties for the working-class vote. In the words of the Gilbert and Sullivan opera *Iolanthe*, first performed in 1882:

> Every boy and every gal
> That's born into the world alive
> Is either a little Liberal
> Or else a little Conservative.

Attlee's father was a Gladstonian Liberal, though his mother was a Conservative. Dalton and Cripps had strong Tory backgrounds, while Morrison's father was a policeman who supported the Conservative Party.

Politics was still the preserve of the landed and middle classes. But there were a few signs of the changes that were to come. A Scottish miner, James Keir Hardie, having been rejected by the Liberals, stood as an independent Labour MP and sat in the 1892 parliament. In 1893 he helped set up the Independent Labour Party. Other socialist groupings were forming at the same time, including the gradualist Fabian Society and the Marxist Social Democratic Federation (SDF). The new unskilled unions which emerged in the late 1880s and early 1890s were more sympathetic than the craft unions to the idea of an independent workers' party. These hesitant steps represented the beginnings of a new politics.

Clement Attlee was born in Putney on 3 January 1883, the seventh child and fourth son in a family of eight. He later described the Attlees as 'a typical family of the professional class brought up in the atmosphere of Victorian England'.[2] His father, Henry, the son of a Surrey miller, had worked his way up an old-established firm of City solicitors to become senior partner and, in 1906, president of the Law Society. His mother, Ellen Bravery Watson, came from a family of doctors. Her father, however, lived off his private income and acted as secretary of the Art Union of London, which issued high-class reproductions of masterpieces. Ellen inherited her father's love of literature and the arts. She and Henry were both committed members of the Church of England and Sunday was strictly observed in the Attlee household, with, as Clement noted later, 'much church-going, special reading and no games'.[3] Discussion of controversial issues, such as Irish home rule, which Henry strongly supported, was usually avoided, because Ellen was the kind of Tory who, whenever politics was mentioned, tactfully changed the subject.

The Attlees lived in a large house with a big garden in a quiet Putney side street. Putney was then an outer suburb, surrounded by market gardens. Standing in the garden, the Attlee children could hear the horses' hoofs beat on the main road to Wandsworth and Putney High Street. Their home provided a happy and secure world, with its set routines, familiar games and occasional exciting excursions to their grandfather's house in Wandsworth or to Kew for strawberry teas. Like many middle-class families, the Attlees usually spent August at a seaside resort; Seaton in south Devon was their favourite. In 1897, Henry Attlee bought a seventeenth-century manor house with 200 acres in Essex. Here, in the holidays, the Attlee children played tennis, cricket and their favourite game of bicycle polo, for which they used sticks and tennis balls.

Unlike the rest of the boys, Clement did not go to school until he was nine. He was painfully shy and small for his age, inheriting clothes from his younger brother, Lawrence. He was taught at home mostly by his mother. Encouraged by Ellen, he learnt some of her favourite poetry by heart, including a number of Wordsworth's shorter poems and parts of Tennyson's *Idylls of the King*. (As he grew up, he wrote verses of his own.) From his sister's French governess he learnt to recite La Fontaine's *Fables* with a good accent and he also picked up some Italian from his mother. For his age, he was a voracious reader and ranged widely in his father's well-stocked library, devouring poetry, history, novels and the bound volumes of *Punch*. While his brothers were climbing trees, he preferred to read on the lawn or indoors on a sofa.[4] When he went away to join his brother Tom at preparatory school, he had a fair grounding in literature and foreign languages but he was still an undersized and somewhat introverted boy.

The Attlees' preparatory school, Northaw Place, near Potters Bar, was a small boarding school of between thirty and forty pupils, notable not for its academic prowess but for its devotion to cricket. Though both the head-master, F. J. Hall, and his deputy, F. Poland, were clerics, according to Clement Attlee, 'the real religion of Hall and Poland was cricket'.[5] Throughout his life, Attlee was an avid follower of the game but not much of a performer. He was happy enough at Northaw Place but learnt very little, apart from an almost encyclopaedic knowledge of the kings of Israel and Judah from the Old Testament, leaving the school with hardly more than a smattering of historical and geographical facts, and not much of a grasp of Latin and Greek. However, at the age of thirteen he managed to pass the entrance examination into Haileybury College.

Haileybury had originally been founded as a school for candidates for the East India Company but was reopened as a public school in 1862, though it still retained some of its imperial connections. When Attlee went there in 1896, it was suffering from a shortage of pupils, probably because of the inadequacy of its teaching. He commented that 'many members of the staff were elderly and had never learnt to teach'.[6] Attlee's career at Haileybury was undistinguished. Though he played games with enthusiasm, his small stature and lack of proficiency meant that he could never aspire to be an athletic star. He was above average in English subjects, especially history, but his weakness at classics and ignorance of science held him back. In his last year, he spoke occasionally at the literary and debating society but because of his shyness found the experience painful. Only in the school cadet corps did he excel. He went to the Public School Cadet Corps Camp at Aldershot, where he proved an outstanding cadet. Though Attlee retained a life-long affection for Haileybury, he got little out of it and left, in his own words, 'mentally very young'.[7]

He went up to University College, Oxford in October 1901. He quickly came to love Oxford, which was not then the industrial town it later became. It was, in William Morris's words, 'a long winding street and the sound of many bells',[8] a place of delight for a young undergraduate intent on enjoying himself. University College was then going through a golden age. In Attlee's first year, it had two presidents of the Oxford Union and a number of distinguished scholars. Attlee found that, even without being good at games (except billiards), a brilliant intellectual or a debating star at the Union, he was able to make friends not only among old Haileyburians but also with other members of his college.

He read widely around his chosen subject, history, particularly his special subject, the Italian Renaissance, but only worked hard for the 'schools' examinations in his last two terms. He failed to get a first but achieved a good second. He attended debates at the Oxford Union but was too shy to take part. In so far as he was political, he rejected his father's high-minded Liberalism, favouring the imperialism of Joseph Chamberlain.

One of his biographers has called Attlee's time at Oxford 'a social interlude rather than an intellectual adventure'.[9] Certainly his university career was unspectacular. One of his tutors wrote about him: 'He is level headed, industrious, dependable with no brilliance of style or literary gifts but with excellent sound judgement.'[10] These were the tortoise-like qualities which he was to deploy so effectively when he became Prime Minister.

Attlee came down from Oxford with little idea what he wanted to do. He was not interested in pursuing a career but vaguely sought 'some way of earning my living which would enable me to follow the kind of literary and historical subjects that interested me'.[11] He took the line of least resistance for a lawyer's son and, in the autumn of 1904, entered Sir Philip Gregory's Lincoln's Inn chambers as a pupil. Attlee found Gregory a hard taskmaster but he learnt from him how to write and draft documents accurately and speedily, a skill which was to be of use to him in government. He passed the Bar exams the following summer and then spent a few months in his father's firm, Druce and Attlee, to gain experience of a solicitor's office. He found the work boring and the working methods old fashioned; he spent much of the time at a small table in his father's room doodling – 'mostly dragons, breathing fire and smoke',[12] – a habit which he continued when chairing the Cabinet.

In March 1906, after a more congenial spell as a pupil of a practising barrister, Theobald Mathew, he was called to the Bar and joined the chambers of H. F. Dickens, the son of Charles Dickens. There was little work for him to do. Attlee appeared in court on only four occasions, once at Maidstone and three times in London. As he admitted later, 'my interest in the law was, to put it mildly, very tepid'.[13] He was more or less a gentleman of leisure, living comfortably at home and continuing to receive the £200 annual allowance which his father had given him when he was at Oxford. It was a pleasant enough existence but one with little purpose.

However, his life was about to take a new direction. In October 1905, while he was still a pupil in his father's firm, he had paid a visit with his brother Lawrence to Haileybury House, a boys' club supported by Haileybury School and run by old Haileyburians in Stepney, in the heart of London's East End. The club provided military recreations and discipline for East End boys aged between fourteen and eighteen. Overcome by his usual shyness, he found it difficult to communicate with the lively young boys, but he was impressed by the spirit of the club and especially by its manager, Cecil Nussey, an old Haileyburian solicitor. 'Good show, that,' Clement remarked, in the clipped speech of an Edwardian gentlemen. 'Might look in from time to time.'[14]

Attlee began to come to the club at least every week, and, within a few months, he took a volunteer commission as second lieutenant, which committed him to help in the running of the club. In the summer of 1906, he attended his first camp at Rottingdean, on the Sussex coast, and enjoyed it immensely. In the autumn of 1907, Nussey resigned as manager and asked Attlee to take over. At first Attlee was hesitant, wondering whether he had the ability to run the club, but he was persuaded that, unless he became manager at least on a temporary basis, the club would be in serious difficulties. Taking the job, which carried a small honorarium of £50 a year, meant leaving Putney and moving into the club itself.

Living in Stepney brought Attlee face to face with the precarious existence of working-class families. He described Stepney as the 'home of under-employment and sweated labour'.[15] The boys' club members mostly followed 'blind alley' occupations. When they reached eighteen, they were usually thrown out of work, without any training on which to fall back. Many of the men were casual dockers or building labourers, who were often out of work. In times of unemployment or sickness, families, without state benefits to draw on, fell into debt and were often ejected from their homes by slum landlords. Stepney was desperately overcrowded, with a population of 300,000 herded into less than 1,700 acres. Yet despite the slums and the poverty, Attlee grew to admire the friendliness, generosity and sheer spirit of the East Enders. As he was beginning to realise, it was the social system and not the people which was largely responsible for the appalling conditions in which they lived.

Attlee's family had a tradition of voluntary social work. His mother was a district visitor for the church. His aunt had left home in order to manage a club for factory girls in Wandsworth. His elder brother helped at boys' clubs, while a sister became a missionary. But the longer he worked and lived in the East End, the less he was convinced that individual good works could provide an adequate answer to the intractable problems of the area. The whole social and economic fabric needed to be changed.

Throughout 1906 and 1907, Clement had long political discussions with his architect brother, Tom, who was himself working at the Christian socialist Maurice Hostel in Hoxton, also in the East End. Although, unlike Tom, he was no longer a practising Christian, he was a firm believer in fairness and social justice. He was also attracted by the ideas of William Morris, especially his attack on the materialism and squalor of the Industrial Revolution and his espousal of fellowship and beauty. Some time during the latter part of 1907 Attlee began to call himself a socialist, a big step for someone of his temperament and background. In many ways, he was and remained throughout his life a conventional member of the professional classes. As his earliest biographer put it, 'it was a desire, not to destroy his social background, but to extend to all the benefits that he himself had enjoyed which impelled him'.[16]

The first decade of the twentieth century was a time of political change. In 1906, after a long period of Conservative rule, a Liberal government, led by Sir Henry Campbell-Bannerman, was elected with a large overall majority. A remarkable feature of the general election was the unexpected arrival in

Parliament of twenty-nine members of the Labour Representation Committee (LRC), which, as soon as the new parliament assembled, assumed the name of 'Labour Party'. The defeated Conservative leader, Arthur Balfour, made the jibe that the Liberal Prime Minister was a 'mere cork' on the socialist tide but it would have been more accurate to say that it was the Labour Party that was a cork on the Liberal tide.

Labour was reliant on Liberal votes. The new Labour MPs owed their presence in Parliament mainly to a secret pact between Ramsay MacDonald, secretary of the LRC, and Herbert Gladstone, the Liberal chief whip, which had given most of the LRC candidates a clear run without Liberal opposition. So far from there being a strong socialist tide, the Labour Party itself was little more than a trade union pressure group set up to protect trade union rights and immunities, though the Fabian Society, the ILP and the SDF were founder members. Individuals could not join the Labour Party directly, but had to attach themselves to one of its affiliates, either a trade union or a socialist group. Middle-class supporters usually joined the Fabian Society or the ILP. It was to these two socialist groups that Clement and his brother now turned.

In October 1907, they paid a visit to the Fabian office at Clements Inn in the Strand. According to Attlee, the secretary, Edward Pease, regarded the two young men 'as if we were two beetles who had crept under the door' and asked them why they wanted to join. The brothers persuaded Pease of the genuineness of their socialist beliefs and were invited to attend a Fabian Society meeting at Essex Hall. The meeting was full of talkative and mostly bearded middle-class intellectuals such as Sidney Webb, George Bernard Shaw and H. G. Wells. Clement murmured to his brother: 'Have we got to grow a beard to join this show?'[17] A more serious objection was that the Fabians seemed engrossed by an internal row about whether to remain a research organisation (the position backed by Sidney Webb and his formidable wife, Beatrice) or whether to become a larger and more active propaganda organisation (for which Wells argued). And, though the Fabians had helped set up the LRC, they had not yet given up the idea of permeating the two big existing parties with their ideas. Attlee joined the Fabian Society (he remained a Fabian for the rest of his life) but he was not satisfied that being a Fabian would actually help his working-class friends in Stepney.

One evening in January 1908 an East End wharf keeper, Tommy Williams, came to Haileybury House to complain about how the Charity Organisation Society had refused to help the parents of one of the boys in the club. 'They believe in charity but I am a socialist,' said Williams. Attlee replied: 'I am a socialist too.' Williams immediately invited him to join the local branch of the ILP. He went to their next meeting and became a member. Sitting in a small east London church hall with ten other members, all working men, he felt very much at home: 'I knew at once this was the right show for me.'[18] Attlee had taken his first step in politics. In two years a lukewarm conservative had turned himself into an ardent socialist.

When Attlee joined the ILP, it had expanded considerably from its beginnings in Bradford in 1893 but was by no means a mass organisation. It had only 22,000 members,[19] and the vast majority of trade unionists were not interested in politics. The ILP had 887 branches but most of them were weak, including the one in Stepney. Indeed within a few weeks, Attlee, with time on his hands, was surprised to find himself elected branch secretary.

Over the next few years, he made a new life for himself as a social worker and political activist. Four evenings a week were spent at Haileybury House and the fifth at the ILP branch. He filled his weekends refereeing the boys' football matches and speaking at open meetings. He made his first Sunday morning speech at the corner of Salmon Lane in March 1908, with his brother Tom, sporting a beard like the Fabians, in the audience. Clement's message was that the Stepney Public Health Committee should ensure a supply of cheap milk to the women and children of the borough. One of his fellow ILP members reported that 'Comrade Attlee was no orator . . . but he put up a good case'.[20]

Attlee served a long political apprenticeship in the East End. He spoke on street corners. He visited local pubs when trade unions held their meetings and tried, usually without success, to convert these working men to socialism. In conjunction with the SDF, Attlee started a local monthly paper, the *Stepney Worker*, which ran for a few issues before the SDF withdrew its support on the grounds that the paper was not revolutionary enough. He began to be invited to speak at meetings across London: in 1909 he spoke at fifty-three public meetings, in 1910 eighty-eight, in 1911 sixty-three and in 1912 seventy.[21] He talked on a variety of subjects including unemployment, socialism and tariff reform, boy labour and trade boards. He twice stood unsuccessfully for Stepney Borough Council and the Limehouse Board of Guardianship. Attlee was inspired by being part of a fighting socialist minority, 'crusaders in enemy-occupied territory',[22] as he put it. At that time, Attlee saw himself as a rank-and-file member with no greater ambition than perhaps one day being elected to a local council.

In November 1908, Attlee's father died after a heart attack at his desk in the City. Clement was left £400 a year, which gave him a degree of financial independence. His father's death also made it easier to give up the Bar, at which he clearly had no future. He was now free to pursue employment either full time or part time in fields which were more attractive and more relevant to his interests. In June 1909, he was hired by the Webbs to act as a part-time organiser of a campaign to put across the message of the Minority Report of the Royal Commission on the Poor Laws.

The minority report, signed by Beatrice Webb and George Lansbury, ILP local councillor for Poplar, and written by Sidney Webb, has been called 'one of the greatest state papers of the century'.[23] In its rejection of poverty and unemployment and its espousal of a comprehensive welfare programme (including a national health service), it was a forerunner of the Beveridge report and the social legislation of the 1945 Labour government. It was rejected by the Liberal government (as was the commission's majority report) so the Webbs decided to launch a campaign in favour of their proposals, using the Fabians, whose younger members were seeking a cause, as their 'shock troops'. Attlee was appointed to organise meetings and provide speakers. When speakers failed to turn up, Attlee had to act as a substitute, once having to address a large gathering of Liberal women on 'Problems of Birth and Infancy'. Although the campaign was unsuccessful in forcing the government to change its mind, Attlee found it enjoyable, with much of the atmosphere of an election. When Beatrice Webb wrote to thank him for his work, she gave him some typically blunt advice: 'What I think you need to make you a first-rate organiser is rather more of the quality of "Push" and the habit of a rapid transaction of business.'[24]

After a few months, Attlee left the campaign to become secretary of Toynbee Hall, which for more than twenty years had been a social and educational university settlement, promoting working-class education and social facilities in Whitechapel in the East End. However, this move was not a success. In Attlee's view, Toynbee Hall was living on its past reputation. Attlee was thankful to leave the settlement at the end of the year and return to his old friends in Stepney and Limehouse. At first, he shared an LCC flat with his brother Tom in Narrow Street, Limehouse and then, when Tom married Kathleen Medley, a Labour councillor in Poplar, Clement moved back to Haileybury House, where he lived until the war.

After Attlee left Toynbee Hall in 1910, he was out of full-time work for nearly two years. However, he assisted a team of researchers providing information on sweated labour for the wages boards, which had been established by Winston Churchill, the president of the Board of Trade, to set minimum wages in low-paid industries. He was also one of the part-time lecturers imaginatively appointed by David Lloyd George, the Chancellor of the Exchequer, to explain the workings of the ground-breaking 1911 Unemployment and Health Insurance Act, which provided for free medical treatment and sickness benefits for low-paid workers, as well as unemployment benefit to those laid off in the building, shipbuilding and engineering industries. Attlee, unlike a number of Labour leaders, was prepared to support the Act, even though it was based on the contributory principle and did nothing to prevent unemployment, because he saw it as a useful advance. He bicycled vigorously around Essex and Somerset, speaking to local meetings and sometimes staying the night with Tory landowners who were surprised to find that the earnest young middle-class lecturer was a socialist.

It was an opportune moment for a committed Labour supporter to have time on his hands. In 1910 two general elections were fought on the issue of the powers of the House of Lords. Attlee was able to help his East End colleague George Lansbury become Labour MP for Bow & Bromley. He worked closely with the suffragettes in their campaign for votes for women. Though he had little sympathy with syndicalist trade union leaders, he supported workers and their families involved in the great wave of strikes which swept the country. He cut up loaves to feed dockers' children during the 1911 dock strike and collected money for the Irish Transport and General Workers' Union strike in 1913. He also led ILP delegations from Stepney to gatherings of international socialists. 'I remember hearing Jean

Jaurès, the French Socialist leader, speak and seeing Anatole France kiss Bernard Shaw,' he later said.[25]

In 1913, Attlee had a lucky break which, ironically, given his initial scepticism about the Fabians, he owed to the Webbs. They had managed to secure funds from a Bombay steel company to create a social science department at the London School of Economics (set up by Sidney Webb in 1895). Attlee was offered a job as a tutor in the department by a selection committee chaired by Webb. Webb told the unsuccessful candidate, the bright young Hugh Dalton, who had already been awarded a research studentship at the LSE: 'We thought that, if we appointed him, he'd stick to it, and that if we appointed you, you wouldn't.'[26] Attlee was well aware that he was appointed not because of his academic qualifications but because of his practical experiences in the East End. 'The salary was small but sufficient for my wants, while the hours of work left me plenty of time for social work and also for socialist propaganda,' was his comment about his appointment.[27]

By 1914, the year war broke out, Attlee could look back on a period full of variety and hard social and political work. In conventional career terms, he could hardly consider himself a great success. He had failed at the Bar, he had left Toynbee Hall after only a year, he had not even tried to convert his part-time job as an official explainer of the National Insurance Act into a full-time civil service job, as some members of his family hoped, and he lacked the oratorical power to become a natural leader of the East End Labour movement. But his years in Stepney had given him a close knowledge of East End life, and he had learned to work easily and well with working-class people. He had also acquired an exceptionally good feel for the grassroots of the nascent Labour Party. As he said, 'the people I admired were those who did the tedious job, collecting our exiguous subscriptions, trying to sell literature . . . They got no glamour. They did not expect to live to see victory, but, uncomplainingly, they worked to try and help the cause.'[28] There is no evidence that the modest, rather lonely thirty-year-old had any other ambition than perhaps to become a councillor, but there all the same Attlee was building himself a strong political base in the East End.

The 1914–18 war proved a turning point in Attlee's life. It not only gave him a greater belief in his own abilities but also, by strengthening the Labour

Party, opened up the possibility of a political career. When war came, Attlee was on holiday in south Devon with Tom and Kathleen. Without undermining their close relationship, the two brothers took different positions on the war. Tom's Christian beliefs led him to a position of principled conscientious objection, against the use of force in all circumstances. By contrast, Clement was not persuaded by pacifist arguments. But, inevitably, he took account of the views of the Labour movement, especially ILP members, most of whom were anti-war. At the outbreak of war between Germany and France, the Parliamentary Labour Party passed a resolution demanding that Britain stay out. However, when on 4 August Germany invaded Belgium and following the expiry of the British government's ultimatum to Germany that evening, the PLP decided not to oppose supplementary war estimates. Ramsay MacDonald, chairman of the PLP and later the first Labour Prime Minister, resigned in protest against this change of policy and was succeeded by Arthur Henderson.

Despite pressures from his ILP friends, Attlee decided not only to support British entry into the war but also to enlist himself. He wrote later:

> I could not accept the ordinary cry of 'Your King and Country need you', nor was I convinced of Germany's sole guilt. On the other hand it appeared wrong to me to let others make a sacrifice while I stood by, especially as I was unmarried and had no obligations . . . I realised that some people had to serve and perhaps be killed and that I was partially trained already. I had no real conscientious objection.[29]

Like many others, Attlee may have been influenced by the unprovoked German attack on neutral Belgium. Once Britain had come into the war, he felt that he had an obligation to enlist, especially as he already had a volunteer commission in the Cadet Battalion of the Queen's London Regiment. At a deeper level, he was a Victorian patriot who felt that, now the country was at war, it was his civic duty to fight.

At first Attlee found it difficult to join the armed forces, both his age (he was thirty-one) and, surprisingly, his volunteer commission proving barriers. It was only through the influence of a brother-in-law of one of his former pupils at the LSE, who had been given command of a newly formed so-called 'Kitchener battalion', that, at the end of September, he managed to secure a commission in the 6th South Lancashire Regiment at Tidworth, Wiltshire. For the rest of the war, except for a year with the Tank Corps, he remained with the South Lancs. He saw extensive active service, as an officer in the Gallipoli peninsula in 1915, in Mesopotamia (now Iraq) in 1916 and, in 1918, with the 5th Battalion in the last stages of the war on the western front in France.

The Gallipoli campaign, an attempt by the British and French to open up a new eastern front in the Dardanelles to help their Russian allies and break the impasse in the west, was a tragic failure. The allies lost 265,000 men, either killed, wounded or missing, including thousands of Australians and New Zealanders. The defending Turks lost 300,000 men.[30] Attlee always believed that the strategic concept of a new eastern front, which was so strongly advocated by Winston Churchill, was sound but that the generals chosen to implement the plan were 'elderly and hidebound'.[31] His experience in Gallipoli marked him for life. He always remembered the heat and the flies and, in the winter of 1915, the frost and the snow. Yet, despite the appalling conditions, he also treasured the comradeship of the trenches.

A few weeks after his arrival, Attlee went down with acute dysentery. Against his wishes, he was embarked on a hospital ship bound for England, and then, following his protest, was put off the ship at Malta. His illness probably saved his life, as two weeks after his collapse his company took part in the big allied attack at Sari Bair and two-thirds of his men were killed. In November, he had recovered enough to rejoin his battalion in the front line at Suvla. He remained there until the final evacuation. His company was chosen to hold the lines until all the allied troops had embarked. Attlee and the divisional commander, General Stanley Maude, were the last two soldiers to leave.

The South Lancs were then switched to the campaign in Mesopotamia and, after disembarking at Basra, went up the Tigris by paddle steamer. After being briefed by Maude, whom Attlee admired, they were sent into action against the Turks at El Hanna in what is now southern Iraq in the early morning of 6 April 1916. Attlee went over the top carrying a large red flag as a warning to the supporting British artillery. The advance rapidly cleared the first two lines of Turkish trenches and Attlee decided to go forward alone to the third trench to plant his flag as a sign to the British gunners to lift their barrage. Unfortunately, as he was sticking the flag in the ground, he was hit by 'friendly fire' from behind, a piece of shrapnel from an artillery shell tearing a hole in his right buttock, while a bullet also went through his left thigh. The wounds were serious and he was immediately evacuated, first to hospital in Bombay and then to Alexandria, arriving in Southampton on 2 June. As with his attack of dysentery at Gallipoli, his wound may have saved his life, as his division suffered heavy casualties in the subsequent attacks, including the death of sixty of Attlee's own company.

By September 1916 Attlee had regained the use of his legs and was posted to his regiment's training battalion in Shropshire. Although he was transferred to one of the newly formed tank battalions and was promoted to the rank of major, he found training soldiers in England frustrating and longed to get back to fighting. Both his age and the fact that he had only seen action on the eastern front told against him. As he wrote to his brother Tom, who was now in prison as a conscientious objector, 'the trouble with us Eastern Front men is that those who know us are at the other end of the world'.[32] Eventually, having arranged a return to the South Lancs in the winter of 1917, he was posted to the 5th Battalion, which was serving in the front line in France as part of the 55th Division, in June 1918. Apart from the heavy shelling, he found conditions on the western front a great improvement on those in the east: 'Food was good and plentiful and one got letters and newspapers regularly. One also returned to rest in comfortable beds and could get baths.'[33]

In August 1918, the Germans began to weaken and the allies went on to the offensive. The South Lancs were in action near Lille. During one sharp engagement, Attlee had to take over another company after its commander had been wounded. On reaching the next German trench, he himself was hit on the back by falling timber. He also developed piles. In October, he was ordered back for treatment, ending up in a hospital on Wandsworth Common, less than half a mile away from his brother, who was imprisoned in Wandsworth gaol. Exhausted, rundown and covered with painful boils on his stomach, Clement spent Armistice Day in hospital. He managed, however, to get himself leave for Christmas, which he spent with his sister in Salisbury. Here a civilian doctor cured him in a few days and, early in

January 1919, he was discharged from the Army, a more mature and self-confident person than when he had joined up in 1914.

Though Attlee had been seriously wounded, he had survived the war without being disabled. He had proved himself a reliable officer, capable of leading his men without panache but effectively and humanely. He was also able to get on with most of his fellow officers, despite his shyness and political differences. On his return to the 6th Battalion in the Gallipoli peninsula after recovering from dysentery, he reached HQ just as the officers were sitting down to dinner. 'It was really like coming home after so much wandering about and uncertainty.'[34]

He never hid his socialist views. Indeed in Gallipoli he sometimes engaged in fierce arguments with fellow officers. The battalion's commanding officer would say: 'Let's have a good "strafe" tonight – have Attlee to dinner,' and they would discuss socialism or some other controversial issue. He wrote to Tom from the ship carrying his battalion to Basra in February 1916: 'I have had numerous strafes on social subjects since I have been on board, some with the CO – a very genial old Tory with a gift of humorous epithet.' The CO described Attlee as 'a charming fellow – just going to play bridge with him – but a damned democratic socialistic tub-thumping rascal'.[35] On the night watches, he would debate issues such as the different forms of trade union organisation with his sergeants.

The war was changing the world, as Attlee noted in his letters to his brother. He was sceptical about the Russian revolution of November 1917: 'Lenin and Trotsky appear to me to be like the Socialist Party of Great Britain type or the wilder types of the Social Democratic Party. I can imagine the state of the country run by the Whitechapel branch of the SDP.' He praised the Labour leaders who supported the war: 'Henderson, Horner and Smillie are doing particularly well I think.'[36] In the second wartime coalition, Arthur Henderson had joined David Lloyd George's War Cabinet. However, in the summer of 1917, he had been forced to resign by his War Cabinet colleagues, after advocating Labour participation in an international socialist conference in Stockholm, which German Social Democrats would also attend. In opposition, Henderson devised a new structure and constitution for the Labour Party (including Clause 4, establishing common ownership as a party objective), as well as a new foreign policy, based upon the League of Nations. In July 1918 the American ambassador wrote to President Woodrow Wilson: 'The Labour Party is already playing for supremacy.'[37] New political opportunities were opening up both for the Labour Party and for the younger generation of middle-class supporters, like Attlee. The tortoise was about to make a move.

2

The hares (1): Bevin and Morrison

In sharp contrast to Clement Attlee's comfortable upbringing, Ernest Bevin was born in rural poverty on 7 March 1881 at Winsford, a Somerset village on the edge of Exmoor. Although his mother, Mercy Bevin, had been married to William Bevin, an agricultural labourer, he was not Ernest's father. When she registered the child's birth, Mercy left the space for the father's name blank.

At a time of agricultural depression, Mercy had to bring up a large family (Ernest had five elder brothers and an elder sister, Mary Jane) by herself. She scraped a living by working as a domestic help in neighbouring farms, acting as the local midwife and occasionally helping out in the kitchen of the village inn. One friend who grew up with Bevin said: 'I'm sure there's no one in this wide world was ever poorer than he and his mother.'[1]

However, despite the struggle to make ends meet, Mercy earned the respect of her fellow villagers by her strong character and independence. She was a committed Methodist at a time when to be a dissenter risked the displeasure of the local gentry and farmers. She sent her children, including Ernest, to the Wesleyan Sunday school run by the village postmistress and spent what little spare time she had raising funds for the building of a new chapel. Ernest was devoted to his mother and was devastated when she died of a fibrous growth on 1 May 1889. After the funeral, the family gathered together at Mercy's cottage for the last time. Fortunately for Ernest, Mary Jane and her husband, George Pope, who was a railwayman, offered the orphan a home 30 miles away near Crediton in Devon.

For the next three years, Bevin learnt to read and write and do simple arithmetic, first at Morchard Bishop Church School, then, when the Popes moved, at Colebrooke Board School (which had been opened in 1879) and finally, when he was nine, at Hayward's Boys' School in Crediton. By the end of his first year at Hayward's he had reached Standard IV, which entitled him to a Labour Certificate.

However, while Attlee remained in full-time education until he was twenty-one, Bevin's formal schooling came to an end in March 1892, when he was just eleven. This makes his subsequent achievements the more remarkable. He was sent out to work as a live-in farm boy. His wage was sixpence a week, paid in a lump sum of six shillings and sixpence every quarter. He worked ten hours a day, stone picking, hoeing, clearing twitch grass, driving cattle and cutting up mangelwurzels and turnips for their fodder. On winter evenings he displayed his newly acquired education by reading out news and articles from the local paper to the farmer and his family around the kitchen fire.

There is a local tradition that it was after a row with his second employer, a sharp-tongued, hot-tempered farmer, that Ernest followed the example of his five brothers and sought his future in Bristol. Though he later denied the story, it is clear that he left Devon in the spring of 1894 with few regrets.[2]

When the thirteen-year-old boy arrived at Temple Meads, Bristol's main station, he must have been both excited and apprehensive. His eldest brother, Jack, had offered him a room in his house but he now had to make his own way in an unfamiliar new world. Bristol was a bustling industrial and commercial centre and widely recognised as the capital city of the West Country. This meant that, even for a teenager without skills, like Ernest, there were jobs to be had. But they were mostly in 'dead end' occupations. As he later explained, 'you had to take what was going. You got a job and you lost it and then you picked up something else and made do with whatever came along.'[3] He was in turn a baker's boy, a kitchen boy, a grocer's errand boy, a van boy and a tram conductor. He got what he later described as his first 'man's job' when he was eighteen, as a drayman driving a two-horse van for a mineral water firm. At last he had relative financial security and independence. Once he had loaded up his van in the morning, he was virtually his own master.

This was a time of self-education, when Bevin's exceptional abilities gradually revealed themselves. He had kept up the habit of chapel-going instilled in him by his mother and it was in Sunday Bible classes at Old King Street Baptist Church, led by a charismatic local minister, the Reverend James Moffat Logan, that he began to ask questions about the big issues of the day, including the Boer War, which Moffat Logan strongly opposed. He also went to the lecture classes organised by the Bristol Adult School Movement. One contemporary wrote: 'My impression is that it was in the Adult School that Ernest Bevin learned how to stand on his hind legs and express himself in public. [He] got the name for being extravagant in voicing social and industrial injustice.' The same witness remembered Bevin attending a Workers' Educational Association trade union study where the subject was agriculture: 'Here again Ernest Bevin was vocal, sitting with papers and books bursting from his pockets.'[4]

During the day, driving his mineral water van round the city and its surrounding villages, he would mull over what he had heard and read. He had grown to be a broad-shouldered, powerful man, determined in manner, emphatic in speech, and with an independent cast of mind, forming his opinions not only from what he learnt but also from his own observations of conditions in Bristol.

Bevin's growing capacity to think, argue and speak impressed his fellow Nonconformists, so much so that he was chosen as a lay preacher and there was even talk of him taking a theological course as a step to becoming a Baptist minister. But his interests were moving away from religion and towards politics and socialism. Deeply angered not only by the poverty and squalor which he saw daily in Bristol's slums but also by the selfish, uncaring attitude of the city's professional and employer classes, he began to look for more radical answers than Nonconformity could provide to these glaring divisions and inequalities.

One day, while driving his van, he passed an open air meeting organised by the Bristol Socialist Society and stopped to listen. He was sufficiently impressed to go later to a branch meeting at the Shepherd's Hall. The Bristol Socialist Society was affiliated to the Marxist Social Democratic Federation (SDF). The SDF's call to the working class to stand up for themselves and its denunciation of the 'reformism', both of the Independent Labour Party and even more of the newly formed Labour Representation Committee (LRC), appealed to Bevin's youthful vehemence. He became a frequent attender at local meetings and rapidly developed into a powerful and fluent advocate of working-class action to bring about a socialist society.

His twenties were a crucial period in Bevin's progress. Joining the Bristol Socialist Society was a symbol of his new commitment to politics. His marriage to Florence Townley, the daughter of a taster at a local wine merchant, gave him love and confidence as well as the security of a house of his own. In 1908, he was chosen as secretary of the Bristol Right to Work Committee, an indication of his growing reputation in the local Labour movement.

The years 1908 and 1909 saw exceptionally high unemployment. With no state unemployment benefit, the impact of a depression on industrial centres such as Bristol was appallingly harsh. According to Bevin, by the winter of 1908 the number of families in Bristol without work had risen to 5,000, while the number of paupers on the derisory poor relief had risen to 10,000. In many houses, children were found with only rags to clothe them, no heating and very little food.[5]

Bevin became an effective lobbyist for the unemployed. At the inaugural meeting of the Right to Work Committee in the Haymarket, hot coffee and bread and butter were provided for more than 600 men. On Christmas Eve he distributed 3,545 loaves to unemployed families. He also took a deputation to see the Liberal MP for Bristol North, the government minister Augustine Birrell, and bombarded the local council with proposals for work-creating projects.

To highlight their plight, Bevin led a procession of the unemployed into Bristol Cathedral for morning service on 9 November 1908. Their ragged appearance and orderly behaviour made a deep impression on the congregation and, faced by growing public support for the campaign, the council agreed to back proposals put forward by the Right to Work Committee, including borrowing money for the construction of a lake in Easterville Park. Emboldened by his success, Bevin stood for the city council as Socialist candidate for the St Paul's ward in the autumn of 1909.

Ernest fought the election on the slogan 'Vote for Bevin who fought for the unemployed'. In his election address, he called for the nationalisation of the docks, advocated the building of 'artisans' cottages' to be let at subsidised rents, and concluded by referring again to the high unemployment and poverty of the winter: 'You will realise the chaos, misery and degradation brought upon us by the private ownership of the means of life. I claim that socialism, which is the common ownership of those means, is the only solution of such evils.' However, despite the vigour of his campaign, he was easily defeated by the sitting Liberal councillor, who retained the seat by 1,052 votes to 663.

The months following his election defeat were difficult for Bevin. His high political profile and reputation as an agitator made him a marked man, especially among local businessmen. A movement to boycott him spread among the hotels and restaurants he served and his sales, and therefore his commission, dropped sharply. Fortunately his employer, although a Liberal who disliked his senior drayman's socialist views, stood by him and gradually Bevin's earnings recovered. Even so, while the boycott lasted the Bevins had a hard time, especially as they now had a daughter to keep. Ernest dropped out of local politics for a while, gave up his secretaryship of the Right to Work Committee and even talked of becoming a missionary.

In fact, his career was about to take a crucial turn. Within less than two years of his setback in the election for Bristol City Council, Bevin, who was to be the greatest British trade union leader of the twentieth century, became a full-time trade union official. In the summer of 1910, a dock strike held up the port of Bristol. Bevin was not a member of the dockers' union but, because of his reputation as the secretary of the Right to Work Committee, he was asked to organise a relief fund for the dockers. He observed that the employers were attempting to use carters, who, although widely employed in the docks, were not organised in any union, to load and unload ships. An organiser of the dockers' union urged Bevin, who as a drayman was himself a carter, to take the initiative in bringing the carters together. In Bevin's opinion, it was right for the carters to join the union, given their common interest. In August 1910, a carters' branch of the Dock, Wharf, Riverside and General Labourers' Union was set up in Bristol, with Bevin as its first chairman. At the age of twenty-nine, Bevin became a trade union member for the first time. His framed certificate of membership, much decorated with scrolls and dated 27 August 1910, was a prize possession and, at the end of his life, hung above the marble mantelpiece in the study of his official Foreign Office flat in Carlton Gardens.

Within six months the branch had 1,000 members, and by September 1911, more than 2,000. He also persuaded the Bristol employers to recognise the branch and to negotiate a comprehensive agreement with the carters covering hours, wages and conditions. A feature of this agreement was the limitation of 3 tons imposed on horses' loads. Previously carters could earn a bonus on every extra ton above three. Bevin persuaded the carters and their employers that it was in their joint interests to ensure that their horses were not overloaded on the steep Bristol streets. In the spring of 1911, his exceptional powers of organisation and communication were rewarded when he was made a full-time organiser at the Bristol office of the dockers' union at a weekly salary of two pounds.

Bevin became a trade union official at a time of greatly increased industrial militancy. Between 1900 and 1909, the average number of working days lost each year through strikes and lock-outs had averaged three and half million. In 1910, however, they went up to twelve million and in 1912 to more than thirty-eight million. During 1911 and 1912, every port, every coalfield and every railway company was at one time or another hit by a strike.[6] The root cause was the failure of wages to keep up with the increase in prices but an important contributory factor was growing ideological support for strike action among activists of both unskilled and skilled unions.

The Dock, Wharf, Riverside and General Labourers' Union, with its general secretary, the fiery Ben Tillett, was one of the leading exponents of the new militancy, helping bring the port of London, the world's largest, to a standstill in both 1911 and 1912. It was Tillett who urged a mob meeting of dockers on Tower Hill to take off their hats and pray to God to strike dead the chairman of the Port of London Authority, Lord Devonport. It was against this turbulent background that Bevin learnt the ropes as a trade union official. In 1911 he was sent from Bristol to south Wales to help organise the ports. Here he was fiercely opposed by employers who refused to recognise unions and by rival unions who were competing for members. It was a rough school but, despite fluctuations in membership, he managed to build up local branches in Cardiff, Barry and Newport. He also had some success in recruiting members in his native West Country, where trade unionism was little known.

In March 1914 Bevin was appointed assistant national organiser, with the brief of replicating on a wider scale what he had achieved in the West Country and south Wales. His office was in London, but for his family's sake he kept on his house in Bristol, where his wife was more at home. His first biographer described Bevin at this time: 'Powerfully built, with the stocky muscular hands of a manual labourer and the rolling walk which is almost as common to draymen as to seamen, Bevin had a natural pugnacity and the physical courage to back it up.'[7] But, although he became a powerful speaker with the confidence to stand up for himself in any situation, he was far more than just a militant demagogue. He understood the need to build up trade union organisation, to win recognition from the employers, and to negotiate terms and conditions for his members which would endure. He was a practical trade unionist with an instinctive grasp of the needs of the workers, but he also had a remarkable ability to relate those needs to a wider vision.

The 1914–18 war transformed the position of the trade unions. For the first time, they were taken into partnership by government. Their leaders, who before the war had been denounced as agitators, were now invited to join important advisory committees. Bevin gained from the war. One of his biographers aptly highlighted the prospects opening up for him: 'Thus, at a time when Bevin's abilities were beginning to win recognition, the scope of activity open to him was transformed, the scale of opportunity enlarged to proportions which promised to draw out, not frustrate, the powers he possessed.'[8]

On the first weekend of August 1914, when demonstrations against Britain going to war were held all over the country, Bevin called for international workers' action at a meeting on the Bristol Downs. Some months before, he had supported a resolution urging all members of the International Federation of Trade Unions to proclaim an international general strike in the event of war. But the German trade unions, fearing reprisals by their own government, did not back the resolution, a hesitation which Bevin saw as a betrayal. However, when hostilities broke out, trade unions in all the major European countries, including Britain, rallied in a wave of patriotic fervour to their national war efforts.

Bevin's attitude towards the war was characteristic. As his speech to the 1915 Bristol Trades Union Congress showed, he was unimpressed by jingoistic outbursts against the Germans. He was also extremely sceptical of the blandishments offered to the trade unions by government ministers, especially the Prime Minister, David Lloyd George, whom he greatly mistrusted, and was strongly opposed to Labour leaders joining the government coalitions of 1915 and 1916.

On the other hand, he was contemptuous of the pacifism of the ILP's Ramsay MacDonald and Philip Snowden, which he saw as self-serving, and he had little use for the militant Clydeside shop steward movement, which he considered dangerously divisive. In his view, the main priority should be to bolster the power and cohesion of the trade unions, so that they could come out from the war stronger.

Bevin played a leading role on the key Port and Transit Committee, set up by the government to organise the ports. He supported action required to help win the war, including eliminating congestion at the ports and preventing strikes. But he also spoke up vigorously on behalf of the dockers and was able to secure reforms, notably the registration of dock workers at Cardiff port. He persuaded the Transport Workers' Federation, composed of thirty unions representing workers in the transport industries and on whose executive he sat, to agree on and campaign for a national post-war programme for transport workers, including the abolition of overtime and reduction in the hours of work.

Bevin impressed Lloyd George, who in 1917 offered him a paid post as full-time labour adviser to the government. Bevin refused the offer because he saw his future not as a civil servant but as a trade union leader. However, he accepted an invitation from the Ministry of Reconstruction to serve on its advisory council and its subcommittees, which included Sidney Webb and the economist J. A. Hobson among its members and which produced a notable report on adult education. In 1917 he also took part in discussions between employers and trade unionists on the future of industrial relations, sponsored by the Quaker philanthropist Arnold Rowntree.

These talks were the first of their kind and, though they did not lead to immediate results (indeed the period after the First World War was dominated by bitter industrial disputes), it could be argued that they began the process which led eventually to the more co-operative industrial relations which Bevin himself did so much to promote when he was minister of labour in the Second World War. The young Bevin spoke frankly of his doubts about the prospects for closer co-operation with the employers. In a report of one of the conferences, it was noted: 'The operatives are frequently regarded by employers as being of a different and inferior order . . . So long as these views continue to exist they inevitably produce an intense class bitterness.'[9] Being involved in such a dialogue was bound to influence Bevin's thinking over the long term.

Another formative experience for a future Foreign Secretary was the journey (his first abroad) that Ernest made in 1915 to the United States, as one of two fraternal TUC delegates to the annual convention of the American Federation of Labor (AFL). He was away from Britain for three months and was greatly stimulated by different immigrant groups he met – the Russian-Americans, the Polish-Americans, the Germans and the Irish – and their different views. He was impressed by Samuel Gompers, the president of the AFL, who was then at the zenith of his reputation as the archetypal trade union boss and apostle of business unionism. Bevin disagreed with Gompers's non-political approach to trade unionism but could not help admiring his self-confident use of power and exceptional bargaining skills. At the end of the fortnight's convention, which took place in San Francisco, Gompers attempted to place an official gift, a heavy gold ring decorated with a naked lady, on Bevin's massive fingers. The ring proved too small and had to be sent away to be enlarged. However, Bevin wore the ring to the end of his life and in 1949 used it to seal the North Atlantic treaty between the USA, the UK and other western European powers.

By the end of the war Bevin was worn out by attending numerous committees and meetings, catching trains up and down the country, living on sandwiches and hastily eaten meals, away from home all week and sometimes at weekends as well. In July 1918 he suffered a nervous breakdown and was not back full time for several months. However, he was now recognised as one of the most able of the younger generation of trade union leaders, a spokesman of his union at TUC and Labour conferences, and its leading representative on many negotiating bodies and government committees. Bevin was a rising star in the trade union and Labour world.

*

Ernest Bevin's great and also exceptionally able rival, Herbert Morrison, was born in relative prosperity on 3 January 1888 at 240 Ferndale Road, Brixton in south London. His parents were cockneys. His father, Henry, was a police constable. Henry had met Herbert's mother, Priscilla, working as a maidservant at a boarding house for doctors at the London Hospital in the East End. As a policeman, Henry Morrison had a secure job with a rent allowance and a pension. Most of his children, Herbert's brothers and sisters, found clerical jobs. So Herbert Morrison could be said to be a member of the lower middle classes and thus to be several rungs higher up the social ladder than Bevin.

However, within three days of his birth, the infant Herbert was totally blinded in one eye, probably as a result of infection. Though he claimed in his autobiography that 'my one eye served me well',[10] the loss of his right eye handicapped and disfigured him for life, making his later achievements all the more impressive. His mother, fearing that Herbert's other eye could be damaged as well, lavished love and attention on the young boy. His earliest memories were 'of the stout, comfortable looking woman who was my mother serving beef with a magnificent batter pudding and getting me to drink milk'.[11] When he and his sister Edie came home from school in the winter, his mother would warm their frozen hands in her armpits. She organised games for her children and joined them in sing-songs.

If Herbert was devoted to his mother, his relationship with his father was far more distant. Henry Morrison was a difficult, often irritable man, who seldom played with his children. He had a weakness for alcohol and young Herbert would be sent to the local public house so that he could warn his mother when his father had had too much to drink. Henry was a staunch Conservative who, in the 1880s, had played his part as a policeman in upholding the law against the demonstrations and marches of an increasingly assertive trade union movement. He was greatly upset when his son later got involved in left-wing politics.

In 1893, Herbert (or Bert, as he was then known) was sent to Stockwell Road Board School, a fortress-like building with fifty to a class. The five-year-old had to be dragged to school by his sister. He hated it. 'That school of mine – I can see it, feel it, smell it now. Dark paint, heavy walls, a feeling that the roof was falling on you.'[12] He was called 'One Eye' by his classmates and left out of school games.

At the age of eleven he was transferred to Lingham Street Church of England School. He became an avid reader. He was a frequent user of the school library, where he would devour the adventure stories of G. A. Henty, R. M. Ballantyne and George Manville Fenn. On the way home, he would buy the penny comics, such as *Comic Cuts* and the *Boy's Own Paper*, which were then flooding the newsagents of London. He was always grateful that he had been made to learn poems by heart – 'no one can become word perfect in Gray's *Elegy*, which was a set piece for recitation, without in time responding to the beauty of the lines'.[13] The outstanding achievement of Morrison's schooldays was being chosen as the school's orator to deliver a set speech on Trafalgar Day – his first public address.

When he was just fourteen, on 17 January 1902, he had to leave his elementary school. In 1960 Morrison said of his educational experience: 'I shall always be grateful for my elementary education – that is, all there was of it . . . I don't have any grievance against the education system that kept me out of the secondary schools which hardly then existed – I was just born at the wrong time.'[14] He later summed up his childhood as unhappy and described himself as introspective and lacking in self-confidence. However, a photograph taken when he was twelve shows an assured, smartly dressed young boy, already with his trademark quiff in place. Perhaps his confident public face even then hid an inner insecurity.

Herbert now had to find work. His father vetoed his first two ideas – becoming a compositor like Edie's fiancé or a clerk in a City firm – on the grounds that these jobs would impose too great a strain on his remaining eye. Instead, he became an errand boy at five shillings a week for his elder brother, Harry, who had recently set himself up as a grocer. When Harry's shop failed, Herbert got another job as an errand boy, this time for the local branch of the well-known grocers and wine merchants Walton, Hassell and Port. His wages were now seven shillings a week but the work was much harder and involved carrying baskets which, fully laden, weighed up to 40 pounds. The shop was only ten minutes' normal walk from his home but at night the journey often took him half an hour or more, so exhausted was he. However, sometimes, he still had the energy to go to the Empress Music Hall or the Brixton Theatre, where he saw Wagner's *Tannhäuser* performed by the Carl Rosa Opera Company.

When he was nineteen, Morrison was promoted to be a junior assistant at Walton, Hassell and Port's Pimlico branch, at Lupus Street, near Victoria. His main task was to keep the premises clean and weigh and wrap the sugar, tea and coffee. He was delighted when the manager allowed him to dress the window. He quickly became the star window dresser: 'To me it was an expression of proportion, of colour, and of balance.'[15]

By day the young Morrison observed Walton, Hassell and Port's customers. By night he read voraciously, mostly in his room above the shop. Morrison's was the first literate generation of his class. For the first time, there was a flood of books, pamphlets and articles available for the intellectually curious. Herbert used to comb the secondhand bookshops for copies of works on ethics, history, economics and sociology. Cheap reprints from publishing firms such as Thomas Nelson and J. M. Dent also helped open up a new world. As Morrison wrote in his autobiography, reading was his further education.

He had been brought up in a conservative household where criticism of the established order, especially the glaring contrast between rich and poor, was regarded as futile and unjustified. Now he studied books from different viewpoints which condemned existing conditions, such as L. G. Chiozza Money's *Riches and Poverty*, Karl Marx's *Communist Manifesto* and the beginning of *Das Kapital* and Robert Blatchford's *Merrie England*. He also admired the writings of George Bernard Shaw and H. G. Wells and the novels of Arnold Bennett. 'This literature was without doubt the basic reason why my thoughts began to turn towards socialism.'[16] These works helped Morrison make intellectual sense of his gut feelings about the injustice and unfairness of Edwardian Britain.

Morrison also spent many hours listening to street corner orators. One of these was a phrenologist who 'read' people's heads for sixpence a consultation. The phrenologist told Morrison that, if he used his time well and continued his reading, he might become Prime Minister. The Brixton Discussion Forum, which met on Sunday mornings to debate a wide range of issues, became the highlight of Morrison's week, so much that he bought a three-and-ninepenny bowler hat from Dunn's hat shop solely to wear to forum meetings. There he learnt to intervene and to argue. He was proud to be accepted as a socialist, quoting liberally from *Das Kapital*.

In October 1906, a few months after the success of the LRC at the general election, Morrison joined the Brixton branch of the ILP but, after a short time, he resigned on the grounds that it was insufficiently socialist. In the summer of 1907, he joined the Westminster branch of the Social Democratic Party (SDP), the Marxist party led by H. M. Hyndman which had left the LRC because it was too right wing.

Morrison told the following story in his autobiography. One day, while walking along Brompton Road to get orders from customers who lived nearby, he saw Philip Snowden, accompanied by his wife, limping (from a bone deformity) along the pavement towards him. Snowden, a leading ILP figure, had just been elected to Parliament as MP for Blackburn and was later to be a Labour Chancellor of the Exchequer. As Snowden passed, Morrison took a sheet out of his order book and scribbled a hasty message: 'When, Mr Philip Snowden, will you move this resolution in the Commons – "That in the opinion of this House there is no real remedy for the problems of poverty short of socialism"? Cease talking reform and advocate social revolution. From Unattached!'[17] After thrusting the piece of paper into Snowden's hand, he hurried away without waiting for the MP's reaction. The nineteen-year-old Morrison may deserve marks for cheek but not for tactical judgement. Even if they had wished to advocate revolutionary solutions (and most of them, including Snowden, did not), the new Labour MPs were far too dependent on Liberal votes to take such a risk.

Morrison's commitment to revolutionary socialism – indeed to any kind of socialist politics – strained further his already tense relationship with his father. His beloved mother died, after a short illness, in January 1907 and, when his father threw his invitation card to an SDP meeting into the fire, he decided to leave home. Later in life his attitude to his father became more understanding but at the time he felt bitter.

In fact, Morrison was himself becoming increasingly tired of the SDP. He argued in vain that it should reaffiliate to the Labour Party, in order to increase its clout. By 1910 he was sick of revolutionary gestures and turned back to the ILP, which had remained affiliated to Labour. He rejoined the Brixton ILP branch, on the grounds that the parliamentary struggle was worth taking a hand in. He also fell under the spell of the leading ILP politician, Ramsay MacDonald, whom he heard speak at an ILP conference.

It was at this time that Morrison himself became a fluent speaker, spouting from his soap-box on south London street corners most nights and two or three times on Sundays. He gradually developed the ability to speak without notes; 'I would have my general line of argument mentally prepared but I used to rely on the inspiration of the moment, the atmosphere of the meeting, or on the comments of that invaluable ally of a public speaker, the heckler, to direct my train of thought'.[18] It was at these outdoor meetings that he first met Clement Attlee, whom he recalled speaking in a quiet and modest manner. Morrison was clearly a far more charismatic debater.

Yet, though Morrison had become an eloquent speaker, he quickly understood that political success depended 'less on street corner rabble-rousing . . . than on the slow but steady construction of an organisation devoted to running a planned programme of propaganda, social work and organisation'.[19] Soon after joining Brixton ILP, he became its chairman, brilliant at starting meetings on time, keeping to the agenda and conducting business with dispatch. His reputation as a born organiser rapidly spread. By the end of 1910 he had been appointed honorary secretary of the South London Federation of the ILP branches.

A change of job (he had become a telephone switchboard operator at the bottling stores of Whitbread's brewery) gave him more time for political organisation. Working from his bed-sitting room, he typed agendas, booked halls for meetings and duplicated circulars. He arranged demonstrations, social gatherings and meetings at which other branches could come together. He organised two high-profile and well-attended debates in 1911: one between Bernard Shaw and G. K. Chesterton and the other between MacDonald and Hilaire Belloc. The MacDonald–Belloc debate was published as an ILP pamphlet with a foreword by Morrison. He had found his metier. As he said, 'the work might not be spectacular but I found it deeply satisfying'.[20]

In November 1912 he stood for the first time as a local government candidate for the Vauxhall ward of the borough of Lambeth. He instantly took charge of the campaign, issuing a highly professional election address and organising a last-minute leaflet on the eve of the poll. Morrison felt confident that the ILP would win all the six seats up for election. But, although two sitting ILP members were returned, Morrison finished bottom of the poll. He was bitterly disappointed – 'I had failed abysmally. The lesson was, of course, valuable for a brash and over-optimistic young socialist.'[21]

In the autumn of 1912, Herbert left the switchboard at Whitbread to become circulation traveller and subsequently deputy circulation manager of the *Daily Citizen*, the first official Labour newspaper. He impressed colleagues by his efficiency and flair. Fenner Brockway, then editor of the *Labour Leader*, the ILP newspaper, wrote: 'He had a genius for organisation, becoming the leader of his team of workers by natural ability, surmounting difficulties which baffled everyone else . . . and all the time as he went about his duties whistling, joking, laughing in characteristic cockney light-heartedness.'[22] Morrison's ambition was to move to the editorial side of the paper. To promote his journalism, he wrote some articles for the *Labour Leader*. However, soon after the war broke out, the *Daily Citizen*, which had lost money from the beginning, collapsed, putting him out of work.

Fortunately for Morrison – and for the Labour Party – a new opportunity opened up. On 23 May 1914, 424 delegates from the unions, LRCs and the ILP, along with British Socialist Party leaders and others, met at Essex Hall in the Strand to set up a London Labour Party. At the first annual conference in November a chairman and secretary were elected. But the secretary, Fred Knee, died on 8 December and Morrison was chosen as a temporary stop-gap. On 27 April 1915, he was elected permanent secretary of the London Labour Party, though by only one vote. Despite this precarious beginning, Morrison went on to build up the most powerful local political organisation in the country.

Like many ILP members, Morrison was 'anti-war'. He was not, however, a pacifist. He was against the particular war in which Britain was involved. He objected to fighting on the same side as the Russian Tsar, and in any case saw little to choose between Britain and Germany. He regarded this war as largely a 'capitalist war' brought about by commercial rivalry and by the secret diplomacy which had linked Britain to France. Views such as Morrison's were unpopular even in the Labour Party. Anti-war meetings were often broken up. After addressing an open air meeting on Hampstead Heath, he was dragged from the platform towards the nearest pond. Only the intervention of the police saved him from a ducking.

When conscription came into force in 1916, Morrison received his call-up notice. Clearly, blindness in one eye made him unfit for military service but, for propaganda reasons, he was determined to appear before the Military Service Tribunal at Wandsworth. Unlike many other conscientious objectors who went to prison, he agreed to work at an alternative service which was of benefit to the nation. He offered to be a dustman in Wandsworth but the tribunal ordered him to work on the land and sent him to Letchworth Garden City in Hertfordshire. The market gardener who employed him there turned out to be a socialist.

Established in 1905 by Ebenezer Howard as an experiment in a new kind of living, Letchworth was a hotbed for radicals, utopians and conscientious objectors. It was a haven for Morrison, who continued in his spare time to carry out his duties as secretary of the London Labour Party. On Saturday evenings, he went to the Skittles Inn, a temperance hall where he learnt country dancing. There he met his first wife, Margaret Kent, a star performer at dancing, who was artistic and attractive but also shy and reserved. His autobiography makes no mention of her. The marriage, which took place after the war, was not a success. Many of Morrison's friends felt that his previous girlfriend, Rosa Rosenberg, a vivacious and intelligent woman, who was fascinated by politics and later became Ramsay MacDonald's secretary, would have made a more suitable wife.

Morrison recorded his feelings as the war ended: 'When the sirens and church bells proclaimed the Armistice I was digging for winter planting at Letchworth. I stopped digging, put my foot on my spade and experienced a quiet and profound emotion; relief that the carnage was over, sorrow for the fallen. It was my own two minutes' silence.'[23]

As a non-combatant, Morrison had come through the war personally unscathed. As secretary of the London Labour Party, he had also kept a significant party organisation alive. Even while operating from Letchworth, he had issued a regular four-page monthly magazine, the *London Labour Party Circular*, which contained a mixture of council and party news and arguments for use against the Conservatives and Liberals. Despite the profound split over the war, he had preserved the unity of the London Labour Party. Morrison now found himself in an excellent position both to build up Labour in London and to promote his own career. Another gifted hare was well placed in the political race.

3

The hares (2): Dalton and Cripps

Hugh Dalton, like Stafford Cripps and Clement Attlee, came from a very different background to Ernest Bevin and Herbert Morrison. Edward Hugh John Neale Dalton was born on 16 August 1887 in the large country house of his mother's family in Glamorgan. Although he had been named Edward after the Prince of Wales's eldest son, Eddy, he was always called Hugh.

Beatrice Webb wrote in her diary that the Daltons were 'upper or upper middle class: old governing class of the 19th century'.[1] Dalton's biographer, Ben Pimlott, questioned whether they were much involved in governing. More accurately, the Dalton family had been minor gentry, merchants and clergy for several hundred years.[2] However, the key factor in Hugh's early upbringing was his father's royal connection.

For fourteen years John Dalton, who had been ordained in 1865, was tutor to the two young princes, Eddy (who died in his twenties) and George (who later became George V). For three years, he acted as the princes' guardian on a training ship, the HMS *Bacchante*, cruising round the world. John Dalton remained close to the royal family for the rest of his life. In 1885 he was rewarded for his services by being appointed canon of St George's Chapel, Windsor and given the tenancy of a fine house in the chapel cloisters, a far cry from Mercy Bevin's humble cottage in rural Somerset. This was the home to which the middle-aged canon brought his young bride, Catherine.

Their son, Hugh, and four years later a daughter, Georgie, grew up at No. 4 Chapel Cloisters, in the shadow of the royal castle at Windsor. When he was four, Hugh went to a children's Christmas party at the castle. Queen Victoria passed slowly along the tables, saying some words to each child. When she reached Hugh, she said: 'What a lot of grapes you've got. I expect you'd like me to go away, so that you can eat them all.'

Hugh replied: 'Yes, Queen.'

Victoria turned to her lady in waiting and said: 'What a loud voice that child has, just like his father.'[3]

A version of this story later repeated by Tories and in the press went that the Queen had remarked: 'What a horrid little boy.' On another occasion, Dalton remembered the Prince of Wales, later Edward VII, coming to tea with his parents and him greedily snatching a muffin off the prince's plate. These stories suggest that Hugh was a spoilt, unruly child. Certainly, his sister, Georgie, found him an oppressive elder brother, and their relationship never became close.

When he was eight, Hugh was sent as a day boy to St George's Choir School. He was rejected for the choir, on the grounds that he had 'absolutely no ear'.[4] He did well at his studies but St George's was not equipped to prepare its pupils for scholarships to the top public schools. So when he was eleven he was sent away to Summer Fields, Oxford, an educational forcing house for upper-class boys. At Summer Fields, Hugh was often ill with asthma and bronchitis, and, though he excelled at mathematics, he was not considered an academic high flyer. However, he was put in for an Eton scholarship in the summer of 1901. He was placed seventeenth out of the seventy entered for the exam, a creditable performance but not good enough for a scholarship.

Dalton always regretted that he failed to get into College, where the scholarship boys were housed. In his autobiography he wrote: 'I would have found more mental stimulus and been a member of a more closely knit society.'[5] He did go to Eton, but as a fee-paying 'Oppidan'. Bad at games, physically lazy and coasting at his studies, he achieved little in his first few years at the school. The big event was a fire, which killed two boys and destroyed the house in which he boarded. Dalton's hair was singed and he 'smelt fire very easily for some time after that affair'.[6]

Dalton enjoyed his last year at Eton. He had been made captain of his house and delighted in the authority this gave him, telling one of his father's dinner parties that 'I have greater power in my house than Sir Edward Grey has in the Foreign Office'.[7] However, he was bitterly disappointed when he failed to get into Pop, the glamorous self-elected society of two dozen senior boys which set much of the style of the school. Being a member of Pop was the badge of honour for the socially ambitious Etonian. Dalton reacted against his exclusion by wearing pumps (reserved for members of Pop) when summoning boys to the headmaster's presence in his role as Head Master's Praeposter. By using his influence with his friends in Pop, he also managed to keep out one candidate 'whose election, since he was in my house, would have caused me local inconvenience and rivalry',[8] an early example of Dalton's love of political intrigue.

It would be wrong to conclude that Dalton got little out of Eton. He did well at mathematics, being one of the school's four Tomline Prizemen in 1906 and winning a closed exhibition to King's College, Cambridge at the end of the summer half. He also made his mark as a declaimer of poetry. 'He has a pleasant voice and spoke clearly and with dignity, although the dignity a little suggested the pulpit,' wrote the *Eton College Chronicle*.[9] Hugh had inherited not only his father's voice but also something of the canon's style as well.

As yet, there was little sign of the socialist rebel that Dalton was to become. Almost entirely sheltered from the reality of Edwardian England, he knew nothing of how his working-class contemporaries lived. Politically, he fancied himself as a Tory imperialist in the Joseph Chamberlain mode. As a leaving present, he gave his housemaster a big book about the Empire.

Dalton's four years at King's were to be the making of him. As he wrote in his autobiography, 'when I went up to King's in the autumn of 1906, it was as though the heavens had opened. A whole new world of persons, interests and emotions now spread before me and I advanced most eagerly into the very midst of it.'[10] Throwing himself enthusiastically into under-graduate life, Hugh became one of the acknowledged stars at Cambridge.

He made some close friends there, above all the poet Rupert Brooke, who died of blood poisoning in the Aegean during the First World War. On his first Sunday at King's, Dalton met Brooke on the steps of the provost's lodge. Brooke was handsome, charming and charismatic. His looks appealed to both sexes. Lytton Strachey, the future author of *Eminent Victorians* and a homosexual, wrote about him to Virginia Woolf: 'Whenever I began to feel dull, I would look at the yellow hair and pink cheeks of Rupert.'[11] Female undergraduates, especially Cambridge Fabians, also greatly admired Brooke. Dalton wrote in his memoirs: 'No Cambridge friendship of mine meant more to me than his, and the radiance of his memory still lights my path.'[12] According to his biographer, there is no evidence that Dalton ever had a sexual relationship with another man but there is little doubt that, throughout his life, his emotions were stirred by handsome young men and that Brooke was the first and the most enduring of his adorations. Though Dalton was no poet, he shared Brooke's passion for poetry. From early in their first term they became inseparable, in and out of each other's rooms all day and talking until late at night.

Together with some other undergraduates, they founded an intellectual and cultural society, called the Carbonari or Charcoal Burners after a nineteenth-century revolutionary group in Italy. The Carbonari met once a week to read papers and poetry to each other. Shortly after Brooke's death, Dalton described the impact of these meetings:

> Rupert and I and one or two others were generally the last to separate, and sometimes the dawn was in the sky before we got to bed . . . For we wanted, half passionately and half humorously, to get everything clear quickly. Hitherto, we had been too young to think, and soon we might be too busy, and ultimately we should be too old. The golden time was now.[13]

In another field of mutual interest, politics, it was Dalton who took the lead. At Cambridge in the first decade of the twentieth century, as at Oxford on the eve of the Second World War, the mood was to the left. The result of the January 1906 general election, which swept the Liberals to power with a large majority and brought into Parliament twenty-nine members of the recently formed Labour Representation Committee, had greatly stirred Cambridge undergraduates. Many joined socialist groups, above all the Fabians.

In January 1907 Dalton joined the Cambridge Fabians, later becoming president. By signing the 'Fabian basis', a statement of the society's principles, he declared himself a socialist. 'I exchanged Joseph Chamberlain for James Keir Hardie – and Sidney Webb,' he wrote.[14] In contrast to Clement Attlee, Dalton's conversion to socialism was not based on any first-hand experience of the poverty and inequality of Edwardian England. In part, it was an intellectual decision to support such Fabian objectives as the extinction of private property in land and the social management of industrial capital, as well as equal citizenship for men and women, then a hot issue. In part, becoming a socialist was a question of style and behaviour. Dalton loved the idea of belonging to a special group, the fashionable progressive vanguard represented by the Cambridge Fabians, the fastest-growing society at the university. It was also a way of cocking a snook at the conventional upper-class Etonians and the games-playing philistines whom Dalton much despised. His fellow King's man and record-breaking Olympic runner, Philip Baker (later Noel-Baker), commented about Dalton at this time: 'He half-deliberately said very socialist things in order to shock.'[15]

It was as a socialist spokesman at the Cambridge Union that Dalton emerged as a university figure. The undergraduate magazine, *Granta*, referred to him as 'Comrade Dalton' or 'Comrade Hugh'. He was developing a fluent speaking style, based on meticulous research but with his own patronising tone which infuriated his Cambridge Union opponents and was to enrage two generations of Tory MPs. In 1908, Rupert Brooke followed Dalton's example and joined the Cambridge Fabians, greatly adding to their social cachet. Together with Ben Keeling, the original organiser and first president of the society, and other university friends including James Strachey, Lytton's brother and some attractive women undergraduates from Girton and Newham, they took the national Fabian summer school by storm. Beatrice Webb was especially impressed by Dalton and noted in her diary that he was 'an accomplished ecclesiastical sort of person – a subtle wily man with a certain peculiar charm for those who are not put off by his mannerism'. In a letter to her sister, she presciently picked him out as a future politician.[16]

Dalton had become one of Cambridge's glitterati, but his academic achievements were less impressive. At the end of his third year, he got a third in part 1 of his mathematical Tripos. He switched to economics for his final year. This was a shrewd decision, because, though he failed narrowly to achieve a first, he was taught by two of the most distinguished economists of the age – A. C. Pigou, professor of political economy, whose work on welfare and inequality Dalton much admired, and John Maynard Keynes, who had recently returned to a fellowship at King's after a spell at the India Office. Dalton was impressed by Keynes's brilliance and his grasp of the real world.

Keynes thought well enough of Dalton to invite him to be a member of a group of undergraduate economists, the Political Economy Club, who read essays to each other. But, despite the King's connection, Dalton was never an intimate of Keynes, who did not rate him as intellectually first class. Thirty-five years later, when Keynes was Dalton's economic adviser at the Treasury, this attitude caused problems.

Dalton's interest in economics and its relevance to social issues such as poverty and inequality helped provide a way forward when he came down from Cambridge in 1910. At the same time as reading, though without much conviction, for the Bar, he enrolled at the London School of Economics, the Webbs' creation which had become the most important centre for economic studies outside Cambridge. In July 1911, he won the Hutchinson Research Studentship at the LSE, which gave him £100 a year, and he began work under Edwin Cannan on the distribution of wealth, focusing on the inefficiency of inequality. This research led to a series of articles, a thesis, which was published in 1920 as a book, *The Inequality of Incomes*, and finally a doctorate in the University of London. In 1913, as mentioned in Chapter 1, Dalton failed to land a full-time appointment in the LSE's Social Science Department, the job going to Attlee, whose practical experience in the East End told in his favour. The LSE made the right choice. Between 1911 and 1914, Dalton continued to concentrate his energies on becoming an academic economist.

In contrast to his time at Cambridge, Dalton was hardly involved in politics at all. After the Webbs' defeat over the minority report, the Fabian Society was on the defensive. As the Labour Party had as yet no individual membership, it offered little opportunity for middle-class potential recruits like Dalton. And, unlike Attlee, he was never attracted by the Independent Labour Party. He hinted in his memoirs that he was drawn to the Liberals, especially to the Lloyd George budget of 1909 and the National Insurance Act, though he rejected the idea of becoming a Liberal candidate, suggested to him by prominent figures in the party.[17]

In May 1914, Dalton married a Fabian, Ruth Fox, whom he had met at the LSE, where she was taking a degree in economics. Intellectually and politically they had much in common. Emotionally it was a somewhat ill-assorted marriage. Ruth was thought by some to be withdrawn and Hugh was more moved by handsome young men than women. A few days after he got back from his honeymoon, he found a letter awaiting him from Brooke, recently returned from a voyage to the South Seas. 'I am as free as wind on Thursday night. Are you? You can shelve your wife.'[18] Although the once inseparable pair had been growing apart as Brooke became a literary lion courted by the Bloomsbury set, Dalton immediately left his new wife to dine alone with his friend. It was the last time they were to meet.

Dalton was shaken and astonished by the outbreak of war. He was also angry. He wrote later: 'I do not believe that I was alone in feeling passionately in August, 1914, that the young generation in all the belligerent lands had been collectively betrayed.'[19] He was, above all, furious with Germany, which he felt bore an overwhelming burden of responsibility for the war. Like Attlee but unlike many ILP members, for example Herbert Morrison, he strongly believed that, after the war had started, it should be fought to the finish and that he should play his part in defeating the Germans. As the war dragged on, his anti-German feeling grew, as he blamed Germany for the deaths of so many of his Cambridge friends.

Early in 1915 Dalton was commissioned in the Army Service Corps, as part of the so-called 'Bantam' Division. Although he was well over 6 feet tall, all the other ranks were 'undersized', too small to be accepted in ordinary units. At the beginning of 1916, the division embarked for France. The Service Corps's role was to supply the front lines with food and equipment so, though Dalton could hear the guns, especially during the battle of the Somme, he was not directly involved in action.

In January 1917 Dalton was granted a transfer, at his own request, to the Royal Artillery and brought home for training. In June he was sent to Italy, and in August he was posted as senior subaltern to 302 Siege Battery on the Carso plateau, north of Trieste, and later to the Isonzo front. Dalton fell in love with Italy and the Italians. Here is his diary extract after the taking of Monte Santo, one of the Austrian strong points: 'Victory has an intoxicating quality in this bright clear atmosphere and among these mountains which it has perhaps nowhere else. All day there seemed to grow a great throbbing Triumph song of the Heroes – incomparable Italians, living and dead.'[20] Dalton described how on the conquered summit an Italian military band, conducted by Arturo Toscanini, played patriotic battle hymns to celebrate the victory, as the artillery exchanged thunderous bombardments.

In late October it was the Austrians' turn to advance. A massive attack was launched against the Italian 3rd Army. The Italian retreat, in which 302 Siege Battery took part, became a rout, as whole Italian regiments surrendered at the battle of Caporetto. In the headlong retreat, Dalton showed courage and initiative for which he was awarded the Italian bronze medal for valour, with a citation which recognised his 'contempt for danger' in successfully withdrawing his guns to safety. Dalton wrote that the medal made him feel both 'very proud and very humble'.[21] For some months afterwards, he was traumatised by the shock of the defeat at Caporetto. As he recovered, besides his intense hatred for the Germans and his love for the Italians, he became determined that, after the war was over, the energies of the young generation should be devoted to putting an end to war for ever.

After a short break home in January, where he met his baby daughter, Helen, for the first time, Dalton's 302 Battery was moved up to the Asiago plateau in support of British divisions. It withstood the last Austrian offensive in June and in October was moved again, to the river Piave for the final successful allied offensive. At 3 p.m. on 4 November an armistice came into force and all fighting ceased. Dalton's post-war book on the Italian campaign, *With British Guns in Italy*, ends with a note of hope: 'The soldier had done his duty, now let the statesmen do no less.'[22]

Like Attlee, Dalton had proved himself a brave and competent officer. The war had given a sharper focus both to his ideals and to his ambitions. He was well aware that the new political opening for the Labour Party back home could also provide opportunities for bright, self-confident, young middle-class socialists like him.

*

A key difference between the backgrounds of Hugh Dalton and Clement Attlee, on the one hand, and Stafford Cripps, on the other, was that Cripps was very rich. Richard Stafford Cripps was born on 24 April 1889, the fifth child of Alfred and Theresa Cripps, members of an exceptionally well-off, upwardly mobile Victorian family. Alfred (later Lord Parmoor) was a barrister who specialised in the then booming field of railway law: *Cripps on*

Compensation was the standard work. During his thirty years at the Bar, his average annual income was about £10,000, putting him among the top earners in the country.[23]

His wife, Theresa, was the sixth of the nine Potter girls. The year after Stafford was born her sister Beatrice married Sidney Webb and together their ideas helped prepare the Labour Party for government. The girls' father, Richard Potter, had made a fortune from the Crimean War by supplying both the British and French armies with wooden huts. The Potters had substantial homes in Gloucestershire, Monmouthshire, Westmorland and London, while Alfred Cripps had a London house in Elm Park Gardens, Chelsea and a country house, Parmoor, with 400 acres in the Chilterns.

When Stafford was four, his mother died suddenly, after a throat infection. She had doted on her child. Alfred noted in his diary: 'His mother thinks he has too great a brain development, and looks to him as the rising genius among her boys.'[24] When his wife died, Alfred not only wrote a memorial volume but also commissioned a portrait of Stafford sitting on her lap. Theresa had set out her wishes for the family, including the children's education: 'I should like them to be trained to be un-dogmatic and non-sectarian Christians, charitable to all churches and sects studying the precepts and actions of Christ as their example, taking their religious inspiration directly from the spirit of the New Testament.'[25]

Christianity was a central part of the Cripps family life, with morning and evening prayers and strict Sunday observance. Stafford was brought up to regard God as a friend and Christ as an exemplary hero, calling him to action. As he wrote in his diary when he was twenty-one, 'I can't conceive what Atheists, Agnostics, and other Doubters have in place of this feeling of absolute security, which is given by the knowledge of his care'.[26]

Contrary to conventional Victorian upper-class practice, Alfred assumed the main responsibility for bringing up his children, supervising their education and acting very much as their mentor. They were encouraged to express their opinions at mealtimes, even when they were challenging his views. Beatrice Webb noted that 'the children revel in high spirits and health'.[27] Another Potter sister, Mary Playne, invited the Cripps children every summer to her country house, Longfords in Gloucestershire. Stafford felt that, after his mother died, Mary virtually adopted him.

1. Alfred and Theresa Cripps with their
five children. Stafford is the youngest.
(Cripps family archive)

2. Clement Attlee in his first
term at preparatory school,
aged nine. He was excep-
tionally small for his age.
(Attlee family archive)

3. The self-confident
Hugh Dalton, also at
preparatory school,
aged eleven.
(Dalton family archive)

4. Herbert Morrison
at twelve, already with
his trademark quiff.
He left school two
years later. (Morrison
family archive)

5. Ernest Bevin,
already working aged
fourteen, shown here
in his Sunday best.
(Bevin family archive)

6. Attlee had a 'good' war. Wounded twice, he was a competent officer and ended up as major. (Attlee family archive)

7. Dalton in Alpine uniform. He served as an artillery officer in Italy and was awarded the Italian bronze medal for valour. (Dalton family archive)

8. Cripps as an ambulance driver in 1914. From 1915 to 1917 he helped manage one of Britain's biggest munitions factories until his health broke down. (Cripps family archive)

9. Bevin (*far left*) in 1925, when general secretary of the Transport and General Workers' Union, shown with other union leaders. (Bettmann/Corbis)

10. Morrison in 1927, as leader of the Labour opposition on London County Council. The next year the Labour Prime Minister, Ramsay MacDonald, appointed him transport minister. (Hulton-Deutsch Collection/Corbis)

11. Major Attlee, shown here after his re-election as MP for Limehouse in 1923. (PA Photos)

12. Attlee (*right*), described by Dalton as 'a little mouse', wins the 1935 Labour
leadership contest, following George Lansbury's resignation.
He is congratulated by his deputy, Arthur Greenwood. (TopFoto)

13. A Labour deputation (*left to right* TUC general secretary Walter Citrine,
Morrison and Dalton) goes to see Prime Minister Neville Chamberlain at the
time of the Munich crisis, 1938. (Hulton-Deutsch Collection/Corbis)

14. In 1940, at a time of supreme national crisis, Labour, having helped bring down the Chamberlain government, joined Winston Churchill's War Cabinet. Attlee (*front row, second right*) was Lord Privy Seal and de facto deputy to Churchill, Bevin (*back row, second left*) minister of labour and national service, and Greenwood (*back row, far left*) minister without portfolio. (Topham Picturepoint)

15. Churchill addresses the crowds on VE Day. Bevin (*second left*) was the most powerful minister in the War Cabinet and Morrison (*far right*) was a highly effective Home Secretary. (Central Press/Hulton Archive/Getty Images)

16. Bevin lays down the law at his Central Wandsworth Labour Party
adoption meeting for the 1945 general election. (Popperfoto/Getty Images)

17. Morrison, one of the architects
of Labour's landslide victory, waves
triumphantly after being elected
MP for Lewisham. (Hulton-
Deutsch Collection/Corbis)

18. Even Attlee, with his wife Vi by his
side, smiles after being returned at
Limehouse. (Bettmann/Corbis)

19. The senior members of the new Labour government, with the Cabinet in the first two rows. It is noticeable that the brave new world is being ushered in by a group largely comprising elderly men. The sole woman is Ellen Wilkinson, minister of education. (Fox Photos/Getty Images)

20. The three leading figures of the Labour Party are clearly delighted by their victory. However, behind the scenes Morrison is calling for a fresh leadership election with a view to taking over from Attlee. (Radio Times Hulton)

21. Attlee joins Harry S. Truman and Joseph Stalin at the Potsdam conference. Bevin, the new foreign secretary, is standing behind Truman. Neither Stalin nor Truman (nor even Attlee himself) expected Attlee to be replacing Churchill at the conference. (Ullstein Bild/TopFoto)

22. The crucial partnership in Attlee's Cabinet is illustrated by this photograph of him and Bevin at the first meeting of the United Nations General Assembly, London, January 1946. (Hulton-Deutsch Collection/Corbis)

23. The ebullient Dalton leaves Downing Street to present his 1946 Budget. Michael Foot wrote: 'Dalton on the crest of the wave . . . had the panache which the government so much needed.' (PA Photos)

24. Bevin looks equally cheerful as he poses with dominion foreign ministers at the British embassy in Moscow, January 1946. In reality, he was increasingly depressed by Soviet intransigence. (Bettmann/Corbis)

Encouraged by his father, brothers and sisters, and by the Crippses' governess, Mary Marshall, Stafford was a precocious boy. By the age of eight he read history books and spoke and wrote to his father in French. He also organised a shop where he sold tea to his father's guests. He was good with his hands, building a boat with his brother Leonard, constructing underground houses and bridging the pond at Parmoor. He was called 'Dad' at home because, according to his eldest brother, Freddie, he was fond of giving advice to the elder members of the family. 'I can see him now sitting up in bed, propped up with pillows, in fullest command of the situation.'[28]

Like Attlee and Dalton, Cripps was sent away to preparatory school, first at Reigate in Surrey, then, as he seemed likely to surpass Leonard, to another prep school at Rottingdean on the Sussex coast before going on in 1901, like his father and grandfather, to the most academic of English public schools, Winchester College.

Cripps did not win a scholarship to Winchester. Indeed, there is no evidence that he tried for one. But he was an unqualified success at the school, being both exceptionally able at his studies and good at games, especially Winchester football, soccer and racquets. He was already the youngest member of the top division, when at sixteen he decided to specialise in chemistry (science had only recently been given equal status to classics in the school curriculum). The headmaster, H. M. Burge, who had been responsible for upgrading science, wrote to Alfred Cripps about Stafford's prospects: 'I have an encouraging report about your boy's work . . . The point is that the boy is developing well and has an intelligent and independent interest in his subject . . . He is a thoroughly good fellow.'[29]

In 1907 Cripps won a New College scholarship in chemistry on the first occasion that it had been offered for this subject. But instead of accepting the award at his father's and his brother's old college, he confidently turned it down in favour of a place at University College London. The examiners for the New College scholarship had been so impressed by his papers that they sent them to Sir William Ramsey, professor of chemistry at UCL, who promptly decided to appropriate the promising Wykehamist student for his own team.

Cripps was an outstanding undergraduate at UCL. He found studying chemistry under Ramsey, who had already won a Nobel Prize for his work on inert gases, immensely exciting. While still a student he took part in Ramsey's experiments and co-authored a paper on gas densities which was published by the Royal Society in 1912. It is clear that, like his brother-in-law Jack Egerton, who married Stafford's sister, Ruth, Cripps could have had a brilliant scientific career. He was also elected president of the UCL Union, mainly because he was good at organising social events. But unlike Dalton, he showed little interest in politics. If he had any political views, he was probably, like his father, a Conservative.

However, in January 1910 a crucial event occurred in Cripps's life – he met Isobel Swithinbank. He was helping his father, who was standing as a Conservative for the Wycombe division of Buckinghamshire in the general election. Alfred Cripps had already stood twice as a Conservative & Unionist candidate, though both times he had failed to win. Beatrice Webb described him as a 'Conservative opportunist'. He had been a Liberal as a young man but was now a Conservative and ambitious enough to be prepared to stand for a third seat, this time against a sitting Liberal MP. Alfred won by an unexpectedly decisive margin of 2,556.

A week before the count, Stafford had been struck by the looks of a tall, fair-haired young girl as she prepared election leaflets for his father. Isobel Swithinbank was the daughter of a leading local Conservative, Commander Harold Swithinbank, and a prospective heiress to a substantial fortune derived from her grandfather, J. C. Eno of Eno's Fruit Salts. Following up this initial sighting, Stafford persuaded Ruth to invite Isobel to a house party at Parmoor for the Henley regatta. Their meeting was clearly a success, for it was followed up by an invitation to Isobel from Ruth to stay at the Crippses' London house, where the young couple met again. They agreed to correspond over the summer while Stafford was away in Hamburg learning German and after Christmas to make up a skiing party at Klosters in Switzerland with Leonard, Ruth and Jack Egerton, with Ethel Slocock, a family friend, acting as chaperone.

A few days after their arrival in Switzerland, Stafford proposed and Isobel accepted. Together with their chaperone, they returned to England to explain their plans to their surprised parents. Isobel was not yet twenty, Stafford was twenty-one. Isobel had no training of any sort. More relevant for an Edwardian upper-class marriage was that Stafford had not yet completed his studies and had little prospect, if he stuck to chemistry, of being able to keep his bride in the style which she would expect.

Polite haggling between the two fathers followed, with most of the cards in Commander Swithinbank's hands. Stafford's letter to Isobel of 4 May 1911 gives the flavour: 'I quite agree with your father, who thinks probably that Pa should give me as much as you get.'[30] Swithinbank also had firm ideas about Cripps's choice of a profession. There could be no question of his becoming an academic chemist. If Cripps was to provide a 'comfortable house for his future wife', then he should either go into business or follow his father's footsteps by making a career at the Bar, with the possibility eventually of going into politics (presumably as a Conservative).[31] The two fathers came to an amicable arrangement. Alfred Cripps was to match the £500 a year which Isobel was to receive on her marriage with a similar annual sum for his son.

Following his first meeting with Isobel, Stafford had begun to read for the Bar. Although for a time he attempted to keep up his scientific studies as well, he had to accept a change of profession if he was to get the agreement of the two fathers to the marriage. Stafford and Isobel's wedding followed on 12 July 1911 at Denham church in Buckinghamshire.

The couple's early married life was relatively uneventful and certainly not political. They settled down at Fernacres Cottage, Fulmer, Buckinghamshire, a substantial property with nine bedrooms and 3½ acres of land. Their first child, John, was born in May 1912 and their second, Diana, in September 1913. Cripps passed his Bar exams with ease in the summer of 1912 and in the autumn entered his father's chambers in the Middle Temple. But, like most young barristers, he found briefs hard to come by. However, by 1914, he was beginning to get some work, including a brief from the Great Western Railway. He had also taken over his father's chambers, following Alfred's elevation to the peerage and promotion to the Judicial Committee of the Privy Council (which meant retiring from the Bar).

When war came, his three brothers joined the armed forces, but Stafford did not. He was not a conscientious objector. His own explanation was: 'I was at the time under medical treatment and, being married, did not think of trying for the Army, as at that time married men were not wanted.' It is true that his digestive problems, which were to plague the rest of his life, had forced him to 'lie up for a month' during the summer of 1914 and might have led him to be turned down by the Army doctors. It is also true that the authorities were encouraging single men to enlist before married men, though Stafford's brother Leonard, who was also recently married, gave up his job and rejoined his old regiment, the 4th Hussars.

However, Cripps did want to make a contribution to the war effort. Together with Jack Egerton, he crossed to France in October to deliver comforts to the troops, and joined the British Red Cross Society (BRCS). For nearly a year he drove ambulances, ferrying wounded soldiers to the port of Boulogne, from where they were evacuated back to Britain. Isobel persuaded her grandfather to donate a 2-ton lorry to the Red Cross to carry hospital supplies. Stafford wrote to Isobel: 'No one who was not there can conceive how dependent the Army were on the BRCS in those early days.' The most arduous job was coal carting: 'On dry hot July days tipping sacks of dusty coal in a small cellar was no joke.'[32]

At the end of May, following the use of gas by the Germans at Ypres, Cripps received an order: 'Hold yourself in readiness to proceed to St Omer at any time as a chemist in connection with their poisonous gases.'[33] He immediately wangled himself a week's leave in England (he had had no leave since arriving in France) but on returning to Boulogne heard no more about the chemical job. However, in September 1915, back home once more on leave, he heard from Egerton, who was now working at the Ministry of Munitions, that chemists were required in the ministry. Cripps applied for a job and, backed by references from Sir William Ramsey, Egerton and his father, was taken on.

After initial training at Waltham Abbey, where he learnt about the manufacture of gun cotton and tetryl, Cripps was sent to Queensferry in Flintshire, to a vast new munitions factory employing more than 7,000 women, as assistant to the factory superintendent, Colonel Waring. For the first time, Cripps found himself in a responsible managerial job. Given the stalemate at the front, there was continuing pressure on the factory to increase output and Cripps worked between twelve and fourteen hours every day, including Sundays, reaching a climax on Christmas Day, when he worked twenty hours. At the end of January 1916, Waring took ten weeks' sick leave, so Cripps took charge. Production increased but, after six weeks, he also had a breakdown from which he took four months to recover. According to Waring, Cripps's breakdown was the direct consequence of his overwork.

During his absence, the Treasury repudiated Cripps's recent promotion to assistant superintendent and refused to give him an increase in salary. In January 1917 Cripps broke down again and was diagnosed as suffering from colitis, an inflammation of the colon. He carried on working at Queensferry until June 1917, when he went into a nursing home. On 1 September his doctors told him that 'it was useless my trying to work again at Queensferry for at least a year as I could only do light work'.[34] Cripps immediately resigned, thus effectively ending his war work.

For the rest of the war, he was an invalid, living with his family in Gloucestershire. In his diary entry for 5 October 1918, he wrote: 'We have lived out of doors as much as possible and have spent nearly the whole of the time in the garden or the field . . . We have started farming in a small way with chickens, pigs, rabbits, cows, bees and hope that the experience will prove of value later on.'[35]

Cripps's illness gave him time to reflect on his political position. Before the war he had been an unreflecting Conservative with only the occasional twinge of social conscience, as when he wrote to Isobel in 1911: 'Coming home this evening, I saw two poor shivering people . . . That's the sort of thing that makes one feel a socialist.'[36] Now, during the last year of the war, he began to shift politically leftwards. 'All my bias at the present moment is towards the policy of the Labour Party,' he noted in his diary.[37]

Through the Webbs he had met Arthur Henderson, the general secretary of the Labour Party and, with Sidney Webb, the architect of its new constitution and its new programme *Labour and the New Social Order*. Cripps was suspicious of the role of trade unions in the party but welcomed its opening up to individual members and especially the new emphasis on 'brain workers': 'The Labour Party since they have decided to admit "brain-workers" have become the representatives of all those who work for their living and in this respect I feel drawn towards them.'[38]

The greatest influence on Cripps remained his father. The effect of the war was to make Lord Parmoor, who had started off as a Liberal and then been elected to Parliament as a Conservative Unionist, more sympathetic to Labour. The war was the key factor: in contrast to his son, Parmoor was strongly anti-war and in 1915 backed calls for a League of Nations. In May 1917, he presided over the initial meeting of the League of Free Nations Association at Central Hall, Westminster and in 1918 was, with two leading Labour figures, Henderson and George Lansbury, a co-signatory of a League of Nations manifesto. In this and other initiatives promoting international conciliation, Parmoor worked closely with fellow Christians, many of whom had joined or were soon to join the Labour Party. After the war, a second marriage to Marian Ellis, daughter of a Quaker MP, and his work with the World Council for Promoting International Friendship through the Churches led him into the new internationally minded Labour Party and the first Labour Cabinet of 1924 as Lord President of the Council.

As the war ended, Cripps was far more sympathetic to Labour than before. But, in contrast to Attlee, Morrison, Dalton and even Bevin, his main priority was to establish himself in his profession rather than in politics. If he was to provide for his wife and growing family in the way which they thought appropriate, then he had to become a really successful lawyer. At the end of the war, the law, not politics, came first.

4

1919–31: Two minority governments, the general strike and a crisis

The decade after the end of the First World War was crucial to the development of the Labour Party – and to the tortoise and hares of this book. Assisted by the expansion of the franchise, Labour now replaced the Liberals as the main opposition party and, under the charismatic leadership of Ramsay MacDonald, twice formed a minority government – in 1924 and 1929. Two other events in this period – the 1926 general strike and especially the 1931 crisis – also had a major impact.

During the 1920s, Clement Attlee, Herbert Morrison and Hugh Dalton were elected as MPs and established reputations as rising Labour politicians. Stafford Cripps did not enter Parliament until January 1931 and then only after MacDonald had recognised his legal brilliance by making him solicitor general. Ernest Bevin was the first of the five to stand for Parliament as Labour candidate for Bristol Central in the 1918 general election, in which the Lloyd George coalition gained an overwhelming victory and Labour won only fifty-seven seats. Bevin was heavily defeated and spent the 1920s building up the Transport and General Workers' Union (which included Bevin's dockers' union) into the biggest in the country, developing the influence of the TUC and becoming the most prominent trade union leader in Britain, which put him in a different league from the other four.

Crucial to the careers of Attlee, Dalton and Cripps were the 1918 Henderson reforms, which opened up local Labour parties to individual membership and enabled professional-class recruits to join the Labour Party directly rather than attaching themselves to socialist groups such as the

Independent Labour Party and the Fabian Society. It became easier for middle-class parliamentary candidates of the calibre of Attlee and Dalton to get themselves selected for winnable seats. It was to Morrison's credit that, as secretary of the London Labour Party, he saw the point of bringing lawyers, accountants and doctors into the party. It was he who persuaded Cripps, then the youngest King's Counsel in the country, to join the Labour Party and a London constituency to accept him as parliamentary candidate (but it was for Bristol East that Cripps was elected to Parliament in a January 1931 by-election).

Morrison and Attlee both started politics in local government, though Morrison always played a bigger role than Attlee. As secretary of the London Labour Party, Morrison masterminded the Labour campaign for the March 1919 London County Council (LCC) election, in which the party won fifteen seats. Attlee, whose job as lecturer at the London School of Economics left him plenty of spare time, stood for one of the Limehouse seats and was only narrowly defeated. However, he avoided blame for the failure and was soon after selected as parliamentary candidate for Limehouse. He also agreed to become campaign manager for Stepney Labour Party in the November borough elections. Labour, which had never before held even a single seat, won a great victory in Stepney, gaining forty out of sixty council seats. The new ruling majority immediately asked Attlee to become mayor, in part because he was neither Jewish nor Catholic (the two predominant factions in the borough) and in part because 'Major' Attlee was 'an officer and a gentleman' and therefore considered somewhat above the party battle, even by the Tories.

He proved an outstanding mayor. Honing his diplomatic skills, he acted as an arbiter between Jewish and Catholic party members. He was able to spearhead a new approach by the council, which set up advice bureaux to inform tenants about their rights, forced slum landlords to repair their properties, appointed health visitors and set up antenatal clinics, thus reducing the infant mortality rate.

The most intractable issue was growing unemployment. Stepney did its best to provide work for unemployed ex-soldiers but local councils needed the assistance of central government if they were to offer long-term jobs. So, as chairman of the newly formed Association of London Labour Mayors,

Attlee led a deputation, backed up by a march of large numbers of unemployed, to 10 Downing Street. The Prime Minister, David Lloyd George, had little to offer the mayors and there was a threat of disorder. However, Major Attlee, stick in hand, promptly marched the Stepney contingent back to the East End, thus 'saving some broken heads'.[1]

Labour's strong showing throughout London in the borough elections, when the party won a majority or became the leading party in sixteen out of the twenty-eight boroughs, brought Morrison much credit. Ten months later, following Attlee's example, he was asked to become mayor of Hackney, where Labour had a majority of only two and the sitting mayor, a respected local businessman, had died. Despite the hostility of the local Tories and his refusal to wear the scarlet mayoral robes, he quickly won a reputation for calm, good-humoured authority, emerging as the real leader of the Labour Party on Hackney Council. The Conservative opposition concentrated their fire on him, while the militant minority on the Labour group attacked him for his opposition to 'direct action'.

Morrison's opposition to direct action brought him into conflict with Poplar Council, which, under the leadership of the ILP left-winger George Lansbury, refused to pay the borough's precepts, legally required by the LCC and the Metropolitan Police, on the grounds that the money should go to the unemployed. Morrison argued that refusing to pay the precepts would not only hold back public services to the less well off such as education, school meals and medical treatment but would risk reprisals by the government, including the appointment of commissioners to run the council and imprisonment of the councillors. In his role as secretary of the London Labour Party, he advised other Labour councils not to follow Poplar's example.

Morrison clashed with Attlee over 'Poplarism'. It was not so much that Attlee supported Poplar's tactics. It was rather that he deplored the vehemence of Morrison's public attack on Lansbury, his East End friend. In his turn, Morrison resented 'Major C. R. Attlee . . . delivering at me a needle-pointed and rather superior lecture, in the manner of major-to-private' at the next London Labour Party conference.[2] Attlee had already fallen out with Morrison in 1919 after the LCC elections, when, according to Attlee, Morrison had approached him to ask him to be an alderman.

Attlee had agreed, only to hear that a City financier friend of Morrison had been chosen. In Attlee's eyes, Morrison had revealed himself as 'not being straight';[3] early on, Attlee marked Morrison's card.

However, notwithstanding Attlee's misgivings about Morrison's character, his reputation as the architect of Labour's advance in London rapidly increased. In 1920 he was elected at his first attempt to a constituency party seat on Labour's National Executive Committee. He lost his seat the following year but promptly regained it in 1922 and remained on the NEC for the next thirty years. In 1922 Morrison was elected to the LCC as the member for Woolwich East, in 1923 he was appointed chief whip and in 1925 he became Labour leader on the council and leader of the opposition. He proved a brilliant leader and a good administrator, outstanding in debate and with shrewd political judgement.

However, it was Attlee who was the first to be elected to Parliament, at the general election of 1922. That year his life had already changed when he married Violet Millar, sister of a Treasury friend of his brother Tom. Clement had got to know Violet during a long holiday in Italy with the Millars in the summer of 1921; he proposed and was accepted only two weeks after their return to England. Vi was thirteen years younger than her 38-year-old husband, and Clement was 'mad as a March hare with joy'[4] when she agreed to marry him. It was to be a highly successful marriage, giving both partners a new strength and security. Vi was little interested in her husband's politics, but he did not mind, seeming to prefer a wife who concentrated on looking after their house and children (they were to have four). On his marriage, Attlee moved from Limehouse to set up home with his bride in Woodford Green, a middle-class suburb only 5 miles by rail from the East End.

In October 1922 the Lloyd George coalition broke up. A general election was held on 15 November. Attlee fought a vigorous campaign in Limehouse against the sitting MP, a well-liked local Liberal businessman (who was supported by the Conservatives). Attlee was not an inspiring speaker but, with the assistance of an energetic young agent, John Beckett, a yellow two-seater car hired for the occasion and a hard-hitting and pithy election address, he succeeded in arousing the interest of the voters. His promise to voters was as follows:

If you return me to Parliament to represent the people among whom I have lived and worked for the last seventeen years, I shall carry the message that they are sick and tired of the injustice which condemns them to toil long hours for low wages, to live in poverty and squalor without the certainty of where the next meal is to come from, and to see their children doomed to endure the same conditions. I shall claim that all shall enjoy the wealth that all produce.[5]

Attlee was returned to Parliament with a majority of 1,899. A horse and cart carried him in triumph through the cheering streets of Limehouse.

At Westminster, he was one of 142 Labour MPs. The Conservatives had won 344 seats, a majority of 73 over all other parties. But Labour was now clearly the main opposition party (the Liberals, split between the supporters of Lloyd George and Asquith, only mustered 115 seats) and had been greatly strengthened in Parliament by the election of leading party figures such as Ramsay MacDonald, Philip Snowden and Sidney Webb. The composition of the Parliamentary Labour Party had changed markedly. In 1918 it had been overwhelmingly trade unionist. In 1922, thirty-two MPs were sponsored by the ILP, while as many as 100 were ILP members (though a number of ILP members were also trade unionists). Both in terms of class composition and geographical spread, the Labour Party was beginning to become a more national party.[6]

The first task of the new PLP was to elect a chairman or leader. The chairman of the PLP in the last parliament had been J. R. Clynes, a competent but uncharismatic trade unionist. Arthur Henderson, who might well have been chosen as his successor, had failed to hold his seat. MacDonald, the anti-war champion and darling of the ILP left, was the obvious alternative. A private meeting of the ILP, attended by Attlee, decided to nominate MacDonald. At the subsequent PLP meeting of 21 November, Attlee supported MacDonald, who narrowly defeated Clynes for the chairmanship. He later wrote: 'Like others, I lived to regret that vote.'[7] However, at the time, despite his own stance, he admired MacDonald for his courage in opposing the war. In any case, in the circumstances of the 1920s with the Liberals still breathing down Labour's neck and Lloyd George waiting in the wings, MacDonald was almost certainly the best choice. No other Labour leader, even including Henderson, would have been nearly as effective as the handsome, eloquent and persuasive MacDonald in broadening the party's appeal and promoting it as the alternative government to the Conservatives.

Attlee was rewarded for his support by being appointed one of MacDonald's two parliamentary private secretaries. The other was Jack Lawson, the miner from Chester-le-Street, County Durham whom Attlee was later to make secretary of state for war in his 1945 government. MacDonald's choice of Attlee was a shrewd move, as he combined membership of the left-wing ILP with an impressive war record. In his new post, Attlee was able to observe MacDonald's rhetorical skills at first hand, though he was less impressed by his leader's habit of privately disparaging his parliamentary colleagues in front of him. He later commented: 'I thought it was quite wrong. I was only his P.P.S.'[8]

He soon made his maiden speech. Coming into the chamber after supper during the debate on the King's Speech, he found that the chief whip wanted a fresh Labour speaker, following a succession of Clydesiders complaining about unemployment in Scotland. On his debut, Attlee naturally decided to concentrate on the big issue in his constituency – unemployment. But his tone was far less strident than the Clydesiders'. He picked up one of the themes of the government programme, waste, and used it to describe unemployment: 'There is one particular waste that is never mentioned, and that is the waste of the manpower of this nation.' He referred with approval to the speech of the Tory MP Nancy Astor, one of the first women in Parliament, agreed with her that housing was crucial to the well-being of the nation and underlined the contribution that the unemployed, many of them building workers, might make to the solution of the housing problem. He concluded by arguing that if, during the war, the government was able to find employment for everyone, then it could also do the same in peacetime:

> It is possible for the government, by methods of taxation and by other methods, to take hold of that purchasing power, and to say that, exactly as they told manufacturers and workers that they must turn out shells and munitions of all sort to support the fighting men, so they must turn out houses and necessities for those who are making the country a country of peace.[9]

Without being eloquent, it was, like most of Attlee's speeches, a competent performance.

*

The 1922 parliament lasted no more than a year. In November 1923 the Conservative Prime Minister, Stanley Baldwin, on the grounds of seeking a mandate for protection (which he saw as the answer to unemployment), called a general election for 6 December. Baldwin's gamble failed. The Tories lost eighty-six seats and their overall majority. The Liberals, this time united, won 158 seats but Labour, with 191, was ahead of them. Attlee increased his majority to 6,185 and Morrison now became an MP.

In Morrison's autobiography, the relevant chapter is entitled 'Pushed into Parliament'. According to him, the London district organiser, R. T. Windsor, came to see him at his home in Clapton to try and persuade him to stand for Hackney South. Morrison apparently told Windsor that he had no parliamentary ambitions and wanted to devote himself to the London Labour Party and to local government, but eventually he allowed himself to be persuaded to put his name forward. What Morrison's account does not reveal is that he had discussed the possibility of standing for Labour at the Hackney South by-election of 1922, following the imprisonment of the former MP, Horatio Bottomley, for embezzlement, and only withdrew when he found that he did not have sufficient support in the Hackney South party. Morrison was more enthusiastic about getting into Parliament than he subsequently claimed.

In November 1923 the Hackney South Labour Party adopted Morrison as its parliamentary candidate. As one might expect, he fought an energetic election campaign, but he was still surprised to win the seat with a majority of 2,821 in a three-cornered fight. He defeated two former army officers, the Tory Captain Clifford Erskine-Bolst and the Liberal Captain George Garro-Jones.

When Parliament met on 8 January 1924, the political world was agog with excitement. Clearly the Conservatives had lost their majority but, with 258 members, they were still comfortably the largest party. Baldwin was entitled to test the resolve of Labour and the Liberals, both of whom had gained seats in the election. Winston Churchill, who had been defeated as

Liberal candidate for Leicester West, overexcitedly proclaimed that the election of a Labour government would be a 'national misfortune such as has usually befallen a great state only on the morrow of defeat in war'. But the Liberal leader, Herbert Asquith, told his followers that 'if a Labour government is ever to be tried in this country, as it will be sooner or later, it could hardly be tried under safer conditions'[10] and made it clear that his party would not join with the Tories to keep Labour out. A few days earlier, at a dinner with the Webbs, the 'big six' of Labour's first generation of leaders (J. H. Thomas, MacDonald, Snowden, Henderson, Clynes and Webb) agreed that, if the opportunity arose, Labour should take office as a minority administration.

On 21 January, Baldwin's government was defeated on its programme in the Commons and the next day George V asked MacDonald to form the first Labour government. MacDonald became Prime Minister and Foreign Secretary and Snowden Chancellor of the Exchequer. Attlee's comment was to the point: 'The electors at the time needed to see a Labour government in being, if they were to appreciate that Labour was now the alternative to a Conservative administration. Refusal on our part to accept responsibility might have given a new lease of life to the Liberal Party.'[11] He became under-secretary to the War Office, an appointment which was welcomed by the Tory paper the *Morning Post*: 'For the War Office, Major Attlee has the recommendation of excellent war service. He was not . . . a conscientious objector.'[12] Attlee, who had hopes of being made chancellor of the Duchy of Lancaster (presumably as a result of hints from MacDonald), was somewhat disappointed with his new post, though he grew to enjoy seeing Army leaders whom he had met during the war.

Morrison, who was told by Thomas that he was going to be minister of transport, was also disappointed, even though, as a new MP, he was not entitled to expect a job. Like Attlee in the previous parliament, he was asked by the Labour whips to speak during the debate on the King's speech. Normally an excellent speaker, Morrison was unprepared and made a rambling and overlong speech, in which, contrary to the conventions governing maiden speeches, he was abusive of his political opponents. A further custom is that the member who follows a maiden speaker is expected to offer fulsome congratulations. Austen Hopkinson from the government benches made the briefest of mentions of Morrison's speech, merely remarking that 'he may take the usual conventional compliment as paid'. Later that evening, Morrison heard a Tory member say woundingly of his speech that it was 'the worst [maiden speech] since Disraeli's'.[13] It was perhaps some comfort to him that Disraeli, despite being howled down in gales of laughter, was twice Prime Minister.

He told the Hackney press: 'Parliament is a very funny place, and the more I see of it the more I admire the Hackney Borough Council.' Morrison's problem was that he had been used to being in control at the London Labour Party and on Hackney Council. Now he was a mere backbencher, expected to support the government on the floor of the Commons and in the lobbies. However, on local government matters, especially the London Traffic Bill, he rapidly acquired a reputation for his mastery of detail and grasp of procedure. He also made a good speech in the censure debate on the attorney general, Sir Patrick Hastings.

It was this debate which brought down MacDonald's 1924 Labour government. The Tories and Liberals accused MacDonald of exerting unconstitutional pressure to make the attorney general withdraw the prosecution of the acting editor of the communist *Workers' Weekly* on a charge of incitement to mutiny. The Conservatives put down a censure motion, while the Liberals put down a less severe amendment, calling for the setting up of a select committee to look into the matter. Hastings made a skilful contribution, in which he showed that, though he had, as was normal on such a political matter, consulted the Cabinet, the decision both to prosecute and to withdraw prosecution was made by him. However, MacDonald had to apologise for giving a misleading answer to a question about his involvement in the withdrawal. He also said that, if either the censure motion or the amendment were carried, the government would call an election. At the end of the debate, Baldwin announced that the Tories would support the Liberal amendment, which was then carried by 364 votes to 198. The next day, MacDonald asked the King for a dissolution.

Despite the Labour government's creditable performance in foreign relations and in aspects of domestic affairs, especially housing, the 1924 election was dominated by the alleged threat from the USSR and international communism. The Tories concentrated their attack on the government's recognition of the Soviet Union and the subsequent treaties between the two countries, mendaciously claiming that Labour was under the thumb of the Soviets.

A few days before the poll, hearing that the *Daily Mail* was splashing the story the next day, the Foreign Office published the so-called 'Zinoviev letter', apparently written by the chairman of the Communist Party of Great Britain and praising MacDonald's entente with the Soviet Union as a step towards revolution and calling upon British communists to set up cells in the armed forces. In 1999, an official inquiry by the British Foreign Office chief historian concluded that the letter had been forged by elements of the British secret service based in Riga and planted on the Foreign Office, possibly with the connivance of Conservative Central Office. MacDonald suspected the letter was a forgery but, partly because he could not be certain, unwisely delayed a statement until two days before the poll. The Tories gained 155 seats, giving them 419 MPs; though its vote went up, Labour lost 40 seats and finished up with 151; while the Liberals, whose successful amendment had precipitated the election, were reduced to a rump of 40 seats, a good example of turkeys voting for Christmas.

Despite the Zinoviev letter and the intervention of a Liberal candidate, Attlee easily held his Limehouse seat, his majority falling by only 164 votes. Morrison was opposed by a single Liberal candidate, and went down to defeat by 1,764 votes. He found audiences at meetings 'attentive, orderly, but much too subdued'[14] and, though he did not get any questions about the Soviet Union or the Zinoviev letter, he had a strong premonition that he would be defeated. Dalton, standing for the Tory seat of Peckham, gained it for Labour against the tide.

Between March 1922 and October 1924, Dalton had stood five times for Parliament and it was only at his fifth attempt that he was successful. He was chosen for Peckham at the last moment, when the prospective Labour candidate withdrew after a stroke. After a rowdy and strenuous campaign in which he canvassed every afternoon and spoke at meetings every night, Dalton won a three-cornered fight with a 147-vote majority over the Conservative candidate after a recount. He wrote in his diary: 'A strange sensation, this victory at last, while others are falling at the touch of the Zinoviev letter.'[15]

Paradoxically, the frustrating delay in entering Parliament may have worked to Dalton's advantage. Though in the unfamiliar and unstable three-party politics of the 1920s, any seat could appear winnable, particularly to someone who, like Dalton, was by temperament an optimist, in his more sober moments he realised that constituencies such as Cambridge, Maidstone or Holland with Boston, which he had fought, were at best Tory marginals, only contested by Labour for propaganda purposes. As Dalton well understood, he acquired merit with party headquarters by taking on the more difficult seats with his characteristic enthusiasm, energy and verve.

In the meantime, he was able to develop his career as a professional economist (in 1920 he was appointed Cassell Reader at the LSE) and to build up a reputation within the Labour Party as a professional 'expert' to whom party leaders such as Henderson and Snowden could turn for advice and assistance. The idea for a capital levy, which Labour put forward at the 1922 election, was largely devised by Dalton. Dalton's unusual combination of political eloquence and economic expertise made him, as Beatrice Webb noted in her diary,[16] a considerable asset to the PLP, so much so that by the end of his first parliamentary session he had been elected to its executive, a position which Attlee was not to achieve until the 1930s. An able 'hare', Dalton was rapidly making up for lost time. (His personal life, however, was blighted by the tragic death of his four-year-old daughter.)

*

The downfall of the first Labour government and the party's subsequent defeat in the 1924 general election led to fierce criticism of the parliamentary leadership, and especially of Ramsay MacDonald. Ernest Bevin, now the trade unions' coming man, would have liked to see MacDonald replaced, preferably by Arthur Henderson, but Henderson refused to run against MacDonald. At the 1925 Labour conference, Bevin, who had led two successful strikes during the life of the MacDonald government, moved a resolution calling on the party not to accept office again as a minority government. He declared:

> If I were in Parliament and called upon to take office and represent a great movement like ours, I would not accept it unless, when I spoke to the

representatives of other nations or addressed our own people, I was able to speak with the power which rested on the knowledge that I had a majority behind me both inside the House and outside in the nation.[17]

Bevin's motion was heavily defeated. That it was moved at all and by a leading trade unionist was an indication of a tide of opinion away from politics towards direct industrial action.

The coal industry was in crisis. The decision in April 1925 by the new Conservative Chancellor, Winston Churchill, to return to the gold standard at the pre-war parity of $4.86 to the pound immediately raised the export price of coal by 10 per cent. This led the coal owners to demand drastic cuts in miners' wages and a longer working day. The miners called on the General Council of the TUC for assistance and, with the help of the rail-waymen, Bevin prepared a plan to prevent all movement of coal. Faced by this threat, Stanley Baldwin agreed to subsidise miners' pay until 1 May 1926, while a royal commission, chaired by Sir Herbert Samuel, was set up to examine the industry.

The trade unions had won a breathing space but the underlying problems remained. The Samuel report, which recommended reorganising the industry on a more efficient basis, including the amalgamation of smaller pits, also said that the costs of production, including wages, must be reduced. It was on the question of which should come first – the cuts in wages or amalgamations – that negotiations between the TUC and the government broke down and the general strike took place. Bevin and other trade union leaders did their best to avert industrial action but it was on Bevin's plan to bring out the key industries and services that the national strike was based.

The workers' response to the call for a general strike was overwhelming. But, although it lasted nine days, it was a failure. The government had the support of public opinion and stood firm against what could be seen as a challenge to the democratic constitution of the country. Interestingly, King George V took exception to suggestions that the strikers were revolutionaries, saying: 'Try living on their wages before you judge them.'[18] The General Council of the TUC, clutching at vague assurances from Baldwin, ordered a return to work. The miners stayed out for six months longer, until they too were forced to capitulate.

In public, Bevin did not admit the obvious – that the unions had gone down to a disastrous defeat. In a speech just after the end of the strike, he said:

> We believe the struggle was inevitable, that the challenge had to be accepted. And whether it was conducted wisely or not, the fact stands out in grand relief that the great bulk of the people were loyal . . . Even the governing class of the country, who in the end know when to retreat for their own safety, will be compelled by this great demonstration of unity to pay greater regard to the consequences of their policies than hitherto. It has produced a new alignment of forces.[19]

This was a rash claim. But over the next decade or so, a more co-operative approach between the two sides of industry gradually emerged, starting with the so-called Mond–Turner talks of 1928–9 between prominent trade unionists (including Bevin) and businessmen. The unions and employers began to accept that they had common as well as divergent interests.

The collapse of the general strike and the subsequent Conservative legislation making general and sympathetic strikes illegal had another, more immediate effect. It reminded trade unionists, especially Bevin, that they needed the Labour Party as much as it needed them. Politics was back in fashion. Attlee, like most other Labour MPs, including Morrison, was pleased to see the end of the general strike as a political weapon: 'It had to come some day and it had to go. A good thing to get it out of the way. The Labour movement got back on the political track.'[20]

The general strike caused an acute personal problem for Attlee which nearly drove him out of politics. It arose from his chairmanship of the Electricity Committee of Stepney Council. At the beginning of the strike, he got the agreement of the TUC that the electricity workers would supply power for local hospitals but, if other consumers tried to obtain power, then the workers would pull their fuses. A local firm, Scammell, used the current and had its fuses pulled. Although Scammell had its own generators, it took out a civil action for conspiracy against Attlee and other Labour members (the vindictive nature of the action was demonstrated by the fact that the firm did not include the Conservative members in the action). The High Court found against the other Labour councillors and damages of £300 – a substantial sum at that time – were awarded against Attlee. Attlee, represented by Sir Malcolm Macnaghten, an old friend from his former chambers who was a KC as well as the Ulster Unionist MP for Londonderry, successfully appealed against the court decision. Attlee had made up his mind that if the appeal failed he would leave politics for his family's sake and find a more remunerative profession.

The 1924–9 parliament began as a quiet period for Attlee in which he had time to see more of his growing family. As a former junior army minister, he spoke in the occasional debate on army matters. He also acted as party spokesman on the legislation setting up the Central Electricity Board and, with his local government experience, took part in debate on Neville Chamberlain's Rating Bill. Then in November 1927, Attlee was appointed a member of a commission set up to examine the prospects for self-government in India. The secretary of state for India, the Earl of Birkenhead, had picked a commission, chaired by Sir John Simon, which, he hoped, would produce a cautious report. Attlee knew nothing about India and was hesitant about leaving his wife with two small children and another child on the way (though, in the event, Vi came with him for most of the second trip to India in the autumn of 1928). MacDonald, who saw Attlee as a safe pair of hands, assured him that his absence from Britain would not affect his future ministerial prospects.

The knowledge of India which Attlee acquired from his membership of the Simon commission was to prove of great value during the wartime coalition and especially after 1945 when, as Prime Minister, he was faced with the decision about Indian independence. As he told his official biographer, 'you've got to go to a place, see it and smell it, before you can say what's got to be done about it'.[21] In the short term, however, his membership of the Simon commission was not helpful to his career. The Indian Congress Party boycotted the commission because there were no Indians on it. As a consequence, those of his colleagues who were interested in India tended to be critical of his presence on the commission. His absence from British politics in a crucial, pre-election period was another disadvantage. The old adage – out of sight, out of mind – applied: when Attlee returned from India, he had found that Hansard had forgotten how to spell his name.

While Attlee's career stagnated, Dalton's went from strength to strength. He was elected to the Parliamentary Executive Committee in 1926 and then, with the support of the miners, to the NEC. He was re-elected every year from 1928 until 1952. His intelligence, speaking talents and ability to appeal to different wings of the party made him very much a rising star. So rapid was his political ascent that, in contrast to Attlee, he began to be tipped as a future party leader.

However, he was unwise enough to quarrel with his agent. The row was referred to the NEC Organisation Committee. A subcommittee attempted reconciliation, criticising the agent for his tactlessness but also blaming Dalton for 'presiding at the party meetings and becoming involved in local disputes'.[22] In June 1928 Dalton tried to press the issue to a resolution but a motion at the constituency General Management Committee meeting to dismiss the agent was narrowly defeated. A few months later, he announced his withdrawal from the Peckham constituency at the next election, a move which most of his more experienced colleagues considered an ill-conceived gamble.

However, Dalton knew what he was doing. He had formed a close political relationship with Arthur Henderson, Home Secretary in the first Labour government and secretary of the Labour Party. With Henderson's assistance he took soundings in the north-east. In September he received the crucial backing of the Durham miners, who supported him for the rest of his parliamentary career, and at the beginning of October he was selected by the Bishop Auckland General Management Committee as a prospective Labour candidate. On 7 October Dalton wrote in his diary: 'Clouds pass away. My position with a safe seat and a place on both executives in this critical year is a very strong one, come what may.'[23]

But he now faced a further hurdle. The Labour MP for Bishop Auckland, Ben Spoor, suddenly died, putting Dalton's future at risk. If he resigned from Peckham to fight the seat, there would have to be a further by-election, which would be unthinkable. However, Bishop Auckland's constituency officers, who, having just chosen Dalton, wanted to keep him, came up with an ingenious solution. Why should not Ruth Dalton, Hugh's wife and a Labour LCC councillor, stand at the by-election and then make way for Hugh at the coming general election? Ruth agreed to act as Hugh's proxy and, with Hugh constantly at her side, more than doubled the Labour majority. During their campaign, the Daltons were shocked by the poverty in the mining villages and Hugh pledged himself to remedy it, a promise which, thanks to the regional policies of the 1945 Labour government, he was eventually able to keep.

Herbert Morrison was out of the 1924–9 parliament but his local government activities kept him in the public eye. In 1925, Labour became the official opposition on the LCC and, as leader of the Labour Party there, Morrison was provided with an office from which he organised the opposition to the Tory majority. With his flair for publicity, he made sure that his work was continually in the news.

Throughout the 1920s Morrison led the campaign for public transport in London to be controlled by local government. As an MP in the 1924 parliament, he had voted against the second reading of the London Transport Bill, which gave the minister of transport powers to regulate services. This brought him into conflict with Bevin, who believed that a national rather than a local government solution would be in the best interests of his members. Morrison also argued against Bevin's idea of having a union representative on the minister's advisory committee. This was the beginning of a destructive feud between the two men which was to endure throughout their political lives and was one of the main reasons why Attlee was able to become and remain leader.

*

The Conservative 1929 election campaign was built round the slogan of 'safety first' and posters of the reassuring figure of Stanley Baldwin. But it was the Labour Party, under Ramsay MacDonald, which gained from the weakening economic situation and especially the rising unemployment. The Liberals, led by the dynamic David Lloyd George, had the most radical programme to tackle unemployment, entitled *We Can Conquer Unemployment* and supported by John Maynard Keynes, but they won only fifty-nine seats. For the first time Labour were returned as the biggest single party, with 287 seats to 260 for the Tories. Baldwin resigned quickly and the King asked MacDonald to form another minority government.

Herbert Morrison, now MP for Hackney South, and Hugh Dalton, MP for Bishop Auckland, joined Clement Attlee in the new parliament. Morrison, widely acknowledged as the party's leading transport expert and also chairman of the party in a successful election year, was an obvious choice as minister of transport. He was delighted to be made a minister, though within a few months he was writing to MacDonald saying that such an important ministry ought to be represented in the Cabinet. Dalton, as a close ally of Arthur Henderson, went with him to the Foreign Office as parliamentary under-secretary. One of the first things he did was to send for two dozen copies of Labour's programme, *Labour and the Nation*, mark the foreign policy section and distribute them to key FO officials, especially those preparing answers to parliamentary questions. He was determined that it should be ministers, not civil servants, who decided policy.

Despite MacDonald's promise to him, Attlee's claims were ignored. He was furious that MacDonald had not taken the trouble to inform him that he was being left out and wrote to the new Prime Minister to complain. MacDonald replied: 'I am in a fix about this Indian affair. Obviously we cannot put members on it into the Ministry. It is a terrible concern for me, but I shall not forget you.'[24] Attlee was not mollified by MacDonald's answer, especially as MacDonald entirely failed to consult either him or the other Labour member on the Simon commission, Vernon Hartshorn, before announcing that India would get dominion status and also proposing a round-table conference of British and Indians, to meet in London. The report of the Simon commission, on which Attlee had worked diligently for almost a whole year, was out of date even before it was published. The report put forward a competent analysis of India's problems and recommended the establishment of responsible government at provincial level, a proposal which was accepted by the British government, but its caution on the central issue of dominion status had been overtaken by events.

Five months after the general election, the Wall Street crash cut off the flow of American funding which had sustained European prosperity. During the first half of 1930, a world depression set in, with unemployment rising inexorably month by month. Oswald Mosley, chancellor of the Duchy of Lancaster, sent MacDonald a cogent memorandum arguing for an immediate package of large-scale public works on the lines suggested by

Lloyd George and Keynes and a longer-term programme of economic reconstruction. However, a committee chaired by the Chancellor of the Exchequer, Philip Snowden, condemned the proposals out of hand. MacDonald prevaricated and an impatient Mosley resigned.[25] The following year Mosley left the party entirely to form the New Party, which in 1932 became the British Union of Fascists.

Attlee's personal frustrations over the Simon commission were to some extent alleviated when, following Mosley's resignation, he was appointed chancellor of the Duchy of Lancaster on 24 May 1930. However, by the time he joined the government, it was being threatened by rising unemployment. Attlee's promotion was part of a wider reshuffle. MacDonald appointed himself to chair a new Cabinet committee on unemployment policy. Attlee's position was stripped of the responsibilities carried out by Mosley; in practice he acted as a general factotum to the Prime Minister, assisting him with the 1930 Imperial Conference and helping the agriculture minister, Christopher Addison (later a close colleague in the 1945 Labour government), pilot the Agricultural Marketing Bill through the Commons.

As MacDonald's part-time economic adviser, Attlee was made a member of the Prime Minister's Economic Advisory Council (EAC), on which Keynes and Ernest Bevin also sat. The Cabinet asked him to prepare a paper on the problems of British industry. Helped by his own adviser, the economist Colin Clark, Attlee argued for industrial intervention by government and the creation of a Ministry of Industry. His report was circulated to Cabinet ministers but, as Attlee tersely noted, 'never reached the stage of being discussed in Cabinet'.[26] Dalton commented in his diary in November: 'Colin Clark comes to see me in the afternoon and gives me a Cabinet paper prepared by Attlee last July. It is not a very distinguished production but it recommended that a Ministry of Industry should be set up to nationalise on socially sound lines – armed with considerable powers.'[27] Dalton pointed out that the only result had been that a top civil servant had been made an industrial adviser.

According to Attlee, he himself refused to wind up debates on unemployment 'until he saw signs of a more vigorous policy'.[28] But there was no evidence that he had any concrete ideas on how to deal with unemployment. It was fortunate for him that, in another reshuffle in March 1931, he was moved sideways to become postmaster general. His five months at the Post Office was to be his main experience as a departmental minister. As the economic situation deteriorated, Attlee immersed himself in improving the department's public relations, in launching a campaign to sell more telephones and in devising plans to loosen Whitehall's control of his department. He much enjoyed his short period as postmaster general: 'We had a great time at the Post Office.'[29]

Meanwhile, Dalton was also having a 'great time' at the Foreign Office. He worked closely with Henderson, the Foreign Secretary, and Henderson's parliamentary private secretary, Philip Noel-Baker, his friend from his Cambridge days. The Labour team had an impressive list of apparently solid achievements to their credit. These included negotiating the evacuation of the Rhineland; signing the optional clause by which member states of the League of Nations accepted compulsory arbitration of disputes; the London Naval Treaty, which was designed to end competitive building between the three greatest naval powers, Britain, the United States and Japan; and preparations for a disarmament conference in February 1932 with Henderson as chairman. Dalton's biographer pointed out that, despite all this activity, these two years of office were for nothing:

> In retrospect, the diplomacy that preceded the end of the Weimar Republic in Germany has a Chekhovian air – overshadowed by a future event [the coming of Hitler] which the actions could scarcely have prevented even if they had foreseen it. The international deliberations of this twilight time seem neither sensible nor foolish but sadly irrelevant.[30]

Focused as he was on foreign affairs, Dalton contributed little on the domestic front, though as a constituency MP the rising unemployment figures were part of his political life. At the end of 1930 he wrote in his diary: 'I am going to Bishop Auckland in the first days of January and hate the prospect of meeting my constituents again. It is all tragically different, so far as economic questions go, from what one had hoped and dreamed a Labour government would be like.'[31] There is the implication here that Dalton's economic ideas were more radical than those of the orthodox Chancellor. Yet Dalton was highly critical of the expansionary plans of Mosley and Lloyd

George and, in October 1930, took the side of the LSE economist Lionel Robbins when he clashed fiercely with Keynes on the EAC, both on the issue of protection and on the stimulatory role of public spending. Following the Wall Street crash and the growing depression, Keynes argued not only for public works but also for a 10 per cent tariff on all goods. Robbins, who was a firm free-trader, enlisted Dalton's support. A few days later, Dalton saw Snowden about the controversy. Snowden spoke 'with withering scorn of Keynes'[32] and Dalton did not demur. When the 1931 crash came, Dalton may have opposed MacDonald and Snowden on political grounds, but, though a trained economist, he never put forward any alternative to Snowden's orthodox economic policies.

*

Herbert Morrison was widely acknowledged to be a highly competent minister. Beatrice Webb noted in her diary on 23 January 1930 that he was 'the only outstanding minister'.[33] He proved a first-rate administrator, assiduous at reading his papers, prepared to listen to advice, yet excellent at making up his mind. He was good in the Commons. Morrison piloted the Road Traffic Bill through Parliament and only the fall of the government prevented him taking a second bill, the London Transport Bill, to a successful conclusion. He devised a new type of body, the public corporation, to run London Transport, an administrative innovation which was to prove a model for subsequent nationalisations when Labour came to power in 1945.

Morrison's ability as a minister was rewarded when Ramsay MacDonald brought him into the Cabinet as its youngest member at the beginning of 1931. However, he was joining a body which was being undermined by the economic situation. Unemployment had risen from about a million and a half in the middle of 1929 to two and a half million by the end of 1930 and just under three million in July 1931. Morrison was himself criticised by Oswald Mosley for failing to launch the massive road-building projects which, in his view, were necessary to reduce unemployment. In fact, Morrison put pressure on Philip Snowden to increase the road-building programme and more money was spent on roads while he was minister than in any other previous administration. However, as a supporter of local government, he resisted Mosley's idea for a national agency for road building, which might have been able to act faster than local councils. Morrison was no economist and did not pretend to have any alternative to the Chancellor's policies.

In August 1931 the Labour government was brought down by a combination of financial crisis and deep division in the Cabinet over proposals to cut public spending, especially unemployment benefits. During the summer the international financial turmoil, which had begun with the collapse in May of Credit Anstalt, an Austrian bank, and had spread to Germany, began to threaten the pound. Then on 31 July a committee chaired by Sir George May, a former secretary of the Prudential Assurance Company, and set up following a Liberal amendment in February calling for independent advice on how best to carry out reductions in national expenditure, forecast a budget deficit of £120 million and recommended slashing cuts in public spending, including one of £67 million in expenditure on the unemployed.

The impact of the May committee's report on the government's fortunes was devastating. It triggered an immediate run on the pound and pressure from international banks. The Bank of England pressed Snowden for rapid budget cuts to re-establish confidence. The government was therefore faced either with what most experts then considered to be the extremely risky step of leaving the gold standard or with preparing a programme of cuts which, as MacDonald himself admitted, were the negation of everything the Labour Party stood for. The Prime Minister tried desperately to get the support of the Cabinet for a retrenchment package but a substantial minority (nine out of twenty members, led by Henderson) refused to accept a 10 per cent cut in unemployment benefit and threatened to resign over the issue.

This dissenting minority was strengthened in its resistance by the opposition of the TUC, in which the general secretary, Walter Citrine, and Ernest Bevin played the leading parts. Sidney Webb told his wife: 'The General Council are pigs. They won't agree to any cuts.'[34] But in fact, Bevin was at least as well qualified to give his views on economics as either MacDonald or Snowden. He had been a member of both the EAC and Lord Macmillan's Committee on Finance and Industry and had been greatly influenced by the expansionary ideas of Keynes. In contrast to Dalton, Morrison and Attlee, Bevin rejected the government's 'deflationary' policy.

As he had argued in an addendum to the Macmillan report, he believed that a unilateral devaluation would be preferable to continued deflation. Contrary to what Snowden had told the TUC, Bevin did not believe that devaluation would lead to complete industrial collapse. He was proved right only a month later when the United Kingdom was forced off the gold standard without the malign results which the Chancellor of the Exchequer had forecast.

On 23 August 1931, MacDonald, faced with irreconcilable division in his Cabinet, resigned as Labour Prime Minister but the following day he was persuaded by George V to form an emergency so-called National Government, with the Conservative leader, Stanley Baldwin, and the acting Liberal leader, Herbert Samuel, serving under him. Only Snowden, J. H. Thomas and Lord Sankey, the Lord Chancellor, remained in his new Cabinet from the Labour Party. MacDonald's action, which he announced to an astonished Labour Cabinet, may have arisen in part from vanity and egoism – the belief that only he could solve the crisis. But he also considered it his duty as a patriot to respond to the pleadings of the King that he should remain at his post in order to carry through the public spending cuts demanded by the banks and thus prevent a financial crash. It was highly convenient for the Tories and the Liberals to retain a Labour Prime Minister to carry out measures which would be unpopular with the working class.

Not surprisingly the vast majority of Labour MPs saw MacDonald's decision as a betrayal of the party. On 24 August Dalton and Attlee were summoned back from holiday to an afternoon conference of junior ministers at 10 Downing Street. Beforehand they lunched together at an Italian restaurant, sharing a bottle of sparkling red Burgundy to fortify themselves for the meeting. Late in the day, Attlee now blamed MacDonald for his indecision on economic matters and was even more critical of Snowden, who he said had blocked every positive proposal for the last two years. At the meeting, MacDonald told the junior ministers that the Labour government was over but he was not asking them to join him in committing political suicide, though perhaps some of them would be willing 'to travel the same road with him'.[35] A few questions were raised, including one from Attlee, who asked what sacrifices, if any, were being asked from recipients of unearned income, before the meeting dispersed. It was already clear from the hostile reception given to MacDonald that few Labour MPs would be supporting their leader.

Later that afternoon, a council of war took place in Henderson's room at Transport House to rally the party against MacDonald. Those present besides Henderson included Bevin, Citrine, Dalton and George Lansbury – but not Attlee. Significantly Dalton was at this crucial Transport House meeting, partly because he was close to Henderson, whom he called 'Uncle', and also because, unlike Attlee, he was a leading personality on the Labour NEC. But the most influential figure there was Bevin, who immediately pledged his support: 'This is like the general strike. I'm prepared to put everything in.'[36]

Though Attlee, Dalton and, above all, Bevin came out against MacDonald and the National Government immediately, Morrison and Stafford Cripps were more circumspect. During the early months of 1931, Cripps had made a considerable reputation for himself as MacDonald's eloquent solicitor general. A fellow Labour MP, summing up his first six months in Parliament, said: 'His is the biggest new reputation of today.'[37] When the August crisis broke, Cripps, typically, was in a clinic in Baden-Baden, the celebrated German spa, where he was recovering from the strain of his first parliamentary session. It was there on the twenty-sixth that he received a telegram from MacDonald, which read: 'Hope you are progressing. Would you like to go on.' Cripps did not reply at once but waited until his return to London two days later. Although both his father, Lord Parmoor, and his uncle Sidney Webb had supported MacDonald's spending cuts package in the Cabinet, Webb wrote to Parmoor on 27 August (who, like his son, had been in Baden-Baden for treatment) that 'he had rallied to Henderson and the party without hesitation'.[38] Webb's attitude may have influenced Cripps's courteous but negative response of 28 August to MacDonald:

> May I be allowed . . . to say that I admire immensely the courage and conviction which have led you and other Labour ministers associated with you to take the action you have taken. My own personal hope is that the rift in the party may be quickly healed . . . I disagree with the policy of the Labour Party

taking any part in a National Government having the programme of the present government.[39]

Morrison's account in his autobiography of his attitude to the formation of the National Government, under the heading 'The 1931 Betrayal', is misleading. According to him, when MacDonald returned from Buckingham Palace and announced that he had accepted the King's request to form a National Government, he was the first to protest: 'Prime Minister, I think you are wrong.'[40] Yet there is evidence from a number of sources that at first Morrison was uncertain about whether or not to join MacDonald.[41] After all, he had been one of the Cabinet majority which had supported the cuts package. He not only owed his Cabinet position to MacDonald but also greatly admired his leadership during the last days of the Labour government. He understood the reasons why MacDonald had decided to lead the National Government and hesitated for a day or two about whether he should follow him. However, MacDonald advised Morrison not to join the National Government, as it could ruin his political career. From MacDonald's point of view, it made sense to have allies inside the Labour Party to support the National Government (which he believed would be short lived) in carrying out the necessary cuts and restoring confidence.

So, after some hours of agonising, Morrison accepted MacDonald's advice and stayed with Labour, though he was reported in the *Daily Mail* of 28 August as saying that he was likely to lose neither his personal admiration for MacDonald nor his belief that MacDonald's action showed exceptional political courage. It was only when MacDonald (having been expelled from the Labour Party) bowed to the Tories' pressure to call a general election, in which he would be in opposition to his old party, that Morrison finally publicly attacked his former leader, symbolically turning MacDonald's photograph in the London Labour Party office to face the wall.

All the protagonists of this book in the end stayed with Labour and rejected MacDonald's National Government. This was not so much because they had an alternative economic policy (though, as has been described above, Bevin was much influenced by Keynes) but more because they believed in the longer-term objectives of the party – a fairer distribution of wealth, social welfare, economic planning and nationalisation. The collapse of the minority Labour administration and the electoral disaster that followed was to result in the emergence of a new generation of Labour leaders, to the top of which Attlee would unexpectedly rise.

5

1931–9: Depression and the coming of war

The result of the general election of October 1931 was a disaster for the Labour Party. The Labour vote dropped from eight million to six million, while its parliamentary representation was drastically reduced from 287 to a paltry 52 members. Only one Cabinet minister, George Lansbury, and two junior ministers, Clement Attlee (who scraped home by 551 votes) and Stafford Cripps (who had a majority of 429) survived. Hugh Dalton and Herbert Morrison were both defeated, while Ernest Bevin, who at Arthur Henderson's request stood in the formerly safe seat of Gateshead in County Durham, lost by nearly 13,000 votes. The Labour Party had been routed by a powerful coalition of forces (the Tories, Liberals and a handful of MacDonaldites) led by its former leader, Ramsay MacDonald.

The events of 1931 had a profound impact on the Labour Party. The Parliamentary Labour Party was reduced to a trade union rump. Nearly half the new PLP were miners and the only region which had a good proportion of Labour MPs was the mining area of south Wales. In normal circumstances, it would probably have taken at least two elections before Labour could make a serious challenge for power. The weakness of the PLP led to an increase in power of the TUC, and especially of Bevin, in the running of the party's affairs. One historian goes so far as to refer to the party in the 1930s as being 'the General Council's party'.[1]

The failure of the MacDonald government, the part played by the international banks in its collapse and the prospect of a long period of opposition had the effect of pushing the party further to the left. There was a powerful feeling of hostility to capitalism and a demand for a strong 'socialist' programme, which would give the party new direction. Above all, there was a sense of resentment at what Labour Party members saw as betrayal by the party's leaders, especially MacDonald and Philip Snowden. They wanted a different kind of leadership, less charismatic, less pragmatic and more accountable to the membership. The way was open for the tortoise.

It was Labour's disasters that propelled Attlee, the tortoise among the hares, into the leadership. Even after the formation of the National Government (and before the October 1931 election) he was well down the pecking order. In September, the PLP voted in a new executive. Henderson as chairman, and J. R. Clynes and William Graham as deputy chairmen, were returned ex officio; Tom Johnston (151), Lansbury (140), Dalton (137) and Arthur Greenwood (131) topped the poll of the thirteen Labour MPs elected. Morrison, although he had been in the Labour Cabinet, and was a member of the National Executive Committee, did not run for the Parliamentary Executive, perhaps because he was still in a state of confusion following MacDonald's formation of the National Government. Attlee, despite having been a junior member of the government, was not a member either of the Parliamentary Executive or of the NEC. As Dalton noted, 'these choices and these votes were a rough measure of our relative standing in the esteem of the parliamentary party at that time'.[2]

The 1931 election result then removed from Parliament all of Attlee's serious rivals, except Lansbury and Cripps, to give him his opportunity. On his way to the first parliamentary party meeting after the election, he received a message from Henderson (the titular leader of the party, who once again had lost his seat) that Lansbury would be proposed as leader, with Attlee as his deputy. If any of the members of the Parliamentary Executive had been returned to Parliament, they would almost certainly have been selected as deputy in preference to Attlee. As one of his biographers pointed out, 'the ill wind for Labour had blown Attlee nothing but good'.[3]

But, arguably, Attlee's breakthrough was not due to good fortune alone. He held his seat in part because of his hard work in the East End. So Dalton, who had only recently been selected for his Bishop Auckland seat, lost by 755 votes, while Attlee, reaping the reward for his close relationship with his constituency, managed to scrape in by 551. Had it been otherwise, Dalton would probably have become deputy to Lansbury.

Lansbury, Attlee and Cripps, the former solicitor general who had only been in Parliament for a few months, shared the leader of the opposition's room in the House. From there they attempted to lead the puny Labour forces. They made a curious trio. Lansbury was popular with party activists but he was already in his seventies and, as Attlee said, 'he was by nature an evangelist rather than a parliamentary tactician'.[4] Cripps was a brilliant lawyer with a first-class mind but he had little previous form as far as Labour politics was concerned. He fulfilled most of the far-flung speaking engagements because only he could afford the travelling expenses. Attlee was frantically busy, manning the front bench and making speeches on subjects such as finance and foreign affairs which he had not previously studied. In 1932 he filled more columns of Hansard than any other member. During the week, he was always rushing from one meeting to another. Lansbury's daughter, who worked as his secretary, called him 'The White Rabbit'.

If the work rate of Labour's new leadership could not be criticised, the direction in which they were leading the post-1931 party was more controversial. Lansbury was a left-wing pacifist. Cripps now talked extravagantly about the need for 'a slap-up socialistic policy for dealing with the whole industrial and financial situation'.[5] Even the cautious Attlee began to sound radical. In a letter to his brother Tom, he wrote: 'We are hard at work on defining policy; my idea is a plan of action to be agreed on, so that when we win next time we shall know exactly what to do, how to do it.'[6] Dalton, who, though out of Parliament, remained an important figure on the NEC, noted waspishly in his diary in October 1932:

> The parliamentary party is a poor little affair, isolated from the National Executive whose only MP is Lansbury; Attlee is deputy leader of the parliamentary party – 'a purely accidental position' as someone puts it – and he and Cripps . . . sit in Lansbury's room at the House all day and all night and continually influence the old man . . . Cripps, who has many good points, including personal charm and political courage, breaks down unexpectedly: his speeches are thought by many to be curiously irresponsible . . . Attlee is a small person with no personality, nor real standing in the movement.[7]

The high water mark of the party's shift to the left was the 1932 party conference at Leicester. In August 1932 the Independent Labour Party, disgusted by the behaviour of MacDonald, decided to disaffiliate from the Labour Party; the minority who were left behind were determined to ginger up the party and, on the eve of the conference, formed the left-wing Socialist League. At conference itself, Sir Charles Trevelyan moved a resolution calling on the next Labour government to put forward a socialist programme immediately on entering office and to stand or fall by it. Henderson urged delegates not to tie Labour's hands in advance but the resolution was carried without a card vote. Against Dalton's advice, a motion to nationalise the joint stock banks was also carried, while Morrison, to avoid defeat (organised by Bevin's union, the Transport and General Workers), had to withdraw his transport plan, because it did not include any provision for automatic trade union representation on boards of nationalised industries.

It was the political novice, Cripps, who rapidly emerged as the darling of the left. Michael Foot, who was a close friend at Oxford of Cripps's son John, explained the attraction: 'His prodigious brain-power, energy and delight in hard work, his stamp of mastery and confidence, made him within a matter of months the most magnetic figure in the party; many were already talking of him as the obvious future leader.'[8] In 1933 he agreed to become chairman of the Socialist League. In this capacity and as one of the leaders of the PLP, he was much in demand at meetings up and down the country.

Cripps's speeches and writings were highly controversial. Influenced in part by ill-digested Marxist ideas and perhaps rather more by the sudden collapse of the MacDonald Labour government, he talked wildly of the need for a Labour government to pass an Emergency Powers Bill on its first day in office and of prolonging the life of a parliament without the need for an election. He foresaw a threat to a Labour government from the armed forces and the City. He told a conference of Labour students: 'There is no doubt that we shall have to overcome opposition from Buckingham Palace and other places as well,'[9] and called for popular support for a general strike to force the government to honour its alliances.

After his 'Buckingham Palace' speech, Cripps was called in front of a committee of the NEC to justify himself. Dalton made a violent attack on him, pointing out that Tory HQ regarded him as 'their greatest electoral asset'.[10] His gaffes had the effect of forcing Labour candidates on the defensive. Cripps shrugged off this criticism, disingenuously claiming that he had been misreported. Dalton's private opinion of Cripps at this time was even more critical: 'I was at first astonished that so intelligent a man could talk such nonsense. He seemed to have no political wits and to leave his first class brains inside his brief-case. Gradually, as attempts at friendly discussion proved unavailing, my astonishment changed to vexation and impatience.'[11]

At the NEC meeting at which Dalton made his attack, one of Cripps's defenders was Attlee, who said that Dalton was 'like a pedagogue addressing a pupil'. Attlee's personal relationship with Cripps was warm. He and Vi went to stay several times at Goodfellows, the splendid Cripps country estate in Gloucestershire. When Lansbury fractured his thigh in December 1933 and was forced to rest for some months, Attlee felt that he could not afford to take over (there was no opposition leader's salary until 1937) and unwisely wrote to Cripps suggesting that he should do the job. Fortunately, Cripps turned down the suggestion and instead generously donated £500, to be used as Attlee's salary until Lansbury's return. He added: 'I shall of course easily earn this sum by non-attendance at Executive meetings, etc.'[12]

Attlee spent nine months as acting leader. Although his speeches did not set the Commons alight, they were usually competent. His eulogy in 1934 on the death of the King of the Belgians was much praised. He led the opposition to the means test and was a prominent member of the joint select committee which produced the report on which the 1935 Government of India Act (a first step on the path to independence) was based. Above all, he began slowly to come to terms with the dangerous international situation, Japanese aggression in Manchuria, the rise of Hitler in Germany and in 1935 the Italian invasion of Abyssinia. His main theme in debates was support for collective security and loyalty to the League of Nations. However, to the disapproval of Dalton and Bevin, he continued to oppose the government's plans for rearmament, including increased spending on the Royal Air Force.

Since the *débâcle* of 1931, Bevin, with the assistance of the TUC general secretary, Walter Citrine, had kept a watching brief over the Labour Party, using the forum of the National Council of Labour (NCL), on which the TUC, the PLP and the NEC were all represented, to issue regular statements of policy. Deeply disturbed by the destruction of the trade unions in

Germany and Austria and concerned about the Italian threat to Abyssinia, Bevin came to Brighton for the 1935 Labour Party conference armed with a joint statement of policy by the NCL and a TUC vote in favour of collective security and in support of sanctions against Italy. He was determined to defeat what he saw as Lansbury's self-indulgent pacifism and the naive Marxism of Cripps (who had resigned from the NEC before conference met). Bevin set out to bring the Labour Party to its senses.

The dramatic debate on sanctions, which took place in the Brighton Dome on 1 October, was opened by a vigorous speech by Dalton. He called on Conference to stand firm against Mussolini's 'barbarous and long-premeditated assault on Abyssinia'. Cripps replied that the League of Nations, which he called the 'International Burglars' Union', was 'nothing but the tool of the imperialist powers' and urged delegates to vote against the NEC resolution. Attlee, who was the only one of the three leaders of the PLP to support the resolution, said: 'Non-resistance is not a political attitude, it is a personal attitude. I do not believe it is a possible policy for people with responsibility.'

The two most notable speeches were made by Lansbury and Bevin. Lansbury, who was given a standing ovation before he even began to speak, put an emotional case for his pacifism. He accepted that it was possible that, if Conference disagreed with him, he would have to resign the leadership but he felt he had to speak out for what he believed in. Bevin's reply to Lansbury was devastating. As one of his biographers wrote, 'he went into the ring to hurt not to score points'.[13] Giving chapter and verse, he accused Lansbury of consistently flouting party policy, while still remaining party leader. Looking directly up at Lansbury, he accused him of placing 'the executive and the movement in an absolutely wrong position by trailing your conscience round from body to body asking to be told what to do with it'. Turning to Cripps and his Socialist League followers, he thundered:

> People have been on this platform today talking about the destruction of capitalism. Lawyers and members of other professions have not done too badly [under capitalism and fascism] . . . The thing that is being wiped out is the trade union movement . . . It is we who are being wiped out and who will be wiped out if fascism comes here.[14]

The resolution in favour of standing firm against the dictators was overwhelmingly carried and a few days later Lansbury resigned as leader. As the general election was expected to be in a few weeks (the Conservative leader, Stanley Baldwin, who had replaced MacDonald as Prime Minister in June, called it for 14 November), there was no time for a full leadership election. Two miners' MPs, David Grenfell and Tom Williams, moved that Attlee should become leader. In Lansbury's absence, Attlee had already led the party for nine months and it seemed logical that he now continue into the general election. It was generally agreed that Attlee's assumption of the leadership in October 1935 was a short-term holding operation until after the general election, when a full leadership election with a wider range of candidates, including Morrison and possibly Dalton, could take place.

Baldwin fought a short but effective election campaign. Tory canvassers could argue that their opponents, who had just shown themselves to be divided, were now led by a little-known, somewhat colourless left-wing socialist. On foreign policy, Baldwin, by trumpeting the government's support for collective security and the League of Nations, had cleverly stolen Labour's clothes, while he attacked Attlee for voting against the defence estimates. The government could also claim that, despite high unemployment in the depressed areas, the economy was steadily improving, especially in the Midlands and the south, and that electing a still convalescent Labour Party was an unacceptable risk. Throughout the twentieth century, 'Don't let Labour ruin it' proved a potent Conservative cry. In the end, Labour won 154 seats, a big improvement on 1931, but still far behind the National Government's total of 432.

After the general election, lobbying among Labour MPs began in earnest for the leadership. By his erratic behaviour at conference, Cripps had virtually ruled himself out and he announced that he was not standing. One of the party's elder statesmen, J. R. Clynes, had narrowly won a Manchester seat but felt that his age (he was sixty-six) precluded him from being a candidate. Just before the party conference, Dalton had invited the Morrisons to his cottage at West Leaze in Wiltshire and, in return for Morrison backing him for the Foreign Office, offered his support to Herbert for the leadership. That left three serious candidates – Attlee, Greenwood and Morrison.

Arthur Greenwood, a lecturer and later a civil servant who had been minister of health in Ramsay MacDonald's administration and who acted as the party's research secretary, had been returned to Parliament for Wakefield in a by-election in April 1932 and had some support, particularly from northern trade union MPs. It was thought that he also had the backing of Bevin. However, he was known to have a serious drink problem. Dalton, who appointed himself Morrison's campaign manager, noisily told MPs that the choice was between a non-entity (Attlee), a drunk (Greenwood) and his own candidate.

Morrison had set his sights on the leadership. In 1934, he had led the party to an election triumph in London, where Labour had gained control of London County Council (LCC). He was backed inside Parliament by some of the brightest and most energetic of Labour MPs such as Dalton, Philip Noel-Baker and Ellen Wilkinson and outside Parliament by intellectual young Turks like Hugh Gaitskell, Evan Durbin and Douglas Jay. Morrison had played a big part during the election, including making the final election radio broadcast. After the election, he made clear what he thought of Attlee as leader: 'Since 1931 we have not yet evolved a clear leadership . . . we ought to have done better . . . Was our appeal wide enough or constructively concrete enough?'[15]

At 11.30 a.m. on Tuesday 24 November, the PLP met in Committee Room 14 of the House of Commons, with Attlee, as the incumbent leader, in the chair. Greenwood, Attlee and Morrison were nominated in that order. An MP favourable to Morrison asked the three candidates whether, if elected, they would give their full time to the job. Attlee replied: 'If I'm elected, I shall carry on as before,' Greenwood said: 'Yes,' while Morrison, shooting himself in the foot, spoke at too great length, saying that he would put himself in the hands of the party: if they thought he should give up the leadership of the LCC, then he would.

The MPs then voted and the result of the first ballot was as follows: Attlee 58, Morrison 44, Greenwood 33. As had been agreed, the bottom candidate dropped out and, on the second ballot, Attlee got eighty-eight votes to Morrison's forty-eight, a decisive victory. What seems to have happened is that Attlee received almost all the votes of those MPs (most of them miners) who had sat in the 1931–5 parliament. They considered he had done a competent job both in Parliament and during the election. On the second ballot, nearly all of Greenwood's votes went to Attlee. Morrison believed that there was a freemasons' plot (Greenwood was a freemason) behind this switch.

More likely, Morrison suffered because he was thought to be anti-union. Bevin, in particular, had distrusted him ever since they had clashed over the issue of automatic trade union representation on the boards of nationalised industries. Recently Bevin had felt that Morrison had been too sympathetic to Lansbury at the Brighton conference because he was fishing for left-wing votes: 'There are too many namby-pambies about. Even Morrison was trying to soft pedal, but no doubt he has his reasons.'[16] Bevin was determined that Morrison should not become leader and, though, at that time, he was not overimpressed by Attlee's abilities, he preferred almost anybody to Morrison. Bevin may not have issued a general instruction to trade union MPs to vote against Morrison, but it is significant that, on the second ballot, almost all the trade union votes switched over to Attlee. Attlee's view was that he won because the party did not want a charismatic leader, who might do another MacDonald; they preferred somebody who would act more like a chairman of a committee.[17]

In a huff after his defeat, Morrison refused to stand for the deputy leadership. He said that he was too busy with the LCC. This was an error because, had he become deputy leader, he would have been well placed to replace Attlee if he had faltered. Instead Greenwood, who was no real threat, was elected unanimously to the deputy position. The election of Attlee depressed Morrison's supporters inside and outside Parliament. After his defeat, Dalton wrote in his diary: 'A wretched disheartening result! And a little mouse shall lead them.'[18] However, immediately after the party meeting, Dalton went to see Attlee to pledge his support. Attlee, displaying that combination of cunning and magnanimity which is an essential part of leadership, gave him a choice of speaking either on foreign affairs or finance. Dalton plumped for foreign affairs, because they 'were going to be very tricky'.[19]

Dalton was only too right. From Hitler's reoccupation of the Rhineland in March 1936, the outbreak of the Spanish Civil War in July 1936, the German annexation of Austria in 1938, the Munich crisis later that year, the

German occupation of Prague in March 1939 and the outbreak of war over Poland in September 1939, international events dominated the political agenda. Dalton was also right that he was best equipped to speak for the party on the subject. Indeed, the period leading up to the war, especially his chairmanship of the party during 1936 and 1937, was arguably Dalton's finest hour.

Working with Bevin, who was then chairman of the TUC, he helped shift Labour policy away from pacifism and towards rearmament and resistance to the dictators. Their task, as they saw it, was to make the Labour movement face up to what Winston Churchill called 'the gathering storm'. Bevin told the Executive Council of his union: 'I cannot see any way of stopping Hitler and the other dictators except by force,'[20] while Dalton, in his chairman's address to the 1937 Labour Party conference, said: 'In this most grave situation, not of the Labour Party's making, our country must be powerfully armed.'[21] It was totally illogical for the party to campaign with great enthusiasm for 'Arms to Spain' to aid the Spanish republicans, while ignoring the equally urgent needs of Britain.

The turning point was the PLP meeting of 21 and 22 July 1937, when by forty-five votes to thirty-nine, Dalton persuaded his colleagues to discontinue their practice of voting against the defence estimates. He argued that the decision on rearmament was perhaps the most important that the party would have to take in the parliament. Although Attlee, Morrison and Greenwood all spoke in favour of Labour's traditional policy of voting against defence estimates, Dalton's persuasive oratory carried the day. Support for rearmament was subsequently overwhelmingly approved at both the 1937 TUC and Labour Party conferences. This change of policy not only strengthened Labour's opposition to appeasement. It also helped prepare the party for participation in the coalition to wage war against Hitler.

The *Daily Express* helpfully suggested that, after such a big shift of policy, Attlee, who had argued against the changes, should resign. In fact, Attlee was probably more sympathetic to the Dalton/Bevin position than he appeared. When he was elected in 1935, he had set up a Party Defence Committee, to discuss such issues as the case for the creation of a Ministry of Defence. Once the policy on rearmament had changed, Attlee refused to allow the issue to be reopened. And in May 1938 he encouraged Dalton to make a sweeping attack in the Commons which exposed the inadequacy of British air defences and the growing superiority of the Luftwaffe and led to the downfall of the air minister. A more valid criticism of Attlee was not that he was a pacifist nor ignorant of what was happening on the continent but that, at a time of great national danger, he carried too far the passive conception of leadership and relied too much on other, more eloquent, advocates to make the running rather than making a stand himself.

On the left, Attlee had to contend with the activities of his former close colleague Stafford Cripps, now turned Marxist rebel. In January 1937 Cripps and the Socialist League (which he helped finance) launched the so-called United Front, with the objective of uniting 'all sections of the working class movement', including the Communist Party of Great Britain and the disaffiliated ILP. This initiative was opposed by Labour's NEC. The Labour leadership was deeply suspicious of any 'front' supported by the Communist Party and promptly disaffiliated the Socialist League. Cripps himself was only saved from disciplinary action by a House of Commons debate on the report of the Gresford mining disaster inquiry. In that inquiry, Cripps had played an impressive role in his legal capacity on behalf of the miners.

There was, at least superficially, a more persuasive case for Cripps's second initiative, the campaign, which he started in January 1939, for a 'Popular Front'. Borrowing the idea from the continent (there were Popular Fronts in both France and Spain), he argued that Labour alone could not win the next general election and that it should bring together a coalition of all anti-appeasement forces, including the Liberals and even dissident Tories. According to Cripps, this was the moment 'to drive out of office the incompetent gang of betrayers who have already brought our country to ruin'.[22]

The NEC, exasperated by Cripps's switch of tactics from a project for narrow working-class unity to an ambitious plan for a far broader coalition, rejected his memorandum, only to find that he had high-handedly already decided to circulate the document to constituency parties. It then became a debate over procedure, a debate which Cripps was always bound to lose. At Labour's last conference before the war at Stockport, he made an unsuccessful appeal against the decision to expel him. His followers, including Aneurin

Bevan and George Strauss, were also expelled but were swiftly readmitted once the war had started. Cripps, by his own choice, remained outside the party. Ironically, his call for a wider unity had, in fact, produced disunity within the party on an almost unprecedented scale.[23]

Why did Cripps behave like this? Here was a man with a brilliant brain, whom many at the beginning of the 1930s saw as a future leader, yet who ended the decade by being expelled from the party. His enthusiasm for Marxist dogma and the certainty which it brought to a dangerous world may have been a factor. But his later espousal of a non-doctrinaire alliance against appeasement showed that he could be flexible and pragmatic. Attlee's conclusion was that in the 1930s Cripps lacked both political judgement and the ability to listen to others. As he wrote to his brother Tom, 'it is a great pity about Stafford, but like all the Potter family he is so absolutely convinced that the policy he puts forward for the time being is absolutely right that he will listen to no arguments'.[24] Above all, Cripps was an individualist who had not yet learned how to be a team player.

At the start of the June 1939 party conference at Southport, Attlee fell ill with a prostate problem. He was in such pain that he was unable to attend the opening session and only recovered enough to make a very short speech on the final day. He returned to London and entered a nursing home where he underwent two operations. He convalesced at Nevin in Caernarvonshire and was still there when war was declared on 3 September. He was not fully fit until the end of the year.

While he was away ill, Ellen Wilkinson, an admirer of Morrison, produced two articles critical of Attlee and boosting Morrison. In an unsigned contribution to *Time and Tide*, she noted that Attlee's absence from conference 'made not the slightest difference to anyone' and that at Southport most people felt that Morrison was the dominating figure.[25] In the same week, Francis Williams, the editor of the *Daily Herald*, wrote an article in his newspaper praising Morrison, Dalton and Bevin without mentioning Attlee or Greenwood.

In Attlee's absence, Greenwood raised the question of Wilkinson's articles at the party meeting and invited her to defend herself. She made a poor showing and was fiercely criticised. Morrison felt obliged to make a short contribution in which he said he had nothing to do with the articles. He was heard in silence. A vote of confidence in Attlee's leadership was carried unanimously, except for Wilkinson, who abstained. The leadership question was raised again at the party meeting in the autumn of 1939, after war had been declared, when Greenwood, Morrison and Dalton were all nominated. Greenwood declared that he would not stand against Attlee, Morrison said he would not accept nomination this year while Attlee was still unwell and Dalton informed his colleagues that he had already made it known the day before that he would not accept nomination. Typically, when asked, Attlee modestly replied that he would never regard as disloyal the nomination of a colleague to displace him.

Despite these intrigues and manoeuvrings (which are well covered in Dalton's diaries), Attlee's leadership was never in real danger. This was in part because he retained a core of loyal support, especially among trade union MPs. There was also no agreement about who should succeed him. Dalton, who had worked so hard and loudly for Morrison in 1935, was no longer backing him. After his successful chairmanship, Dalton may himself have had designs on the leadership. In any case, he felt that Morrison spent too much time at the LCC and too little at Westminster. Cripps, after the behaviour that led to his expulsion, was obviously out of the picture. Despite his drink problem, Greenwood had his supporters, especially after some fine anti-appeasement speeches, including the one for the opposition on the out-break of war when the Tory MP Leo Amery cried out across the chamber: 'Speak for England!' But Greenwood remained faithful to Attlee.

Still, there was no real enthusiasm for Attlee. For some of his colleagues he was still a stop-gap figure, in place because they could not agree on anyone else. In the private session at Stockport, Bevin, despite his insistence on loyalty, was critical of the Labour leader. Attlee's main problem was that he was not much of a speaker. His speeches were usually well researched. As on the death of George V, he could pay a graceful tribute and, on occasions, he could make a sharply critical parliamentary contribution. But he was almost never inspiring and, as the international situation worsened, his followers increasingly felt that they needed inspiration.

The other side to the story is that, under Attlee's leadership, the Labour Party was making progress towards becoming capable, if not yet of winning an election, then of participating in government. A beneficial effect of

Attlee's collegiate style was that it enabled other leaders to emerge. Dalton complained in his diary that 'at annual conferences, when Morrison and I were the principal performers, we can build up the self confidence, unity and morale of the Party in a most surprising way and then, a few weeks later, others having resumed their feeble sway, down it all sags again'.[26] He ignored the fact that Attlee did not at all resent the arguably superior talents of Dalton, Morrison, Bevin and Greenwood. And if only Cripps had not ruled himself out, Attlee would have been happy to work with him as well. He saw himself as providing the framework within which these able men – the hares – could flourish as part of a team.

By 1939, the Labour Party had a so-called Immediate Programme, which combined plans to expand social welfare and economic prosperity with a strategy of nationalisation, including the public ownership of coal, electricity, gas and the Bank of England. This was to form the basis of the 1945 manifesto, *Let Us Face the Future*. Above all, with its support for rearmament, Labour was emerging as an anti-appeasement, patriotic party, able to ally with dissident Tories, such as Winston Churchill and Anthony Eden, and the Liberals to provide resistance to Hitler. The tortoise and the hares were about to combine to help save the nation.

6

1940–45: Winston's ministers

The Second World War transformed the prospects of the Labour Party. From being a party of almost permanent opposition, it became a full partner in the great wartime coalition government which it had helped bring about. Its ministers, especially Ernest Bevin and Herbert Morrison, showed themselves to be outstanding. During the war, and especially after Dunkirk, the tide of opinion turned decisively against the Conservatives and Conservative ideas, though Clement Attlee and his colleagues tended to underestimate the extent of the change. Paradoxically, the party which believed so strongly in peace was boosted by war.

On 1 September 1939, Hitler invaded Poland. On 3 September Britain, after some equivocation, declared war on Germany. Neville Chamberlain decided to strengthen his government by making Winston Churchill First Lord of the Admiralty, with a seat in the War Cabinet, and Anthony Eden secretary for the dominions, outside the War Cabinet. He also asked Arthur Greenwood, as acting leader of the opposition, if Labour would be prepared to join his government. Greenwood consulted Attlee, who was still convalescing in north Wales. Attlee's response, like Greenwood's, was a firm refusal, a stand which was unanimously supported by the Parliamentary Executive. Dalton told R. A. Butler, under-secretary at the Foreign Office, that, though Labour supported the war, it could not enter a government which was led by Chamberlain.[1] Labour's leaders had no confidence that the appeaser of Munich could ever transform himself into a successful war leader.

Hitler overran Poland in three weeks and shared the spoils with the USSR, which had invaded from the east. The next six months was the period of the 'phoney war' (except for the winter war between the Soviet Union and Finland), with the British and the French standing on the defensive in the west. The French troops stayed behind the Maginot line, while the French government requested the British not to initiate any attacks on Germany, in case the Germans retaliated by bombing French factories. Instead, the British dropped pamphlets on Germany. Chamberlain seemed to believe that Hitler could be brought to his knees by a combination of propaganda and economic blockade.

Meanwhile, Attlee, on his return from illness, made it clear that Britain should reject any peace proposals from Hitler which would allow Germany to keep its conquests. On 8 November he set out Labour's 'Peace Aims' to a special conference of MPs and prospective Labour candidates. He called for a fight to the finish with Hitler. War had to lead to the establishment of a new order. Looking ahead, he advocated a strengthened League of Nations which would keep the peace. A new settlement in Europe was needed – adopting a federalist tone, he said: 'Europe must federate or perish.'[2] Then in January 1940 the Labour leader gave an eloquent radio broadcast in which he explained why Labour was supporting the war:

> I believe that in this contest we are fighting for something greater than the safety of our own country. We are fighting the battle of civilisation against barbarism . . . If we really wish to build a new world wherein justice, mercy and truth shall replace brute force . . . we must also build a new Britain worthy to lead the world away from anarchy and strife into the paths of peace.[3]

On a very cold winter's day in January 1940, Attlee toured the British line in northern France. He came back concerned about the lack of adequate Allied resources to meet a German breakthrough. After a visit to Paris with Dalton and Philip Noel-Baker in February, he was even more worried about the pacifism and defeatism of the French politicians he met; Léon Blum, the socialist leader, whose courage Attlee admired, was the outstanding exception.

Then events suddenly speeded up. On 4 April 1940 Chamberlain foolishly told the Conservative Party that Hitler had 'missed the bus'.[4] Once again, he had underestimated the Nazi dictator. On 8 April Hitler brought the 'phoney war' to an abrupt end by invading two neutral countries, Denmark and Norway. The bungling Allied response led not only to military defeat in Norway but to the fall of the Chamberlain government. In early May Attlee, as leader of the opposition, called for a two-day debate on the conduct of the war. Clement Davies, a Liberal MP, tried to persuade Attlee to put down a motion of no confidence but Attlee's view was that the Tories would be more likely to revolt if the debate took place on a motion for the adjournment. It was to be the most dramatic and far-reaching in its political consequences of any parliamentary debate in the twentieth century.

On Tuesday 7 May at 3.48 p.m., Chamberlain opened the debate, with an unconvincing defence of his government's handling of the Norwegian operations. Instead of ignoring the taunts of opposition MPs about 'missing buses', he unwisely tried to justify himself. His only positive piece of news was his announcement that Churchill, chairman of the Military Co-ordinating Committee, was authorised to give guidance and direction to the Chiefs of Staff Committee. Attlee, who followed Chamberlain, criticised the appointment for overloading Churchill: 'It is like having a man commanding an army in the field and also commanding a division,'[5] said the former Army major.

Attlee attacked the government not only for its incompetent handling of the Norwegian campaign but also for its overall conduct of affairs:

> The people find that these men, who have been consistently wrong in their judgement of events, the same people who thought that Hitler would not attack Czechoslovakia, who thought Hitler could be appeased, seem not to have realised that Hitler would attack Norway. They see everywhere a failure of grip, a failure of drive, not only in the field of defence and foreign policy but in industry.[6]

Turning to Tory MPs, he reminded them of their responsibilities:

> They have been content, week after week, with ministers whom they knew were failures. They have allowed their loyalty to the chief whip to overcome their loyalty to the real needs of the country. I say that the House of Commons must take its full responsibility. I say that there is a widespread feeling in this country not that we shall lose the war . . . but that to win the war, we want different people at the helm from those who have led us into it.[7]

It was a competent, though not commanding, performance.

More damaging to Chamberlain was criticism from his own side. The MP for Portsmouth North, Admiral of the Fleet Sir Roger Keyes, resplendent in his full admiral's uniform and with six rows of medals on his chest, said he was appearing in uniform for the first time in the House of Commons because he wished to speak on behalf of the fighting sea-going navy, who were deeply unhappy with the hesitation and delay of the naval staff. When he sat down, there was thunderous applause. The most wounding speech that day came from the Conservative MP for Birmingham Sparkbrook, Leo Amery, who had been a protégé of Joseph Chamberlain, Neville Chamberlain's father. After being highly critical of the government, he called for new men 'who can match our enemies in fighting spirit, in daring, in resolution and in thirst for victory . . . We are fighting today for our life, for our liberty, for our all; we cannot go on being led as we are.' He concluded by quoting Oliver Cromwell's injunction to the Long Parliament: 'You have sat too long here for any good you have been doing. Depart, I say, and let us have done with you. In the name of God, go.'[8]

That evening and next morning, the lobbies and corridors of Westminster were abuzz with gossip. The question for the Labour Party was whether or not to press the debate to a vote. If a substantial number of Tories could be persuaded either to vote with Labour or to abstain, Chamberlain's position would become untenable. On the other hand, if only a handful voted against the government, then the Prime Minister's hand would actually be strengthened. Labour leaders, especially Attlee and Dalton, were in touch with the Tory rebels in order to estimate how many would vote against the government. Dalton, who was influenced by the failure of any Tory MP to vote against the Munich settlement (though thirty abstained), told the meeting of Labour's Parliamentary Executive, held at 10.30 a.m. on Wednesday 8 May, that he thought a vote at this stage would consolidate the government majority.

In his autobiography, Herbert Morrison claimed sole credit for the Labour Party's decision to force a division. He wrote that 'neither Attlee nor almost any member of the Labour Party Front Bench Committee had considered what to do in this important occasion'.[9] Attlee's account is more persuasive: 'Next day, I recommended to the party that we should vote against the motion for the adjournment. I told them that it must be closely understood that this was a vote of censure and that if it brought the government down we must be prepared to assume responsibility.'[10] If there was any hesitation on Attlee's part, it was about whether enough Conservative MPs would vote in the 'No' lobby. On this point, a letter written on the morning of 8 May by the Liberal leader, Sir Archibald Sinclair, about the strength of the Tory rebellion is revealing:

> As a matter of fact a strong movement did develop among them yesterday, and it is Attlee's opinion, as well as my own – which we expressed to Amery and Dick Law [Conservative MP for Hull South West] in an informal conversation in the corridor – that if they could undertake to produce twenty votes in the lobby we should divide the House.[11]

This letter suggests not only that Attlee was much concerned with what should happen at the end of the debate but that he already had a shrewd idea that it would be worth dividing.

What is clear is that Morrison's speech, opening the second day's debate, was more effective than Attlee's the day before. Harold Nicolson, well-known author and man of letters, and then National Labour MP for Leicester West, wrote in his diary that it was 'a very damaging attack.'[12] The strongest part was the conclusion in which he made a fierce attack on the Prime Minister (Chamberlain), the Chancellor of the Exchequer (Sir John Simon) and the secretary of state for air (Sir Samuel Hoare): 'I cannot forget that in relation to the conduct of British foreign policy between 1931 and 1939, they were consistently and persistently wrong . . . I have the genuine apprehension that if these men remain in office we run the grave risk of losing this war.' The sting in the tail was his announcement that Labour intended to divide the House of Commons at the end of the debate: 'I ask that the vote of the House shall represent the spirit of the country and give a clear indication that we instantly demand that this struggle be carried through to victory, with all vigour and capacity by ministers in command.'[13]

Chamberlain was obviously wounded by Morrison's announcement of the decision to divide because he rose immediately to call for national unity. Unwisely, he spoiled this patriotic appeal by a partisan call to his 'friends' ('and I have friends in this House') to support him in the division lobby. Throughout the afternoon and evening, the debate went badly for the government.

Britain's leader in the previous world conflict, David Lloyd George, concluded his speech by calling on Chamberlain to resign: 'I say solemnly, that the Prime Minister should give an example of sacrifice, because there is nothing which can contribute more to victory in this war than that he should sacrifice the seals of office.'[14] Stafford Cripps, recently returned from a four-month-long world trip, which included India, China, Moscow and the east coast of the United States, and now, in contrast to his position for most of the 1930s, strongly in favour of a widely based coalition, backed up Lloyd George's speech by criticising Chamberlain for his call to his friends:

> I never thought that I should be present in the House of Commons when in a moment so grave a Prime Minister would appeal upon personal grounds and personal friendship to the loyalty of the House of Commons. I trust that those revealing sentences which he spoke will show that he is unfit to carry on the government of this country.[15]

Replying on behalf of the government, Churchill, whom Lloyd George had earlier urged not to be used as an 'air-raid shelter to keep splinters from hitting his colleagues',[16] made a skilful defensive speech. But even he could not stem the tide of cross-party opinion (including influential figures such as the Liberal Clement Davies, the Tory rebel Harold Macmillan and Churchill's friend Robert Boothby).

*

When Churchill sat down at 11 p.m., the House divided. The result of the division was 281 for the ayes and 200 for the noes, a sharp reduction in the government's majority from a possible 213 to 81. Forty-one government supporters had voted in the Labour lobby and there were about sixty deliberate abstentions. Hugh Dalton wrote: 'When I went into our lobby it seemed to be full of young Conservatives in uniform – khaki, Navy blue and Air Force blue all intermingled.'[17] Duff Cooper, the former Conservative minister who had resigned over Munich and who voted against the government, saw a 'young officer in uniform, who had been for long a fervent admirer of Chamberlain, walking through the opposition lobby with the tears streaming down his face'.[18]

The big reduction in the government's majority at such a time of national crisis was a devastating blow to its authority. That night, Chamberlain called Churchill to his room in the House to tell him that he did not think he could continue as Prime Minister. But Churchill, even though a likely successor, urged Chamberlain to fight on. Two meetings the following day were crucial to the downfall of Chamberlain and the accession of Churchill to the premiership. At the first meeting – with Churchill, the Foreign Secretary, Viscount Halifax, and the Conservative chief whip, David Margesson – Chamberlain made it clear that he believed that it was essential for the war effort to bring Labour in and that, if they maintained their refusal to serve under him, he would have to resign. In an attempt to tilt the succession in Halifax's favour, he suggested that Churchill might find it more difficult to get Labour support than Halifax, whom Clement Attlee, in one of his sharp remarks, once described as 'all hunting and Holy Communion'.[19] Halifax, however, said that, as Prime Minister in the Lords, he would be in a hopeless position. If he were neither in charge of the war nor the leader of the Commons, he would be a cipher, with all the responsibility and none of the power. Churchill would, therefore, be the better choice. The chief whip added that feeling in the House had been moving towards Churchill. Churchill did not demur.

The second meeting took place at 6.15 p.m. between Chamberlain, Churchill and Halifax on one side of the Cabinet table and Attlee and Arthur Greenwood on the other. Chamberlain, strongly supported by Churchill, began by urging the Labour leaders to accept office under him. However, Attlee made it clear that Labour would refuse to serve under Chamberlain: 'Our party won't have you and I think I am right in saying that the country won't have you either.'[20] He was then asked if Labour would take part in a coalition with some other Conservative as its head. Attlee said that he thought that they would but that he would ask the National Executive Committee, which was meeting at Bournemouth before the start of the party conference, two questions: first, would they enter a government under the present Prime Minister; second, would they come in under someone else. He agreed to give Chamberlain the answers by telephone the following afternoon.

At dawn the next day (10 May) Germany invaded Belgium and the Netherlands. Chamberlain was tempted to use this news as an excuse to delay his resignation. However, early that morning he was told by one of his close colleagues, the Lord Privy Seal, Sir Kingsley Wood, that the German onslaught on the Low Countries made it all the more essential that there should be a coalition government and that he should go. More important, the Labour Party also held firm. Attlee, after a morning meeting with Sir Archibald Sinclair, who was arguing for delay, issued a statement (drafted by Dalton) in which he and Greenwood called for an urgent and drastic reconstruction of the government. The ball was now firmly in Labour's court.

Attlee and Greenwood, accompanied by an excited Dalton (who told Attlee in the taxi from the Commons to Waterloo about his preference for the Ministry of Economic Welfare), caught the 11.30 a.m. train to Bournemouth for the NEC meeting. The meeting, which took place in a smoke-filled hotel basement, unanimously reaffirmed its refusal to serve under Chamberlain but agreed that Labour should take its 'share of responsibility, as a full partner, in a new government which, under a new Prime Minister, commands the confidence of the nation'.[21] In other words, Labour's answer was 'no' to the first question which they had been asked – and 'yes' to the second.

Before catching a late afternoon train back to London to negotiate his party's way into government, Attlee telephoned Chamberlain's private secretary at 10 Downing Street from the hotel call-box and read out Labour's resolution to him. Attlee's 5 p.m. message was immediately given to Chamberlain, who was presiding over a meeting of the War Cabinet. Chamberlain reported Labour's answers to his colleagues and then announced that 'in light of this answer, he had reached the conclusion that the right course was that he should at once tender his resignation to the King'.[22] Chamberlain then went to Buckingham Palace, handed in his resignation and advised the King to send for Churchill. Just after six o'clock on the evening of 10 May 1940, the King asked Churchill to form a government.

When Attlee and Greenwood arrived at Waterloo later that evening, they were met by a naval officer who told them that Chamberlain had resigned and that the new Prime Minister, Churchill, wanted to see them. They went to the Admiralty, where Churchill formally asked Attlee if the Labour Party would join the government. Attlee agreed straight away. Churchill then offered Attlee more than a third of the places in the government, with two out of five seats in the War Cabinet. He asked Attlee to let him have a list of his colleagues so that they could discuss jobs. As he wrote in *The Gathering Storm*, 'I mentioned Mr Bevin, Mr Alexander, Mr Morrison and Mr Dalton as men whose services in high office were immediately required'.[23] Attlee rang Bournemouth to report progress and went home to bed.

Despite holding only 167 seats in the House of Commons to the government's 418, Labour had pulled off an extraordinary coup. Attlee and his colleagues had set up the debate over the conduct of the war and engineered the vote which had provided the catalyst for the devastating government revolt against Chamberlain. Equally important, by making their presence in a national coalition so indispensable to the successful prosecution of the war, they had created for themselves a *de facto* veto against Chamberlain continuing in office. In the end, it was Attlee's telephone message which did for Chamberlain. The Labour Party may not have been directly responsible for making Churchill Prime Minister. Indeed Dalton and Morrison preferred Halifax (at least until Hitler's onslaught on the Low Countries on 10 May). But by not favouring either man, Labour undermined the main argument used by Chamberlain against a Churchill premiership, which was that he would find it difficult to get Labour Party support. In that sense, Labour's decision (or non-decision) at Bournemouth made Churchill's assumption of power easier.

On Saturday 11 May Churchill and Attlee agreed on the leading ministers in the coalition government. Attlee and Greenwood were to be the two Labour members of the War Cabinet, the others being Churchill (as Prime Minister and Minister of Defence), Chamberlain and Halifax. Churchill, concerned to shore up his Conservative flank, wished to make Chamberlain leader of the Commons and Chancellor of the Exchequer. Attlee vetoed this idea, though understanding the case for keeping Chamberlain in the government as Lord President of the Council, as well as a member of the War

Cabinet. Other appeasers, including Sir John Simon and Sir Samuel Hoare, were shunted aside.

The most important Labour appointment, apart from the two members of the War Cabinet, was Ernest Bevin. Churchill had expressed his admiration for Bevin in his wind-up speech in the Norway debate, and believed that it was essential to have Britain's leading trade unionist in the government. At 11 a.m. on the Saturday, Attlee rang Bevin at Transport House. He first asked him what he thought of Labour joining the coalition. Bevin replied: 'In view of the fact that you helped bring the other fellow down, if the party did not take its share of responsibility, they would say we were not great citizens but cowards.' Attlee then asked if he would be prepared to join the government. Bevin said: 'You have sprung it on me.' Attlee replied that it had been sprung on all of them but 'we want someone from the industrial movement from outside Parliament to come in, not merely to run a department but to help the state in this critical hour'.[24] Bevin asked for time to think it over; he walked over to the Commons to meet Attlee at 3 p.m. At the start of the conversation he made it clear that he would serve if he had the support of his union executive, the TUC and the NEC. When Attlee told Bevin that Churchill wanted him to be minister of labour, Bevin replied that if the ministry remained 'a glorified conciliation board it will be a waste of time'.[25]

Over the next few days, Bevin worked out how he could convert the old ministry into a powerful new organisation controlling manpower, so central to the running of the war. In taking the post of minister of labour and National Service he laid down a number of conditions, the most significant of which was that his ministry should not only be an institution to supply personnel but would also 'make its contribution to the actual organisation of production so as to secure the right utilisation of labour'.[26] So anxious was Churchill to bring Bevin in that he straight away accepted Bevin's conditions. Thus began the Churchill–Bevin partnership, which was to prove vital to winning the war, and the Attlee–Bevin partnership, which after 1945 became the linchpin of the Labour government.

Morrison's response to the arrangements Attlee and Greenwood had negotiated with Churchill was negative. When, at the NEC meeting on the Saturday afternoon, he heard the news about the War Cabinet, including the appointment of Attlee and Greenwood, he muttered to a party official: 'These aren't the people to represent the party.'[27] Dalton reported Morrison as saying that this did not sound like a government which would stand up any better than the last one and that he was inclined to stay out. It was obvious that Morrison thought he ought to have been in the War Cabinet, and was not attracted by the prospect of becoming minister of supply, although Dalton tried to persuade him that he should take the job. In the end, he accepted the post: 'I searched my own mind and conscience very closely and decided it was my duty, not only to the party but to the country to render what service I could.'[28] At such a time of crisis, Morrison could hardly refuse.

With the German invasion of the Low Countries and with an attack on France apparently imminent, both Churchill and Attlee were anxious to complete the government quickly. Attlee remembered 'how at a critical stage in the Dardanelles campaign . . . decisions were delayed because of the long-drawn-out bargaining between the Conservatives and the Liberals over the formation of Asquith's coalition in 1915. I was resolved that I would not, by haggling, be responsible for any failure to act promptly.'[29]

In the major jobs, Labour had done well. Attlee and Greenwood were in the War Cabinet, Bevin at the Ministry of Labour, and Morrison at Supply; A. V. Alexander, a leading member of the Co-operative Party, succeeded Churchill as First Lord of the Admiralty; and Dalton, as he wanted, was appointed minister of economic warfare. The miners' MP David Grenfell became secretary for mines, while Sir William Jowitt (later Lord Jowitt) was solicitor general. Labour was weaker in the junior ranks, partly because of the shortage of suitable recruits. Attlee displayed a firm hand in choosing the Labour members of the coalition. Dalton's diary noted: 'A says he left out Pethick [Frederick Pethick-Lawrence, financial secretary to the Treasury from 1929 to 1931] because too old . . . and Phil [Noel-Baker] because too unbalanced in his judgements, increasingly so these last few months. Also a balance had to be maintained between bourgeois and working-class MPs.'[30]

On Sunday 12 May, Attlee and Greenwood drove down to Bournemouth to report to the NEC on the downfall of Chamberlain and the shape of the new coalition government. Harold Laski, professor at the London School of Economics and a leading left-wing member of the NEC, remarked that it felt 'as though the cook and the kitchen maid were telling us how they had sacked the butler'.[31] Attlee also met the TUC, which promised its support both for the new government and for Bevin's participation in it. The following day, he moved an emergency resolution at the opening session of the party conference, calling for endorsement of the unanimous NEC decision that the party should participate in a coalition government under a new Prime Minister. In his speech, Attlee said he had told Churchill that the Labour leaders were going into government not as individuals but as representatives of the Labour movement. He reminded the delegates that they were meeting at a time of the gravest crisis:

> Right along the line in Holland, Belgium and in France, there is an onrush of the Nazi hordes, and our men . . . are struggling to withstand that onrush . . . we have to stand today for the souls in prison in Czechoslovakia, in Poland, yes, and in Germany . . . Life without liberty is not worth living. Let us go forward and win that liberty, and establish that liberty for ever on the sure foundation of social justice.[32]

Attlee addressed the conference in his usual matter-of-fact tone but on this occasion his sincerity and courage more than made up for his lack of style and he left the hall immediately after his speech to return to Parliament with the cheers of the delegates ringing in his ears.

By 2.30 p.m., when Attlee took his place beside Churchill on the government front bench, the news had come through from Bournemouth that he had won an overwhelming victory, with 2,450,000 votes in favour of the NEC resolution and only a hard core of 170,000 (mostly pacifists and fellow travellers) against. When he entered the Commons, Attlee was congratulated not only by his own party but also by the anti-Chamberlain Tories. But when the new Prime Minister, Churchill, entered the chamber, he was cheered mainly by Labour MPs. It was Chamberlain's entrance which drew the overwhelming majority of Tories cheering to their feet. Churchill was going to need all his eloquence, both to rally the country and to unite his own party. He made a magnificent start with his first short speech to the House of Commons:

> I have nothing to offer but blood, toil, tears and sweat . . . You ask: What is our

policy? I will say: It is to wage war, by sea, land and air, with all our might and with all the strength that God can give us; to wage war against a monstrous tyranny, never surpassed in the dark, lamentable catalogue of human crime.[33]

This time the whole House cheered.

Over the next few weeks, Churchill's government was confronted by a daunting succession of catastrophes on the continent. The Low Countries were overrun; the British Expeditionary Force was cut off and forced to evacuate its troops back to Britain from Dunkirk; and, even more disastrous, the French will to resist collapsed. From 17 June, when the newly formed Pétain government requested an armistice from the Germans, Britain stood alone against Hitler.

Between 27 May and 1 June, 335,000 British and French troops were evacuated from the beaches of Dunkirk. The number rescued was far greater than Churchill had expected, though Attlee with his direct Gallipoli experience, when British troops had been safely evacuated, had been more optimistic. As the Dunkirk drama was being played out, a struggle which would decide the fate of Britain was taking place within the War Cabinet. The issue was whether to continue the war or to try and negotiate peace terms with Hitler.

The Foreign Secretary, Lord Halifax, took a pessimistic view. The minutes show that at a War Cabinet meeting at 9 a.m. on Sunday 26 May, he told his colleagues that 'it was not so much now a question of imposing a complete defeat upon Germany, but of safeguarding the independence of our own empire'.[34] He argued that the conversation he had had the day before with the Italian ambassador about keeping Italy out of the war should be broadened into a general conference about peace and security in Europe. Churchill replied that peace and security could not be achieved under a German domination of Europe and that he was strongly opposed to being sucked into negotiations which might compromise British liberty and independence.

Churchill told his colleagues later that day: 'We would rather go down fighting than be enslaved to Germany.'[35] His problem was the weakness of his position in the War Cabinet. He felt that he could not afford to risk the possibility of Halifax's resignation at such a critical time, especially as he was also uncertain of Chamberlain's position. His only reliable allies in the War Cabinet were Attlee and Greenwood, with the valuable assistance of Sir Archibald Sinclair, the secretary of state for air, whom Churchill had asked to attend as the representative of the Liberal Party.

Attlee, laconically, and Greenwood, more volubly, strongly opposed any approach to either Mussolini or Hitler. At a War Cabinet meeting in the afternoon of 27 May, Attlee said that the Foreign Secretary's strategy would be 'very damaging to us' as it would inevitably lead to Britain asking Mussolini to intercede to obtain peace terms, while Greenwood argued that, if it got out that Britain had sued for terms at the cost of ceding British territory, 'the consequences would be terrible'.[36]

The debate came to a head on Tuesday 28 May, when the War Cabinet discussed a message from the French government, then led by Paul Reynaud, which asked for a direct approach to Italy by France and Britain. At the 4 p.m. meeting, which took place in the Prime Minister's room in the House of Commons, Churchill reaffirmed his opposition, saying that 'the French were trying to get us on to the slippery slope'.[37] He said that once Britain got to the conference table with Hitler, all the forces of resolution which were now at her disposal would vanish. He added that nations that went down fighting rose again but those that surrendered tamely were finished. Attlee resolutely backed up the Churchill position by saying that there was a grave danger that 'if we did what France wanted, we should find it impossible to rally the morale of the people'.[38]

The War Cabinet then adjourned. In the interval, Churchill met all the ministers of Cabinet rank outside the War Cabinet (almost thirty in number). Dalton, who was present at the meeting, wrote in his diary: 'He was quite magnificent. The man, and the only man we have, for this hour . . . He gave a full, frank and completely calm account of events in France . . . We must now expect the sudden turning of the war against this island.' Referring to the subject of the War Cabinet discussions, Churchill said:

> I have thought carefully in these last days whether it was part of my duty to consider entering into negotiations with That Man. But it was idle to think that, if we tried to make peace now, we should get better terms than if we fought it out . . . And I am convinced that every one of you would rise up and

tear me down from my place if I were for one moment to contemplate parley or surrender.[39]

There were loud cries of approval around Prime Minister's table, in which, according to Dalton (an expert in the making of loud noises), Leo Amery, Lord Lloyd (secretary of state for the colonies) and Dalton himself were the loudest.

When the War Cabinet reassembled, Churchill immediately reported what had happened at the ministers' meeting, emphasising that they had expressed the greatest satisfaction when he told them that 'there was no chance of our giving up the struggle'. Rubbing in his advantage, he added that he did not remember having ever before heard 'a gathering of persons occupying high places in political life express themselves so emphatically'.[40] Chamberlain had already fallen in behind the new Prime Minister. Halifax now knew he was beaten. Eight months later, Churchill would be strong enough politically to sack him as Foreign Secretary (replacing him by Anthony Eden) and send him to the United States as British ambassador. Churchill, firmly supported by the two Labour leaders, had won his first decisive victory. The British, strengthened by the almost miraculous number of troops evacuated from the Dunkirk beaches, would fight on.

After the fall of France came the 'Battle of Britain', which was fought and won in the skies. In August and September, a mere 2,500 young British, Commonwealth, Polish and Czech pilots preserved Britain from German invasion, thoroughly justifying Churchill's words in his famous speech to the House of Commons on 20 August: 'Never in the field of human conflict was so much owed by so many to so few.' (Though one fighter pilot is alleged to have quipped: 'That must refer to mess bills.')[41]

But, if the successful outcome of the Battle of Britain prevented Hitler from knocking Britain out of the war, the imbalance of land forces between Britain and Germany made a full-scale British military attack on the mainland of Europe quite out of the question. So, by the end of 1940, there was a strategic stalemate which was only broken by external events – Hitler's invasion of the Soviet Union in June 1941 and the Japanese attack on Pearl Harbor in December 1941, which brought the United States into the war as Britain's ally.

At home, public opinion shifted decisively to the left or at least against the Tories.[42] Pre-war Conservatives such as Chamberlain were blamed by soldiers returning from Dunkirk for the inadequate supply of tanks and aircraft. There were fierce criticisms of the appeasers in the press. A book, *Guilty Men*, a left-wing polemic written by three journalists (including Michael Foot), in a few days sold more than 200,000 copies. At the same time, measures such as the introduction of rationing of food and clothing, welfare improvements like free milk and free school meals, and the increase in the rate of tax on excess war profits from 60 per cent to 100 per cent strengthened the support for egalitarian ideas. 'Fair shares for all' became a popular slogan. Despite Churchill's popularity and a political truce (there was a formal agreement between the three parties to avoid contests in parliamentary by-elections during the war), the tide of opinion worked in Labour's favour, especially with Ernest Bevin's towering presence in the government.

Bevin was Labour's giant, almost as dominant in his sphere as Churchill was as a war leader. As he told a delegate conference from 150 unions on 25 May, 'if our movement and our class rise with all their energy now and save the people of this country from disaster, the country will always turn with confidence to the people who saved them'.[43] His idea was to turn the Ministry of Labour into a powerhouse. He told one of his biographers: 'They say Gladstone was at the Treasury from 1860 to 1930. I'm going to be minister of labour from 1940 to 1990.'[44] Bevin was fifty-nine when he became minister of labour. He had no experience of government or Parliament. But by a combination of willpower, creative intelligence and sheer persuasion, he succeeded in making his ministry one of the vital departments in winning the war and in getting his pre-eminent position in the government accepted throughout the country.

On the second day in his new office, he gave his permanent secretary four sheets of paper on which he set out his vision for his ministry. The key to it was Bevin's claim that the responsibility for all manpower and labour questions must be concentrated in his own hands. The War Cabinet immediately accepted his idea. Although the Emergency Powers Act, which was passed through Parliament in a single day, gave him the power to direct labour, Bevin preferred to proceed, if possible, by consultation and co-operation. He asked for – and got – the co-operation of the trade unions; he established a joint consultative committee of both sides of industry; and he created a Factory and Welfare Division inside his department to concern itself with the health, safety and living conditions of employees.

Using a judicious mixture of persuasion and compulsion, Bevin succeeded in mobilising the labour force, so that by September 1943 more than twenty-two million men and women out of a population of thirty-three million between the ages of fourteen and sixty-four were serving in the armed forces and Civil Defence or were employed in industry, an expansion of 3¾ million in four years. The armed forces had increased by nearly four million, munition industries by nearly two million and the less essential industries reduced by more than 3¼ million.[45] It was an impressive achievement. At the same time, unemployment virtually disappeared, living standards rose and, despite the banning of strikes, the position of trade unions was greatly strengthened.

Churchill much respected Bevin. According to Lord Beaverbrook (not always a reliable witness), Churchill said that, if the Germans landed in Britain, he would set up a Committee of Public Safety, composed of himself, Bevin and Beaverbrook, to lead the British resistance.[46] In the critical days of 1940, Churchill recognised the fighting qualities and determination of Bevin. When Chamberlain, who was dying of cancer, resigned from the government in September 1940, Churchill invited Bevin to join the War Cabinet. Bevin told Dalton: 'Of course, I'm very new at this game and I didn't know what to say when the PM asked me last night. But I thought it would help the prestige of the trade union movement and the Ministry of Labour if I went in.'[47]

Apart from Churchill himself, Bevin became arguably the most powerful member of the War Cabinet. Although he left the direction of the war to Churchill, his influence ran over economic and social policy and even sometimes foreign policy. In every sense, he was a big man – with the possible exception of Clement Attlee, he was the one man in the War Cabinet capable of standing up to Churchill. He had 'the same courage, the same independence, the same confidence to be himself, warts and all, without pretence or inhibition in any company'.[48]

His private life was little changed, except that the Bevins moved for a time to the Strand Palace Hotel so that Florence should not be alone during the Blitz. Later, they rented a flat at 20 Phillimore Court, Kensington. His hours were absurdly long; Florence took the Prime Minister to task about holding Cabinet discussions after midnight (which may have suited Churchill, who took afternoon naps, but hardly anyone else). By the autumn of 1943, Ernest's health was beginning to cause concern. 'I'm all right *here*,' he would say to his friends, tapping his head. 'It is *this* that's letting me down,' and he would bang his broad chest with his fist.[49] But, apart from taking a short holiday with his wife in the north of Scotland, he refused to let up.

The other highly successful Labour minister was Herbert Morrison. After a few months at the Ministry of Supply (in which he never felt comfortable), Churchill promoted him in October to become Home Secretary and minister of home security. The reason Churchill gave Morrison his promotion was because of the damaging impact which the German bombing of London – the so-called Blitz, which began in September 1940 – was having on morale, especially in the East End. Morrison, with his unrivalled London local government experience, was the obvious choice to improve security and offer reassurance. On the day after his appointment he issued the following statement: 'In these times, under such an assault, no man can promise you safety . . . But what can be done to ward off danger, to lessen hardship, and to organise some measure of rest and decent living for those of you who suffer directly, I am determined to do . . . Give me a little time, a reasonable chance, and I will be ready to answer to you for my efforts.'[50]

At the end of September 1940, it was estimated that nearly 200,000 people were sleeping rough in the London Underground without proper facilities. Morrison got bunks installed and sanitation, running water, and canteen facilities organised. He persuaded the War Cabinet to announce a programme of deep shelters for 100,000 people. He pioneered steel table shelters for use inside houses – the so-called Morrison shelter. He introduced compulsory fire-watching to alert the brigades before fires in cities spread and he reorganised the fire services on a national basis. By the summer of 1941, Morrison had given Britain's home defences a sure foundation. It was widely regarded as a brilliant performance.

As Home Secretary, he tried to maintain a balance between security and civil liberties. He suppressed the communist paper the *Daily Worker* on the grounds that it was trying to undermine the war effort. When the Soviet Union became Britain's ally he lifted the ban. But he resisted pressure from Churchill to close down the *Daily Mirror* after it published a cartoon which seemed to imply that the lives of seamen were being sacrificed to increase petrol profits. Despite widespread criticism, he released the interned fascist leader Sir Oswald Mosley on medical grounds and bravely faced down public attacks on his decision, including some from Labour MPs and trade unions. Bevin was furious about Mosley's release. When in 1943 the *Daily Mail* asked him about his achievements at the Home Office, he said: 'We have kept for ourselves a high standard of free speech. No country in the world has a higher standard of civil liberty.'[51]

Morrison's promotion to the War Cabinet in November 1942 was recognition by Churchill of his reputation as a minister. However, his elevation was not welcomed by Bevin, who habitually interrupted Morrison's interventions in Cabinet with a stream of audible sneers and jibes. In 1943 he helped block Morrison's attempt to become party treasurer by backing Arthur Greenwood, who narrowly defeated Morrison. Bevin had made up his mind that Morrison was not to be trusted and there was little that Morrison could do about it.

Morrison had virtually no home life during the war. His wife, Margaret, went down to the West Country to escape the bombing and he rarely visited her there. During the week, he slept in the basement of the Home Office or at the Howard Hotel near the Aldwych. At the weekend, he visited friends in the country, including Ellen Wilkinson, who was his junior minister and rumoured by some to be his mistress. (In 1947, while education minister, Wilkinson died following an overdose of barbiturates, which she was taking for depression.) Morrison liked to relax with families and their children; 'he was the easiest and most pleasant of guests,' said one of his hosts.[52] As a teenager, Shirley Williams, who would later become a Labour Cabinet minister, met him during the war when she sat next to him in an air raid shelter. He was impressed by her intelligence and invited her to the Home Office and subsequently they would have lunch together once a month. Williams spoke of his ebullience and humour and said that he had a genuine belief in the advancement of women in politics.

As Lord Privy Seal and deputy leader of the Commons, Attlee worked from 11 Downing Street (which was the traditional home of the Chancellor of the Exchequer). In addition, he had a bath and bedroom upstairs, although he often had to retreat to a bed in the basement. He saw his family at their home in Stanmore some weekends. More often, he toured factories, military headquarters and cities to boost morale.

Attlee got up at 7.30 a.m., walked across to the Oxford and Cambridge Club in Pall Mall for his breakfast, and took a short stroll in St James's Park before returning to Downing Street for Cabinet committees. When Parliament was sitting, he usually lunched at the House and spent some of the afternoon there, before returning to Downing Street for further Cabinet committees or discussions with ministers. After dinner at the Oxford and Cambridge Club, he usually returned to Downing Street for work on Cabinet papers. At midnight he heard the latest radio news bulletin before going to bed.[53]

Attlee believed that the Churchill coalition was vital in winning the war and he was determined to keep it together. One of his biographers described his role as follows: 'He had to conciliate Conservative backbenchers, reassure Labour, mediate between Labour and Conservative ministers and even between quarrelling Labour ministers, and manage Churchill's political and personal idiosyncrasies.'[54] He was crucial to the coalition government. Apart from Churchill, only Attlee was continuously a member of the War Cabinet throughout the war. Only Attlee was a member of the three big Cabinet committees – the War Cabinet itself, the Defence Committee, and the Lord President's Committee, which he himself had proposed to run the civil side of the war. In 1942, Attlee was appointed deputy Prime Minister. During Churchill's long absences abroad in the United States, in north Africa, at international conferences such as Tehran and Yalta, Attlee was acting Prime Minister; in all, he acted as Prime Minister for a total period of at least six months. It was a valuable apprenticeship.

When Attlee presided over the Cabinet, everything changed. A member of the coalition government was asked about the contrast: 'When Attlee takes the chair, Cabinet meetings are business-like and efficient, we keep to the agenda, make decisions and get away in reasonable time. When Mr Churchill presides, nothing is decided; we listen enthralled and go home, many hours later, feeling that we have been present at an historic occasion.'[55]

Attlee played an indispensable role in oiling the wheels of the wartime coalition. His problem was that, in contrast to Bevin and Morrison, the good things which he did were mostly behind the scenes, while his public persona showed him at a disadvantage. Quite often, he had to deputise for Churchill in the House of Commons. Harold Nicolson, admittedly a big Churchill fan, was critical of Attlee's performance – 'like a snipe pretending to be an eagle', he noted in his diary.[56] In May 1943 he wrote to his wife, Vita Sackville-West, after Attlee's statement about the Allied victory at Tunis: 'I cannot convey to you the absurdity of that small man. As someone remarked afterwards, "it is difficult to make a defeat sound like a victory; but to make such a victory sound like a defeat is a masterpiece in human ingenuity".'[57] It was the same at Labour Party conferences, where more eloquent speakers such as Morrison and Dalton and more outgoing personalities like Bevin tended to outshine Attlee. As the tide of war began to turn in the Allies' favour, Attlee was also criticised for his loyalty to Churchill and the coalition and for his failure, as critics such as Laski and Bevan saw it, to press for more socialist measures. Laski even approached Bevin to ask him to run against Attlee for the leadership. But Bevin turned him down flat.[58]

Attlee gave his Labour colleagues strong support. In a sense, he acted as Labour's chief shop steward. He worked very closely with Bevin, in particular; when early in 1942 Churchill appointed Lord Beaverbrook minister of production, giving him overall responsibility for manpower as well as production, Attlee not only backed Bevin's vehement opposition but also faced down Churchill. It was Beaverbrook, not Bevin or Attlee, who resigned. The relationship between Attlee and Bevin, which had not been particularly warm before the war (indeed Bevin was highly critical of what he regarded as Attlee's failure to give a lead on foreign affairs), now became exceptionally close. Bevin came to respect Attlee's judgement and lack of vanity and recognised in him those qualities of integrity and loyalty on which he himself set such store. It was after experiencing the skill and firmness with which Attlee presided over the War Cabinet during Churchill's absences that he began to refer to him as Labour's Campbell-Bannerman (after the modest Liberal Prime Minister who had kept the brilliant Liberal Cabinet of the 1900s together).[59]

Attlee also gave Morrison support when he ran into criticism over the release of Oswald Mosley and backed him against Churchill when he took a permissive line on press censorship. However, the Labour minister who owed most to Attlee was Dalton. As we have seen, from the first Dalton had his eyes on the Ministry of Economic Welfare. Attlee not only intervened with Churchill to ensure that the ministry went to Dalton. He also supported the plan for the Special Operations Executive (SOE), the organisation set up to foster resistance in occupied territory, to be put under Dalton's wing. Yet again Attlee's intercession proved effective. As one of Churchill's aides told Dalton, 'if C.R.A. digs his feet in he will win'.[60]

Dalton was an energetic minister but, with his abrasive personality, he made enemies, especially among Tories, many of whom resented what they saw as his betrayal of his class. One of Churchill's closest confidants, Brendan Bracken, took delight in scheming against Dalton. When Churchill made Bracken minister of information, Bracken launched a campaign to get the SOE put under his control. Though Attlee continued to speak up on Dalton's behalf, Bracken's trump card was the support of the Prime Minister, who found Dalton uncongenial: 'Keep that man away from me. I can't stand his booming voice and shifting eyes.'[61] In February 1942 Dalton, who, ironically, much admired Churchill, was moved to the Board of Trade, a promotion which was to prove a blessing. His greatest achievement there was to develop a 'location of industry' policy to create jobs in the pre-war high unemployment areas, such as the north-east, where Dalton's constituency was situated.

Dalton's egoism led to the temporary breakdown of his marriage. During the Blitz he remained in his office, showing little concern for his wife, Ruth, who narrowly escaped being bombed in their flat. After a time, she left for a job in the north, sickened by his disregard for her.

The year 1942 was a low point for the coalition and Churchill, and for the loyal Attlee as well. Although the entrance into the war of both the United States and the Soviet Union had shifted the strategic balance decisively in the Allies' favour, a series of British military defeats led to a storm of criticism of the government's performance, including a no-confidence debate in the Commons. In the Far East, two British battleships, the *Prince of Wales* and the *Repulse*, had been sunk by Japanese aircraft in December 1941. On 15 February 1942, 130,000 British, Indian and dominion troops surrendered

Singapore to a Japanese force half their number. In north Africa, Tobruk surrendered to Rommel in June 1942 with 33,000 men taken prisoner; Churchill, who was at a White House gathering with Franklin Roosevelt when the news about Tobruk broke, commented: 'Defeat is one thing; disgrace is another.'[62]

It was against this background of bad news that the extraordinary but brief emergence of Stafford Cripps as a 'man of destiny' was played out. After being expelled from the Labour Party, Cripps had spent the beginning of the war on an extended trip to India, China, the United States and the Soviet Union, where he met as many of the leaders of these countries as he could. On his return to Britain, Lord Halifax, Churchill and the rest of the War Cabinet, including Attlee, decided to send him on a special mission to Moscow in May 1940, on the grounds that contact with the Soviet Union was most likely to be established by a leading left-winger. However, the Soviets refused to accept the mission unless he was made ambassador and so Cripps spent the next eighteen months in Moscow trying to build relations. Even after the German invasion of the Soviet Union in June 1941, and despite the presence at the Moscow embassy of his wife, Isobel, and his two daughters, Peggy and Theresa, he found the experience a frustrating one, being virtually ignored by the Soviet leaders.

At the beginning of 1942, Cripps returned from Moscow to find that the public were quite wrongly crediting him with having brought the Soviet Union into the war. Churchill, seeing him as a potential political danger, offered Cripps the Ministry of Supply but without a seat in the War Cabinet, so Cripps refused. On 8 February Cripps made a radio broadcast in which, after referring to the hardships being endured by the Soviet people, he called for 'unstinted sacrifice' by the British. He told listeners: 'I have felt in this country since my return a lack of urgency.'[63] The Cripps message struck a chord, particularly with progressive opinion. According to Mass-Observation, Cripps immediately became the only credible successor to Churchill, apart from Anthony Eden; Attlee, Bevin and Morrison were hardly mentioned. The press, especially the *Times*, were strongly in favour of Cripps being given a seat in the War Cabinet.[64]

On 19 February Churchill brought Cripps into the War Cabinet in Attlee's position as Lord Privy Seal and with Churchill's role as leader of the

House of Commons as well. Attlee was compensated for this change by becoming secretary of state for the dominions and, more important, deputy Prime Minister. Arthur Greenwood, with his long-standing drink problem, was sacked. Here Attlee, in allowing his faithful deputy to go, showed his ruthless side. In mitigation, it should be said that his energy had been concentrated on shoring up Bevin's position against Lord Beaverbrook and also on fighting his own corner. In any case, he had always had good personal relations with Cripps and had regretted his expulsion from the party. Early in March, Cripps agreed to go on a personal mission to India, on behalf of the War Cabinet, carrying with him a plan for future Indian independence to be negotiated with both the Hindu majority and the Muslim minority. The mission did not succeed, mainly because the War Cabinet was not prepared to agree to the Congress Party's demand for an immediate Indian government. However, despite the mission's failure, Cripps's public standing at home remained high.

It is improbable that Cripps really expected to topple Churchill; it is more likely that he hoped to run the war as a kind of Winston–Stafford duumvirate. Dalton wrote in his diary:

> The entry of Cripps as LPS [Lord Privy Seal] is very interesting. If he has grown out of being a bloody fool, he will be first class, and, in any case, if things go badly for a few months, his stock, now artificially inflated, will fall heavily and he will have to bear a large part of the responsibility.[65]

Cripps was not a success as a leader of the House (he tended to lecture MPs instead of trying to charm them) and he unwisely tried to interfere in the running of the war. When he failed to persuade Churchill to give up his special role as minister of defence in favour of a so-called War Planning Directorate, it was clear that he would have to go. Cripps himself accepted that the Prime Minister was entitled to run the war in his own way. He was, however, persuaded by Attlee and Eden to put off resigning while major battles were about to be fought in north Africa.

The victory of British and dominion forces at El Alamein in November 1942, followed a few days later by the successful landing of American and British troops in north Africa, effectively dished Cripps. Churchill dismissed him from the War Cabinet, though, with the support of Attlee, he was made minister of aircraft production, in which his outstanding administrative talents were fully used. If 1942 proved to be somewhat of a disaster for Cripps, his relations with Labour ministers became closer, especially with Attlee, opening the way, as the war reached its end, to his return to the Labour Party – and the third and most successful phase of the Cripps saga.

Churchill described General Montgomery's victory at El Alamein as 'the end of the beginning'.[66] Arguably the Anglo-American landings in north Africa on 8 November and certainly the surrender of the German 6th Army at Stalingrad on 30 January 1943 were more important. The tide of war had at last turned decisively in favour of the Allies. Italy was invaded in 1943 and in 1944 the brilliantly successful Normandy landings opened the way for the liberation of France.

The church bells which Churchill ordered to be rung throughout the British Isles to celebrate victory in north Africa also symbolised a new time of hope, when people's thoughts could at last begin to turn to the future. Churchill had declared the guiding principle of the coalition government to be 'everything for the war, whether controversial or not, and nothing controversial that is not *bona fide* needed for war'. But after El Alamein, political pressure mounted for domestic reconstruction and reform.

The publication of the Beveridge report on 1 December 1942, coming three weeks after El Alamein, was perfectly timed. It set out a comprehensive programme of social security from 'the cradle to the grave'. It proposed a National Health Service and family allowances, as well as a high level of employment for which the state would take responsibility. The report was almost universally welcomed and its author, William Beveridge, a former civil servant and director of the LSE, became overnight a popular hero: he said that it was 'like riding on an elephant through a cheering mob'.[67] Some 635,000 copies were sold, an astonishing number for a government White Paper.

For the Labour ministers, the Beveridge report offered both a great opportunity and a dilemma. Attlee and his colleagues were strongly in favour of the report, which they saw as a central part of their programme. But their hands were tied by the hostility of Churchill and the Tories to its implementation before the end of the war. Attlee wrote to Churchill: 'I doubt whether in your inevitable and proper preoccupation with military problems you are fully cognisant of the extent to which decisions must be taken and implemented in the field of post war reconstruction before the end of the war . . . I am certain that unless the government is prepared to be as courageous in planning for peace as it has been in carrying on the war, there is extreme danger of disaster when the war ends.' The War Cabinet Minutes of 12 and 15 February 1943 show a fierce debate between the parties, with Labour arguing for implementation and the Tories, led by Churchill, refusing to budge. In the end, the War Cabinet agreed to plan for the Beveridge report but not to legislate.[68]

Attlee, Bevin and Morrison tried to persuade the Parliamentary Labour Party not to vote against the government's formula but two excessively cautious speeches, one by the Lord President of the Council, Sir John Anderson, and the other, even more negative, by the Chancellor of the Exchequer, Sir Kingsley Wood, incited Labour backbenchers to rebellion. Morrison, who had played a leading role inside the Cabinet in support of Beveridge, made a skilful winding-up speech in which he pointed out that the coalition government had accepted the majority of Beveridge's principles. But ninety-seven Labour MPs voted against the government and only twenty-three supported it, of whom twenty-two were ministers. Typically Attlee's response to this rebellion was low key. He wrote to his brother Tom: 'The Beveridge report was not a good show though Morrison was first class. On these questions so many of our fellows good men not mischief makers tend to lose their hearts to the exclusion of their heads . . . However no doubt it will all blow over.'[69] Bevin was, however, furious at what he saw as the disloyalty of his colleagues and from February 1943 to May 1944 refused to attend parliamentary meetings, as if he was representative in the War Cabinet not of the PLP but of the trade unions, which was, of course, partly true.

Attlee was fiercely attacked at the June 1943 Labour Party conference for his stand on Beveridge (even though he had argued strongly for it inside the War Cabinet) and there were calls for an end to the coalition, which, in the eyes of many activists, was preventing Labour fully exploiting the tide of public opinion. They pointed out that the successes of independent and unofficial left-wing candidates (including the Common Wealth Party) at by-elections demonstrated how the mood had turned drastically against the Conservatives and towards reconstruction and reforms. At the December 1944 party conference feelings were so strong that the Labour left were able to carry a wide-ranging resolution against the platform, calling for the transfer to public ownership of land, large-scale buildings, heavy industry and all forms of banking, transport fuel and power.

In his down-to-earth, rational way, Attlee had given his answer to the critics: 'I doubt if we recognise sufficiently the progress our ideas have made.' He added: 'The people of this country will not forget that some of the most onerous posts in government have been held by Labour men who have shown great ability, ability to administer and courage to take unpopular decisions.'[70] He was right. Bevin and Morrison had clearly demonstrated themselves to be outstanding ministers, while, in a more modest fashion, Attlee had carried out his many roles in the coalition government (including managing his own colleagues) with unobtrusive skill. The tortoise and the hares had combined with Churchill to help save the country. They were now well placed, even more than they realised, to win power for the Labour Party on its own.

7

1945: Landslide year

Nineteen forty-five was the year of Labour's great election victory, when, for the first time, the party won a majority – a massive majority – in Parliament. Recognising their substantial contribution to the success of the coalition government, particularly on the home front, it was to the Labour leaders and not Winston Churchill that the British people turned in the expectation of a better life once the war was won. Clement Attlee speedily assembled an impressive administration, built around his main colleagues – Ernest Bevin, Herbert Morrison, Hugh Dalton and Stafford Cripps – and presented a full programme, based on the Labour manifesto *Let Us Face the Future*, to the new parliament. However, the government had almost immediately to face up to one of the financial and economic crises which were to be such a burden to it.

As victory drew nearer, the discipline which had masked party differences throughout the war began to loosen. Oliver Lyttelton, one of Churchill's closest colleagues, put it neatly in his memoirs: 'Defeat unites together, victory opens the seams.'[1] As MPs looked forward to the post-war world, their divisions became more obvious.

Inside the Cabinet, Labour ministers, especially Morrison, became increasingly pressing on issues of reconstruction, so much so that Churchill drafted a note to Attlee complaining of 'the force and power of your representatives'.[2] Two months later, in a magisterial rebuke which he typed out himself, Attlee castigated Churchill not only for the self-indulgent way in which he chaired Cabinets but also for the unwarranted attention he gave to his two Conservative 'attack dogs', Lord Beaverbrook and Brendan Bracken (Dalton referred to them as M (Max) and B (Brendan) after the latest sulphur drug, the precursor of antibiotics). Attlee wrote:

The conclusions agreed upon by a committee on which have sat five or six members of the Cabinet and other experienced ministers are then submitted with great deference to the Lord Privy Seal [Beaverbrook] and the minister of information [Bracken], two ministers without Cabinet responsibility neither of whom has given any serious attention to the subject. When they state their view it is obvious that they know nothing about it. Nevertheless an hour is consumed in listening to their opinions.[3]

In October 1944, the Labour Party's National Executive Committee had announced that Labour would fight the next election as an independent party. When Churchill, with Attlee in agreement, moved the prolongation of the parliament for a year that same month, he said: 'I have myself a clear view that it would be wrong to continue this parliament beyond the period of the German war.'[4] Conservative MPs, hoping to ride on Churchill's coat tails to election victory, wanted a poll as soon as possible after Germany was defeated (the German surrender took place on 7 May 1945). But Churchill, 'distressed', as he wrote later, 'at the prospect of sinking from a national to a party leader',[5] and worried about the expansionist ambitions of the Soviet Union, proposed to the Labour leaders that the coalition should be continued at least until the defeat of Japan (the war with Japan was expected to last well into 1946).

Attlee and Bevin were sympathetic to Churchill's argument that, with the international situation so uncertain, it was unwise to break up the coalition immediately. But Morrison, who earlier had advocated a continuation of the coalition after the war (mostly because he had expected a Tory victory), was now in favour of its end and an election in October, when a new register of voters would be ready. In his role as chairman of the Labour Campaign Committee, he voiced party feeling in favour of terminating the coalition.

Churchill had delayed making a decision while Attlee was in the United States attending the San Francisco conference that set up the United Nations. Immediately on his return, Attlee had a long and friendly late night meeting with Churchill at No. 10. Churchill produced a draft letter which offered the choice of an immediate election or the extension of the coalition until the end of the war with Japan. After talking to Bevin, Attlee suggested adding a sentence which said that, if the coalition were extended, the government would do its best to implement the proposals for security and full employment which had already been presented to Parliament. Attlee told Churchill that this addition would give him a better chance of persuading the Labour Party at its coming conference to stay in the coalition.

However, when the NEC met at Blackpool on 20 May, the day before the conference opened, the tide of party opinion was running strongly against a continuance of the coalition. So, in introducing Churchill's letter, Attlee characteristically confined himself to setting out the pros and cons, though Bevin argued for continuing the coalition until the end of the Japanese war. Morrison, backed up by the chief whip, spoke strongly against and carried the meeting by a big majority. Attlee, with the help of Morrison, then wrote a letter to Churchill putting the case for an election in October and explaining Labour's unwillingness to prolong the coalition until after the defeat of Japan. On receiving Attlee's letter, Churchill (who felt that Attlee had let him down), went to Buckingham Palace to tender the resignation of the coalition. Parliament was to be dissolved on 15 June and the general election held on 5 July. Meanwhile, a Conservative 'caretaker' administration would remain in office.

Labour's Blackpool conference, which Dalton described as 'dramatic',[6] signalled the end of the great coalition in which Labour had played so distinguished a part. It also marked the beginning of the general election campaign and provided an excellent showcase for the party. Dalton wrote: 'We have a finer body of Labour candidates, including a large number of young service candidates, than ever before.'[7] The service candidates included John Freeman (Watford), Kenneth Younger (Grimsby), Denis Healey (Pudsey & Otley) and Roy Jenkins (Solihull), who, resplendent in uniform, made the telling point that Labour now represented the entire nation.

Morrison opened a three-day debate on the Labour manifesto. Michael Young, the party's research secretary, who prepared the document, remarked that it 'almost wrote itself'.[8] The passages on social security, the National Health Service and full employment had already been prepared for the coalition government by Whitehall. In calling for planning, Labour's leaders were able to refer to the system of state controls which had been established during the war. The most controversial parts dealt with nationalisation: Labour proposed to nationalise the Bank of England, fuel and power, transport, and iron and steel. Morrison sensibly advised the party not to make a general case for public ownership but to argue the merits of nationalising particular industries. Morrison's speech was cheered to the echo by the conference and highly praised in the press. The *Daily Express* wrote: 'He was the present idol of the delegates and undoubted leader of the party today.'[9]

Attlee and Bevin made speeches on foreign policy, both of which were well received, especially Bevin's. According to Morgan Phillips, national secretary of the party, Bevin spoke on foreign affairs because he happened to be the most senior minister available. Whatever the reason, he made a constructive and original speech which wrongly convinced some observers that he was staking a claim for the Foreign Office. In fact, he had his eye on the Chancellorship.

As described in the Prologue of this book, the party chairman, Ellen Wilkinson, and her successor, Harold Laski, tried to persuade a number of leading MPs that Attlee should step aside in favour of Morrison. Dalton's view was that a change of leadership was out of the question at this time. He added that, if Attlee did stand down, many MPs would prefer Bevin to Morrison. Immediately following the conference, Laski wrote a letter to the party leader asking him to resign, which elicited Attlee's crushingly brief reply (see p. 3). In his letter, Laski had accused Attlee of lacking 'a sense of the dramatic, the power to give a lead, the ability to reach the masses, the definition of great issues in a great way'.[10] Laski's criticisms of Attlee were justified, but the Labour leader now demonstrated that his virtues of integrity, reasoned argument, and coolness under pressure, could prove formidable.

On 28 May, before the campaign began, Churchill invited former members of the coalition government to the Cabinet Room for a farewell party. Churchill, with tears streaming down his face, said that they had all come together, and had stayed together as a united band of brothers in a very trying time. History would recognise this: 'The light will shine on every helmet.' He added that, when he went to meet Stalin and Truman at Potsdam, he wanted to take with him 'my good friend, Clem Attlee'.[11] A week later, on 4 June, when Churchill made his first radio election broadcast (this was an election dominated by the radio), his tone had completely changed. The great statesman and war leader had been replaced by the polemical politician. 'Socialism', he thundered, 'is inseparably woven with totalitarianism.' If a Labour government carried out its programme, it would require some form of Gestapo, 'no doubt very humanely directed in the first instance'.[12] As a description of a party and its leaders with whom he had been in a popular coalition only two weeks before, this was absurd. Mass-Observation reported 'the disappointment and genuine distress aroused by his speech'.[13]

Attlee's response the following night was far more in tune with the mood of the voters. His beginning was 'more in sorrow than in anger'. He continued:

> When I listened to the Prime Minister's speech last night, in which he gave such a travesty of the policy of the Labour Party, I realised at once what was his object. He wanted the electors to understand how great was the difference between Winston Churchill the great leader in war and Mr Churchill the party leader of the Conservatives . . . The voice we heard last night was that of Mr Churchill, but the mind was that of Lord Beaverbrook.[14]

Attlee paid a generous tribute to Churchill the war leader, quietly but firmly rejected his attack on the Labour Party, outlined Labour's policy at home and abroad, and concluded by projecting Labour as a great democratic party 'which most nearly reflects in its representation and composition all the mainstreams which flow into the great river of our national life'.[15] It was a devastating riposte, heard by forty million people, and was the making of Attlee as a campaigner.

In contrast to Churchill's one-man band, Labour's election campaign was a team effort. Whereas the Conservative Party concentrated nearly half its broadcasting time on Churchill, the Labour Party allocated its slots after the nine o'clock news to ten different people. Attlee began the broadcasts and Morrison wound up; in between came Bevin, Dalton, Cripps, A. V. Alexander, Jim Griffiths and others.

Churchill's campaign was a quasi-royal procession. Crowds lined the streets to cheer the great man as he passed in an open car. Attlee's election tour (through the West Midlands to Lancashire and down through Newcastle, Yorkshire, the eastern counties and back to London) was a more modest affair; as Roy Jenkins put it, 'he chugged around in a family saloon with his wife at the wheel from one moderate sized meeting to another, with no spectators on his journeys'.[16] Attlee noted that the contrast, which was widely reported in the press, turned out to be an asset. The hero of the opposition press was Bevin, the vigour of whose speeches appealed to the popular newspapers. Bevin's attacks on Beaverbrook attracted a good deal of attention, as did his promise that Labour would build four or five million houses. Cripps, welcomed back to the Labour fold, was much in demand as a speaker. Pointing to the success of the wartime coalition, he advocated planning as the way to achieve full employment in peacetime. Dalton spoke at the constituency meetings of thirty-two candidates, many of whom were young, good looking and university educated; twenty-nine of them won their seats.

As chairman of the Campaign Committee, Morrison played a dominant role. From an office in Transport House, he helped co-ordinate publicity; one and a half million copies of *Let Us Face the Future* and 100,000 copies of pamphlets on his and Bevin's ministerial work were published. He worked closely with the *Daily Mirror*; Zec, the brilliant *Mirror* cartoonist, gave advice on Labour's posters, including 'Vote for Him', aimed at women whose husbands and sons were in the forces. At the same time as masterminding the national campaign, Morrison was also co-ordinating the London campaign and fighting a new seat. His old seat, Hackney South, was redistributed, so he moved to the Tory-held suburban constituency of Lewisham East, which was close to his Eltham home. At weekends, he visited constituencies outside London. He went to Lancashire and north Wales, and the north-east. The voters were in a serious mood and Morrison was a star attraction.[17]

On 14 June, Laski, chairman of the party, issued a statement which said that, if Attlee accepted Churchill's invitation to attend the 'big three' conference at Potsdam, he should do so only as an observer. Laski's statement was unauthorised. It was seized on by Churchill and followed up by Beaverbrook and the *Daily Express* as demonstrating that, if Labour were elected, foreign policy would be run by the NEC. Laski was now a target.

When he made a later speech at Newark, a local paper wrongly claimed that Laski had advocated the use of force to bring about a socialist state. Some Tories thought that they had found the 1945 equivalent of the Zinoviev letter, which had so damaged the Labour government in the 1924 election.

However, unlike Ramsay MacDonald, Attlee responded promptly and skilfully. In reply to a letter from Churchill, Attlee pointed out that it had reached him at 11.30 p.m., after it had been issued to the press. Tongue in cheek, he apologised to Churchill for sending his reply to the press before it could reach the Prime Minister. He continued: 'Much of your trouble is due to your not understanding the distinction between the Labour Party and the Parliamentary Labour Party ... Despite my very clear statement you proceed to exercise your imagination by imparting into a right to be consulted a power to challenge actions and conduct.'[18] The judgement of the two academics who wrote the Nuffield College survey of the 1945 election was that Attlee had the better of these exchanges with Churchill and rose in public estimation: 'He had the air of a sound and steady batsman, keeping up his wicket with ease against a bowler who was losing both pace and length.'[19]

Throughout the campaign, Churchill misjudged the mood of the voters. As Morrison noted, they were quietly thoughtful.[20] In beautiful summer weather, Labour candidates addressed well-attended meetings, eager to hear what they had to say. Roy Jenkins, who was fighting the safe Tory seat of Solihull, recalled 'two or three twilight open-air meetings outside pubs which had just closed, when great seas of faces looked up seeking a message appropriate to that time of relief, exhaustion and hope'.[21]

Churchill protected the Tories from being associated only with pre-war unemployment and the appeasement of Hitler and Mussolini. But, to most people, he was seen as the heroic war leader rather than a credible post-war reformer. It was to his loyal coalition partners, Bevin, Morrison and Attlee, that the voters turned, in the expectation they would best be able to implement the social gains promised by the coalition government.

Labour put to the electorate a moderate and by now familiar programme of full employment, social security, a health service and more housing, which closely reflected their needs. Though Labour did not highlight its nationalisation programme, there was little opposition to the pragmatic, piecemeal public ownership which they proposed. In the words of Michael

Young, 'There was a real sense in 1945, one which was well understood by the voters, that it was the Labour Party's leaders, not Churchill, who were speaking for the nation and its concerns.'[22]

Most people still thought that Churchill would win the election. A poll in the *Daily Express* showed that 54 per cent believed that the Conservatives would win, compared with only 38 per cent for Labour. Yet a Gallup poll of voting intentions in the *News Chronicle*, based on enquiries made in 195 constituencies between 24 June and 27 June, revealed that 47 per cent were going to vote Labour and 41 per cent Tory.[23] This prediction of a Labour landslide was largely ignored (opinion polls had not yet acquired their subsequent importance), although it proved to be almost spot on.

When the votes were counted, Labour had won 47.8 per cent of the vote to the Conservatives' 39.8 per cent. First-past-the-post translated this into a massive Labour overall majority of 146 in seats, with Labour having 393 members of Parliament compared to the Conservatives' 213. Labour's big advance compared to the 1935 election took place mainly in the London suburbs, the west Midlands and East Anglia. In class terms, what happened in 1945 was that 'the working classes of the declining areas of heavy industry joined forces through the ballot-box with much of the more prosperous working class in the Midlands and the south-east, and a substantial section of the urban middle classes'.[24] More than two million middle-class voters swung to Labour, along with a majority of new and service voters. Labour, as Arthur Greenwood argued, represented for the first time a genuine 'cross-section of the national life'.[25]

Labour had won not only an overall majority in terms of seats, but one which was big enough to give it an impregnable position for the life of the parliament. Inspired by Labour's victory and fortified by the failure of Morrison's attempted coup (see pp. 3–4), Attlee moved with commendable speed to construct a government. His most important appointments were to make Bevin Foreign Secretary, Dalton Chancellor of the Exchequer and Morrison Lord President of the Council and leader of the House of Commons.

His decision to give Bevin the Foreign Office was governed by the need to keep Bevin and Morrison apart and to put Labour's outstanding statesman in the post, which was likely to be exposed to increasing pressure from the

Soviets. However, Edmund Dell, in his survey of Chancellors since the war, concluded that the switch of Bevin to the Foreign Office was a tragedy for the conduct of economic policy and one of Attlee's worst mistakes.[26] Dell argued that Bevin, with his commanding position in the government and in the Labour movement, would have been far better equipped to insist on bringing policy commitments in line with the nation's resources. It was certainly the case that Dalton as Chancellor was no match for Bevin in arguing whether Britain could afford its world role.

There is less debate about Attlee's choice of Morrison as Lord President and leader of the Commons. Morrison was also given the role of chief co-ordinating minister on the home front and, in Attlee's absence, the Prime Minister's deputy. A lesser man might have borne a grudge against Morrison for the attempt to oust him on 26 July. But Attlee understood that Morrison, with his administrative flair, was the best man to run Labour's programme. He was a great success in the job and rapidly became, in the words of Morrison's biographers, 'the most important single dynamo in the government's machine'.[27]

Stafford Cripps's appointment was another example of Attlee turning a blind eye to political manoeuvring against him. Attlee had given Cripps consistent support, even during the 1930s when Cripps sided with the far left against the Labour leadership. During the war Attlee welcomed him to the coalition, even though he was an independent. When Churchill sacked Cripps from the War Cabinet after El Alamein, Attlee fought successfully to retain him as minister for aircraft production. At the end of 1944 Cripps approached Attlee about rejoining the Labour Party; the Labour leader wrote him a warm message: 'It is a real joy to me that we shall be again together in the party in the New Year.'[28] When Cripps backed Morrison in his attempt to seize the leadership, instead of castigating him for his ingratitude, Attlee responded by offering him the Board of Trade. Although the new Prime Minister did not rate Cripps's political judgement (he reputedly described him as a 'political goose') he respected his integrity and brains. In addition, Cripps's success as minister for aircraft production during the war made him an obvious choice for the Board of Trade, where he was able to take the lead in encouraging industrial production and exports, as well as stimulating regional employment.

Attlee's boldest gamble was to make Aneurin Bevan minister of health. Until he entered the Cabinet as its youngest member (aged forty-seven), Bevan was the archetypal rebel, 'always arguing for the most extreme position and kicking against the constraints of political leadership and discipline'.[29] Born in Tredegar, Monmouthshire, he became a miner at the age of thirteen and chairman of his local lodge at nineteen. In 1926 he was appointed a full-time union official and in 1929 he was elected as Labour MP for Ebbw Vale. Blessed with natural wit and a silver tongue, he quickly made his mark in the House of Commons. In the great causes of the inter-war period he was always on the side of the radical left of the party. During the 1930s he was a close ally of Cripps and in 1939 was expelled from the party for a few months (though, unlike his mentor, he quickly returned to the fold).

During the war Bevan emerged as the most formidable critic of Churchill and the coalition government, including its Labour ministers. About Churchill he wrote: 'His ear is so sensitively attuned to the bugle note of history that he is often dead to the more raucous clamour of contemporary life.'[30] He accused Ernest Bevin of finding it 'easier to deceive the people than to offend the Tories'[31] and described Attlee as bringing 'to the fierce struggle of politics the tepid enthusiasm of a lazy summer afternoon at a cricket match'.[32] In 1944 he was nearly re-expelled from the party, after a ferocious attack on Bevin.

In his interview at 10 Downing Street with Bevan, Attlee made it clear to the former rebel that he was starting with a clean sheet: 'You are the youngest member of the Cabinet. Now it is up to you. The more you can learn the better.'[33] According to Bevan, Attlee also said: 'I understand that you have much experience of negotiation. I am offering you the post where you will deal with health, housing and local authorities.'[34] Cynics suggested that Attlee wanted Bevan in his Cabinet to shut up a dangerous critic. But a more important reason was that Attlee recognised Bevan's outstanding ability and wanted to give him the opportunity to use his talents constructively, by helping build the National Health Service.

Dalton described the 1945 Labour administration as 'a well-balanced government, with a number of strong and combative personalities, and Attlee held it together with much tact and patience'.[35] Attlee had had the best training for being Prime Minister it was possible to have. He understood about administration and how governments were run. As deputy Prime Minister to Churchill, he had presided over the Cabinet on many occasions, especially in the later stages of the war, and received praise from all quarters for his performance. Attlee saw his role in Cabinet as more an impartial chairman, whose job it was to facilitate business and get decisions. Usually he did not express an opinion, confining himself to collecting the views of his colleagues and then summing up: 'Well, I think the decision of the Cabinet is this, that or the other. Any objections?'[36]

Attlee relied on the heavyweights in the Cabinet, especially Bevin, Morrison, Dalton and Cripps (his 'hares'), to give his government ideas and direction. As Bevin's biographer, Alan Bullock, put it, 'there were half a dozen men in the government with more obvious talents than his own; it was Attlee's strength as a Prime Minister that he turned this to his advantage'.[37] In Cabinet meetings, he went first to Morrison, co-ordinator on the home front, and finished with the Foreign Secretary, Bevin. Although Attlee was abrupt with most other ministers, he allowed Bevin latitude not only to roam, often brilliantly, over external affairs but to intervene on domestic matters as well. At the end of Cabinet meetings, Attlee usually asked Bevin to stay behind. The close personal relationship between the two men, which had begun during the war, was the linchpin which held the Labour government together. Attlee said: 'My relationship with Ernest Bevin was the deepest of my political life. I was very fond of him and I understood he was very fond of me . . . Ernest was the living symbol of loyalty . . . once he gave his trust to you he was like a rock.'[38] Bevin sustained Attlee. Attlee gave Bevin consistent support, especially when he was under attack from the left on foreign affairs. 'In fact,' as Michael Foot remarked, 'often enough, Bevin was Attlee.' He continued: 'It would be folly to overlook the powerful authority of this composite figure.'[39]

Not surprisingly, given Morrison's designs on Attlee's job, relations between these two were much less close. Morrison's view of Attlee was that in Cabinet he doodled when he should have been giving a lead. He found Attlee's reticence and lack of charisma maddeningly inappropriate for a political leader and continued to believe that he would do better. Attlee knew what Morrison thought of him but that did not stop him respecting Morrison's ability. He understood that Morrison was indispensable to the government.

To a considerable extent, Dalton's importance arose from his job. Although Morrison had an ill-defined role co-ordinating economic planning, the Chancellor of the Exchequer was bound to play a big part in Cabinet, especially with the massive economic problems facing the country. Despite his economic expertise, Dalton initially had cold feet about the Chancellorship (see pp. 7–8), but his fascination with his new job, combined with his mastery of the House of Commons, gave him, for a time, a new status as a politician. This was increased by the Prime Minister's ignorance of economics. Douglas Jay, Attlee's economic adviser at No. 10 and wartime aide to Dalton at the Board of Trade, wrote: 'Attlee made no claim to understand technical fields such as economics, which he engagingly regarded as a subject similar to medicine, in which one consulted qualified experts and if necessary took a second or third opinion.'[40] Attlee was sometimes irritated by Dalton's booming voice and what he saw as his deviousness. But, in 1945 and for the next eighteen months, he relied not only on Dalton's economic judgement but also on his infectious self-confidence to lend the Labour government energy and drive.

Cripps was Attlee's second opinion on economic matters and the Cabinet's Christian conscience. He was one of three ministers (with Dalton and Bevin) overseeing the negotiations of the American loan. He was also a key member of Morrison's Lord President's Committee, which was responsible among other matters for the nationalisation programme. His hard work as a notably pragmatic president of the Board of Trade, concerned to promote exports and industrial efficiency, added to his stature.

At the beginning of 1946, Attlee, like Churchill before him, sent Cripps to India, this time with two other Cabinet ministers, to try and negotiate a plan for independence. Cripps's scheme, which represented the last chance for a united India, broke down on Congress and Muslim intransigence. The failure of his mission did not diminish his reputation or Attlee's regard for him. In contrast to his feelings towards Morrison and Dalton, Attlee liked Cripps. He described Cripps as having 'the egotism of the altruist', as opposed to Bevin, who had 'the egotism of the artist'.[41]

Kenneth O. Morgan, the historian of the Labour government, has pointed out that it was 'a Cabinet of veterans'.[42] The advantage was that many of them were highly experienced ministers. Five of them – Attlee,

Bevin, Cripps, Greenwood and Morrison – had been in Churchill's War Cabinet, while others, such as Dalton, A. V. Alexander, Lord Jowitt, James Chuter Ede, Ellen Wilkinson, George Hall and Tom Williams, had been lesser ministers in the coalition government. The downside was that most of them were approaching old age. Of the Labour Cabinet of twenty, Viscount Addison, leader of the House of Lords and dominions secretary, was seventy-six, Lord Pethick-Lawrence, secretary of state for India, was seventy-three and twelve of the others were over sixty, including Bevin and Attlee. And that was in 1945 when the government started. Bevin was already suffering from heart problems and Cripps from chronic colitis. It was an elderly group to be responsible not only for the difficult task of implementing Labour's ambitious social programme but also for responding to a succession of major financial economic and international crises.

Morale in the Parliamentary Labour Party was high on the morning of 15 August 1945, when the King opened the new parliament. That afternoon Attlee, the new Prime Minister, announced the surrender of Japan, following the dropping of the atomic bomb by US planes on Hiroshima and Nagasaki (which had been agreed by Churchill). On 16 August, the four-day debate on the King's speech opened. As was customary, a government backbencher, John Freeman, the new Labour MP for Watford, moved the address in reply to the speech from the throne. Dalton, perhaps carried away by Freeman's good looks, said that it was 'a faultless act which I shall always remember'.[43] Wearing the dark green uniform of the Rifle Brigade, young Freeman concluded: 'We have before us a battle for peace, no less arduous and no less momentous than the battle we have lived through in the last six years ... Today may rightly be regarded as "D-Day" in the Battle of the New Britain.'[44] Later that afternoon, Attlee took Freeman to introduce him to Churchill in the Smoking Room. According to Dalton, Churchill was so moved that he wept.

In the debate on the King's speech, Churchill, who as leader of the opposition responded to the movers of the address, was in brilliant form. In a sense, it was the last of his great wartime prime ministerial speeches, mostly devoted to the war and foreign affairs, including defending the decision to use the atomic bomb.

Hugh Gaitskell, the new Labour MP for Leeds South, described Attlee's speech as 'not very inspiring but he did quite well within his own limits'.[45] Attlee paid a generous tribute to Churchill: 'In the darkest and most dangerous hour of our history, this nation found in Mr Churchill the man who expressed supremely the courage and determination never to yield which animated all the men and women of this country.' He then warned that there were difficult years ahead which would require 'no less effort, no less unselfishness and no less hard work'.[46] He explained the government's plans for orderly demobilisation and the need for fairness and planning, and outlined the heavy programme which had been set out in the King's speech, including improved welfare, a national health service, a housing drive and nationalisation of the Bank of England and of the coal industry. On a procedural motion at the end of the debate, Labour won by 329 votes to 42. Dalton, who had for most of his parliamentary career been in opposition, wrote that 'the names of the government supporters in the Aye lobby read, to me, like a triumphant reverberating roll-call'.[47]

Labour was riding high in Parliament, but the precariousness of Britain's post-war financial and economic situation soon hit the government. On 21 August, only a week after the Japanese surrender, President Truman signed a document which brought the Lend-Lease agreement between the United States and the United Kingdom abruptly to an end. Lend-Lease, described by Churchill as 'the most unsordid act in the history of any nation',[48] had enabled the UK to receive weapons, materials and food without charge. It had helped the UK to fight the war without having to pay for two-thirds of the money needed to fund a total external deficit of £10 billion over the six years of war. In 1945, external aid was enabling the British to overspend their income by £2.1 billion a year. By the end of the war Britain had exhausted a quarter of its assets and was deep in debt. Without Lend-Lease or a loan to replace it, the UK was bankrupt. In the stark words of Lord Keynes, Dalton's chief economic adviser at the Treasury: 'The country was facing a financial Dunkirk.'[49]

The Labour Cabinet sent Keynes to Washington to negotiate a loan. Keynes started too optimistically with the belief that £1.5 billion could be obtained, without strings or interest, as a free gift. Bevin was more sceptical: 'When I listen to Lord Keynes talking, I seem to hear those coins jingling in my pockets, but I am not so sure that they are really there.'[50] Bevin was right.

The US negotiators were not impressed by British references to their outstanding contribution during the war or by witty lectures from Keynes. They were intent on ensuring British involvement in the Bretton Woods free trade system and on supplanting the UK in world markets, as well as insisting that sterling must be freely convertible into dollars as soon as possible.

For virtually every weekday evening until mid-December the 'big five' – Attlee, Bevin, Cripps, Dalton, Morrison – met in the Cabinet Room to try and oversee the negotiations. It was soon clear that a free gift was unobtainable and that a loan would only come on US terms; the British bargaining position was, as Douglas Jay said, 'hopelessly weak'.[51] By the end of October, a dangerous gap was opening up between Keynes, who had become more realistic, and the senior Labour ministers, who felt that Keynes had become too close to the Americans. The Cabinet minutes show that, after two long sessions of Cabinet on 6 November, the British team in Washington were issued with more credible instructions. Bevan, who wanted to try negotiating 'at a higher level', and Emanuel Shinwell, minister of fuel and power, who said: 'Let us have the loan, but don't let us tie our hands,' led the opposition but were not able to suggest a realistic alternative. Dalton wrote in his diary: 'Bevin, Cripps and I were in firm coalition.'[52] According to the Cabinet secretary's note, Bevin was especially eloquent:

> I believe our bluff is called. We can't ask them [the British people] to face another 3 years of even tighter living – with industrial unrest. We are in Shylock's hands . . . No alternative now but to accept this unless you are ready to demand these further sacrifices from the British people.[53]

Attlee made the occasional intervention but otherwise acted a neutral chairman.

On 6 December, after the agreement of the British Cabinet on the 5th, the US loan agreement was signed in Washington. It comprised a loan of $3.75 billion, to be repaid over fifty years with interest payments of 2 per cent per annum beginning in the sixth year (there was provision for waiving the interest if the UK got into difficulties). In addition, all American claims arising out of Lend-Lease were set aside, amounting to an additional credit of $650 million, making a total credit from the United States of $4.4 billion. Although the amount was a great deal less than had originally been asked for, it was still, as Keynes said in his last speech in the House of Lords (he died in April 1946), a 'substantial' sum.[54] The main difficulty for the British was that, in addition to the acceptance of free trade, they had to accept the convertibility of sterling into dollars a year after the loan had been agreed by Congress (15 July 1947), even though Labour ministers doubted if it would be possible to honour this obligation.

Just before the agreement was signed, Jay advised Attlee to refuse the convertibility condition, even though this would result in extreme austerity at home, and seek what help the government could get, be it from the Commonwealth and/or American private banks. Attlee dismissed this piece of advice out of hand. Jay wrote that he soon realised Attlee was right, because the blow to industrial recovery, exports, investment and employment would have been far worse than having to accept the convertibility commitment (which probably could not be met anyway).[55]

There were other developments which would continue to dog the government throughout its existence. The first was the atomic bomb. On 9 November 1945 Attlee flew to Washington, accompanied by Sir John Anderson, a Tory frontbencher and chairman of the advisory committee on questions involved in the use of atomic energy, to talk to Truman about atomic matters. During the flight, Attlee recommended Wisden, the cricketing bible, as good bedtime reading and remarked on the similarities between selecting a cricket team and choosing a Cabinet. In Washington, Attlee addressed the joint houses of Congress; his aim was to try and reassure US politicians about the democratic credentials of his government.

But the main purpose of his visit was to persuade Truman to give control of the bomb to the UN and to ensure that the United States would continue to share atomic information, which the British thought had been secured by the Quebec agreement of 1943. But, as over Lend-Lease, Attlee discovered that the end of the war had changed things. Though Truman agreed to set up a UN Commission on Atomic Energy and promised 'full and effective cooperation in the field of atomic energy', in practice the Americans refused to give the British the atomic information which they required. Attlee warned the US ambassador, Averell Harriman, that if the McMahon Bill, which forbade the transmission of atomic information to any other country, went through Congress, Britain would build atomic plants for military as well as civilian use.

In early 1947 a subcommittee of the Cabinet took the formal decision to make the atomic bomb. As Bevin had made clear at an earlier meeting, the main reason for making a bomb was to keep Britain at the top table: 'We have got to have a bloody Union Jack flying on top of it.'[56] Attlee carefully confined discussion of an atomic bomb, reporting neither to Cabinet nor to Parliament, easing secrecy slightly in May 1948 with the announcement to the Commons that 'research' on atomic weapons was under way.

Meanwhile, the new Foreign Secretary was having to get used to dealing with the Soviet Union. The Council of Foreign Ministers, which had been set up by the Potsdam conference, met in London in September but broke up unable to agree on anything, even the text of a final communiqué. Bevin's private secretary, Pierson Dixon, explained the Soviet behaviour: 'The Russians see that the war has left us financially and economically weak and dependent on the US. They also know the American phobia about the British Empire and calculate that we cannot rely on American support when defending our imperial interests.'[57]

Dixon was right when he said that the war had severely reduced Britain's power and resources. The question was whether this was a temporary difficulty, as most Cabinet ministers (including the 'big five') supposed, which with help from the United States and the Commonwealth could be alleviated, or whether, as turned out to be the case, this was part of a long-term pattern of declining power which could only be resolved by a big reduction in overseas commitments.

8

1946: Annus mirabilis

Hugh Dalton called 1946 an 'annus mirabilis' for Labour. Boosted by the prospect of the American loan (due to come into operation in July 1946), the government pushed ahead with its programme. By the end of the 1945/6 session, Parliament had passed: an Act setting up the National Health Service, which still survives more than sixty years later; a National Insurance Act establishing a comprehensive system of social benefits on the lines proposed by the Beveridge report; a second National Insurance Act to provide compensation for industrial injuries; the New Towns Act; and Acts nationalising the Bank of England, the coal industry, civil aviation and cable and wireless. In total, eighty-three Acts were put on the statute book in that session. The results of local elections, parliamentary by-elections and public opinion polls all showed that support remained strong for the party. Labour and its ministers were riding high.

Before the coming of television, parliamentary debates were an important means of political communication. Two debates in December 1945 provided a favourable prelude for the government. Winston Churchill had put down a motion of censure, mainly to head off criticism of his performance as leader of the opposition. Some of his supporters thought he was too often absent from the House and that when he did attend he let the government off too lightly, as over the second reading of the Bank of England Bill, when the Conservatives abstained, on the grounds that public ownership of the bank raised no question of principle. In his censure speech, Churchill reverted to the extravagant rhetoric of his election broadcasts, accusing the government of putting sectional political interest before the national interest and of attempting to turn the country into a socialist state by nationalising 'all the means of production, distribution and exchange', with the consequence that 'this island will not be able to support above three quarters of the population which now inhabits it'.[1]

Clement Attlee's reply to this absurd charge was, in Roy Jenkins's words, 'taut, deflating and witty'.[2] He began by referring to Churchill's election broadcast: 'I have not forgotten the right honourable gentlemen's broadcast, nor have the people of this country.' At this thrust, there was a roar of approval from the Labour benches. Attlee then said that the real reason for the censure motion was not the so-called irresponsibility of the government's socialist programme but the criticism of the opposition front bench by its backbenchers. In his speech, Churchill had raised many issues – finance, housing, trade and industry, demobilisation. Why had he not raised these issues when they were being debated in the House? 'My only regret', said Attlee, tongue in cheek, 'is that he was not there dealing with those subjects at the proper time.' Churchill had criticised the government's demobilisation plans, but, as the Prime Minister pointed out, it was only carrying out the strategy already agreed by the coalition.

Point by point, Attlee dissected Churchill's arguments; he even showed, to the delight of the Labour MPs, that most of Labour's nationalisation measures had had all-party support. The problem for Churchill, said Attlee, was that, having run on his own personality and achievements, he had been rejected by the voters: 'This country does not like one-man shows and, therefore, will not accept this motion of censure as anything more than a party move of a politician in difficulties and will not accept the cry of "the people against the Socialists".'[3] Of course Labour, with its big majority, was always going to win the vote. What was important for the government, for Labour MPs and for the Prime Minister's standing in Parliament was that Attlee had comprehensively beaten Churchill in debate and had thus, as the new Labour MP for Cardiff South, James Callaghan, said, 'cut Churchill down to size'.[4]

The debate on the American loan was more difficult for the government. Dalton, Stafford Cripps and Ernest Bevin spoke for the government. But twenty-three Labour MPs, including Callaghan, Barbara Castle (who was Cripps's parliamentary private secretary) and Michael Foot, voted against the government, as did seventy Conservatives, including Robert Boothby, the member for East Aberdeenshire, who described the agreement as 'an economic Munich'. However, the Conservative front bench had no answer to the question posed by Dalton towards the end of his speech: 'To those who are critical of these arrangements, I venture, in conclusion, to put one blunt question: What is your alternative?'[5] Churchill claimed that a Conservative government would have got better terms but admitted that, without the loan, Britain would be in trouble. At the end of the debate, the opposition front bench once again abstained.

Although the US Congress took some months to ratify the agreement, the Labour government proceeded on the basis that it was going to get the American loan. It therefore went ahead with implementing Labour's programme, as set out in *Let Us Face the Future*; 'socialism on credit', one critic called it.[6] The key figure here was the Lord President of the Council, Herbert Morrison, and the key committee was the Future Legislation Committee, with Morrison in the chair. This was the kind of strategic work at which Morrison was highly skilled: 'Herbert played it like a game of racing demon. He would deal with thirty or forty bills, calling on each minister in turn to explain his bill, how long it was, how much time it needed – Herbert went at great speed.'[7] As we have seen, in the first session three great reforms of the social services were introduced, as well as four nationalisation acts. The *Manchester Guardian* (as it was then called) commented: 'Herbert Morrison is omnivorous for work himself and he is enormously enjoying the job of piling work on the House of Commons.'[8]

Among Morrison's responsibilities was that of economic planning and co-ordination. In practice, although an official steering committee on economic development was set up to report to the Lord President's Committee, British economic planning (in contrast to the French system) amounted to little more than an extension of wartime controls, above all over essential raw materials. The Treasury, with all the fiscal and monetary instruments at its disposal, remained aloof, seeing Morrison's planning responsibilities as a threat to its authority. Relations between Dalton and Morrison, close before the war, were strained by these departmental pressures.

Morrison was more successful in overseeing Labour's nationalisation programme. He was the acknowledged party expert on public ownership and, through the Socialisation of Industry Committee, which he chaired, he influenced the structure and timing of individual nationalisations. Emanuel

Shinwell said that Morrison was 'interfering' but agreed that his interventions were helpful because he was 'so well informed'.[9] With the exception of road transport and iron and steel (about which Morrison himself had doubts), most of Labour's nationalisation acts were relatively non-controversial. It was widely acknowledged that coal was in a mess and that the railways were extremely run down; electricity and gas were, to a great extent, in municipal ownership anyway. In addition, Labour ministers were usually able to quote in evidence committees of inquiry set up by pre-war or wartime governments. The official opposition often did not oppose nationalisation legislation (not only for the Bank of England, but also, for example, cable and wireless and civil aviation). It was significant that *The Industrial Charter*, a Conservative Party pamphlet produced in May 1947 by leading Tories such as R. A. Butler, Harold Macmillan, Oliver Lyttelton and David Maxwell Fyfe, accepted the public ownership of coal, railways and the Bank of England. In the difficult post-war conditions, public ownership of industries vital to the economy seemed like a sensible, pragmatic answer, not only to Labour supporters, but to a broad swathe of political opinion.

Above all, Morrison was an exceptional leader of the House of Commons. He got Labour legislation through Parliament, kept his own backbenchers enthusiastic and involved, and respected the rights of the opposition. In the afternoon, he was almost always available in Parliament: 'He would settle in his room in the Commons and hold open court for MPs barging in with their troubles,' said one colleague.[10] It was generally agreed that he was far more approachable than Attlee. Indeed Attlee seemed to recognise his own shortcomings in this sphere by referring MPs and even ministers to Morrison. The Lord President set up a liaison committee between Labour backbenchers and government, as well as establishing party backbench policy groups. He suspended standing orders to give Labour MPs more freedom. And, in part to speed up business, he arranged for all bills, except finance bills and any bill of constitutional importance, to be sent to standing committees, thus boosting the role of backbenchers. On all sides, his work as leader of the house and party manager was widely respected. Anthony Eden called him 'the linchpin of the post-war Labour government'.[11]

If Morrison was the dominant figure in getting Labour's overall programme through parliament, Aneurin Bevan was the most important

Cabinet minister in the implementation of its social programme. Bevan's main achievement was the creation of a free and comprehensive National Health Service. The key elements of his bill were: an Exchequer-funded system; nationalised hospitals run by regional boards, accountable to the minister of health; general practitioners paid by capitation fees (but with a basic salaried element); municipally run health centres; the abolition of the sale of practices; and as a sop to consultants, fee paying by patients in NHS hospitals and elsewhere. Bevan's plan built on previous health service schemes, especially the wartime White Paper, but it went further, above all in the reorganisation of local authority and voluntary hospitals into one, national system.

On this issue, the minister of health met opposition from some Cabinet colleagues. Morrison, with his local government experience, argued strongly on democratic grounds for the preservation of local and voluntary hospitals. Why should power go to non-elected regional bodies? Although Bevan had some sympathy with this argument, he believed that nationalisation of hospitals was essential if the new service was to be properly planned and co-ordinated. Crucially, Attlee gave his support. In May 1946 the National Health Service Bill was carried overwhelmingly on second reading, the Liberals voting with the government. The parliamentary correspondent of the *Manchester Guardian* reported on Bevan's speech at the beginning of the debate:

> He had a most flattering reception from the government benches, and an hour and a quarter later he sat down to salvo after salvo of cheers from the same quarter . . . He had a manuscript, but why, Heaven knows. He completely ignored it. Here was a real parliamentarian acting on the House through living speech.[12]

The fiercest opposition to Bevan's proposals came from the British Medical Association. He had bought off the royal colleges (Surgeons, Physicians and Obstetricians) with the concessions on private patients. But for nearly two years the BMA refused to yield, on the grounds that under the scheme doctors would lose their independence: 'I have examined the Bill,' thundered Dr Alfred Cox, a former medical secretary of the BMA, 'and it looks to me uncommonly like the first step, and a big one, towards National Socialism as practised in Germany.' Dr Solomon Wand, an influential member of the BMA council, threatened: 'If every doctor or most doctors refused to take service under the Act, then the Act cannot be worked.'[13] As the date (5 July 1948) for the start of the National Health Service approached, both sides – the minister of health and the BMA – played a game of brinkmanship. In the end, Bevan offered an olive branch in the form of an amendment forbidding the establishment of a full-time salaried service and permitting the fixed, salaried element in the payment of GPs to be ended after three years if the individual doctor wished. The BMA gave way. About 90 per cent of doctors joined the NHS from the beginning, while, two months later, 93 per cent of the population had signed up. It was a triumph for Bevan and an unforgettable moment both for the Labour government and for the country as a whole.

Bevan was arguably less successful in dealing with another of his responsibilities – that of housing, at least in 1945/6. In the 1945 election campaign Labour had laid great emphasis on housing needs, especially of workers and their families, and Bevan was criticised for his ministry's failure to get a grip on house building. But from 1947 onwards, local authorities were building an average of 200,000 houses a year and more than one million new houses were completed between August 1945 and December 1951. Even so, the Tories made effective political capital out of their promise to build 300,000 houses a year.

The 1946 National Insurance Act provoked much less controversy. Introduced by another Welsh miner, Jim Griffiths, it has been called a 'cornerstone of Labour's welfare schemes'.[14] Together with the establishment of family allowances in 1947, the 1946 Industrial Injuries Act and the 1948 National Assistance Act, it fulfilled Labour's manifesto pledge to implement the Beveridge report's recommendation of a comprehensive system of social security from the cradle to the grave.

From the end of July 1945 to January 1947 probably the most prominent Cabinet minister was Hugh Dalton. In the months after Labour's election victory, he was riding 'a high tide of success'.[15] The American loan agreement afforded the Chancellor a breathing space in which he could begin both to build up the economy and to help implement the party programme. Dalton also took it upon himself to provide the sparkle and gusto which was missing from Attlee's style of leadership. As he said, 'it was one of my constant aims to radiate confidence all through the Labour Party, to rid it of inferiority complexes, and to keep the parliamentary troops behind me in good heart'.[16]

He certainly impressed the left-winger Michael Foot, who, as MP for Plymouth Devonport, was one of Labour's new intake. Foot wrote: 'Dalton on the crest of the wave . . . had the panache which the government so much needed. His spirit of aggression against the Tories satisfied the most exacting standards. The song in his heart was no egotistical solo; it settled to a socialist anthem.'[17] The Chancellor infuriated the Conservatives by his barbs against them. It was characteristic of Dalton that he began his speech moving the second reading of the bill nationalising the Bank of England by waving a copy of the Labour manifesto in the faces of the opposition. Dalton's Tory baiting delighted the Labour MPs behind him. But when events turned against him, he did not have the fund of parliamentary goodwill and respect on all sides of the House that might have cushioned him against a fall.

In his October 1945 Budget speech, in which he had cut income tax, he said that it was part of the mission of the government to close, from both ends, the gap which separated the standard of living of the great mass of citizens from that of a privileged minority. The editor of the *Times*, R. M. Barrington-Ward, wrote in his diary: 'Heard Dalton open his first Budget. He did it very well. His style is bland, arch and unctuous. His jokes are frightful. But he is lucidity itself. A little soak-the-rich by-play, but nothing much.'[18] In his second Budget, in April 1946, he announced an increase in civil department spending of £145 million 'due to the fulfilment of the pledges that we gave to the electors'.[19] This included more for education, more for school milk and meals (milk was to be free from August 1947), more for housing, £38 million for the introduction of family allowances in August 1947, more for old age and widows' pensions (the higher pensions to begin from autumn 1947) and £10 million more for development areas. In the years ahead, he announced that expenditure on social services would 'certainly and properly increase'.[20]

As to how the new welfare state was to be paid for, Dalton claimed that, despite the increased social spending, eighteen shillings and fourpence out of every pound spent (92 per cent) was already coming from revenue. He also expressed the hope that increases in social expenditure would be more than offset by reductions in spending on defence and on overseas expenditure tied to defence.

In his August 1945 memorandum in which he had warned of a 'financial Dunkirk' following the ending of Lend-Lease, Lord Keynes had said that, apart from substantial aid from the United States, two other conditions that would allow the UK to escape a catastrophe were a concentration on the expansion of exports and drastic and immediate economies in overseas expenditure.[21] Dalton did not ignore Keynes's warnings. In his Budget speech, he told the Commons that in 1946 there would be a deficit on the balance of payments of £750 million, which represented the excess of overseas expenditure (including the maintenance of troops abroad) over receipts from exports. In public at least, he appeared confident that action would be taken both to increase exports and to reduce defence and overseas expenditure, so that, when the date for convertibility arrived (15 July 1947) the UK would be able to meet its obligations.

In private, Dalton was much less sanguine. In February 1946 he had circulated to his colleagues a fierce warning by Keynes on the overseas deficit, accompanied by a paper of his own. He had also had a promising discussion with Attlee. The Daltons (Ruth had returned to live with him at No. 11) had spent a weekend with the Attlees at Chequers. Attlee was apparently considering a British withdrawal from the eastern Mediterranean and the Middle East, which would have led to large and speedy economies in defence expenditure. However, when he went to the Paris peace conference in July instead of Ernest Bevin, who had collapsed with a heart attack, he saw Soviet intransigence at first hand and this caused him to modify his backing for immediate cutbacks in defence. Bevin believed that, at a time when the direction of US policy was still so uncertain, it was essential for Britain to hold its ground against Soviet pressure not only in Europe but in the Mediterranean and the Middle East as well. Oliver Harvey, a deputy under-secretary at the Foreign Office, minuted: 'If we went out, the Russians would go in.'[22] For the remainder of the year, Attlee's initial scepticism about this thesis was replaced by support for Bevin, to Dalton's discomfort and to the detriment of Britain's financial and economic prospects.

In November 1946 a left-wing amendment to the King's speech, signed by fifty-six Labour backbenchers, was moved by Richard Crossman, calling for an alternative foreign policy to that of both the Soviet Union and the United States. He called upon the government to repudiate Winston Churchill's Fulton, Missouri speech, in which Churchill had said that an 'iron curtain' had descended over the greater part of eastern and central Europe 'from Stettin in the Baltic to Trieste in the Adriatic' and had urged what amounted to a western alliance of the United States and Britain to deter the Soviet Union. In the King's speech debate, Attlee was non-committal about Churchill's speech, being more concerned to defend Bevin (who was in New York at the Council of Foreign Ministers) from what he said were 'grossly unfair attacks'. At the end of the debate, a number of Labour MPs abstained. Bevin was extremely upset, especially as he was out of the country, but it only strengthened his determination not to give in to Soviet pressure.

Nineteen forty-six was a good year for the government. But the crisis that arose in the summer over bread rationing was a warning of how vulnerable an economically weakened Britain was to external events. In the spring of 1946, an acute shortage of food hit the world. The former US President Herbert Hoover, following a world tour, estimated that twenty-seven nations held less than two months' food supplies. When the British Cabinet discussed the problem on 9 May, the minutes show that ministers were concerned about two areas under their responsibility – India, in which famine threatened, and the British zone of Germany, which had only a fortnight's grain stocks. Britain, which still had food rationing, could not cope with the growing crisis and turned to the United States, which had big stocks of food and no rationing.

Attlee sent Herbert Morrison to ask for US help. The Americans agreed in principle that the British zone of Germany was part of the world food problem and that India should be treated as a special famine case. But, in return, Morrison had to promise that Britain would give up its claim to 200,000 tons of wheat supplies due to it in September, thus making bread rationing in the UK almost inevitable. This was awkward for the government, especially as the minister of food, Sir Ben Smith, had resigned, ostensibly on the grounds of old age but actually because Morrison had been sent to the United States and not him. Also a difficult by-election in the Bexley constituency was pending. On 27 June, with Attlee taking the lead, the Cabinet authorised the new Minister of Food, John Strachey, to tell the Commons that bread rationing would come into operation on 22 July, which was the day of the by-election.

Three days before bread rationing was to start, Morrison behaved in a most curious way. Attlee, Dalton, Bevan, Jack Lawson and the chief whip, William Whiteley, were all at the Durham Miners' Gala when Attlee received a message from Morrison to say that he proposed to call a Cabinet meeting the following morning (Saturday) to reconsider the bread rationing decision, on the grounds of better news about the Canadian wheat crop. Attlee refused to allow Morrison to call a Cabinet for Saturday, because, as he told him, with so many Cabinet ministers absent in the north-east it would be unrepresentative. But he agreed that a Cabinet meeting should be held at 9.30 a.m. on Sunday, with the absent ministers travelling back for it. After a long discussion and with Morrison, Strachey and Bevin arguing for a suspension of the policy, Cabinet decided to go ahead with bread rationing.[23] Clearly Morrison, having negotiated the agreement with the United States over wheat supplies, felt he would be blamed for bread rationing. But to reverse the policy at such a late stage looked like panic. And it was little short of an overt challenge to try and call a Cabinet meeting in Attlee's absence.

The Cabinet minutes show that the Prime Minister, supported by Dalton and Bevan, dug in his heels. He was satisfied, he said, that the introduction of rationing as a measure of insurance was still amply justified and that not to proceed with it at the eleventh hour would cause dismay among the government's supporters. In 1946, over a difficult issue, the tortoise exerted his authority and, despite significant opposition, carried the Cabinet with him. The following year was to present a series of more formidable challenges which were to threaten Attlee's position and shake the government to its foundations.

9

1947: The crisis year

Nineteen forty-seven was the year of crises. The first three months were dominated by a fuel crisis, exacerbated by the coldest winter of the twentieth century. In August, following the convertibility of sterling on 15 July, there was a major financial crisis, the most severe since that of 1931, which brought down the MacDonald government. The near collapse of the government's financial and economic policies led to a political crisis, which included an attempt by Stafford Cripps, backed by Hugh Dalton, to make Ernest Bevin Prime Minister. Then on 13 November, following his unpremeditated leaking to a journalist friend of the main taxation proposals of his Budget, Dalton resigned as Chancellor of the Exchequer and was replaced by Cripps. The government's reputation for competence was badly damaged by these events and, though it gradually recovered its balance, after 1947 it was 'never glad confident morning again'.

On 20 January, a great freeze, brought by east winds, set in. Snow, ice and fog gripped the country for the next eight weeks, with temperatures continuously below freezing. In the eastern counties whole towns and villages were cut off. Throughout the country factories were forced to close. The icy conditions prevented the transport of coal by rail or road, and north-east gales kept Tyne colliers from bringing coal to power stations in the Thames and the south of England.

On 'Black Friday', 7 February, Emanuel Shinwell, the minister of fuel and power, told a shocked House of Commons that the fuel resources of the nation had virtually collapsed. Many power stations had run out of coal; electricity supply to industry was to be cut off in large parts of the country, including London, the Midlands and the north-west; and domestic consumers were to be deprived of power for much of the day. Unemployment, which before the fuel crisis had been down to 397,000 or a mere 2.5 per cent of the workforce, leapt up to 2.3 million or 15.5 per cent by 22 February. The Conservatives made the most of it. Over bread rationing it had been 'Starve with Strachey'; now it was 'Shiver with Shinwell'. The crisis, said a former Conservative Cabinet minister, Viscount Swinton, was due not to 'an act of God, but the inactivity of Emanuel'.[1]

Although the exceptionally cold weather made the fuel situation worse, Swinton's jibe about Shinwell's inadequate performance as minister was justified. Douglas Jay, the Prime Minister's economic adviser from September 1945 to July 1946, had warned Clement Attlee about the danger of fuel shortages as early as November 1945. In a series of minutes during 1946 he continued his warnings; his last note on the subject was on 6 July, before he resigned to fight and win the Battersea North by-election for the Labour Party. Jay stressed that decisions taken at the end of 1945 and in early 1946 would determine coal supplies and stocks twelve or eighteen months ahead. As he wrote in his memoirs, 'what was needed immediately was much greater weekly recruitment into the coal mines. This would affect the labour force, which would then affect production, and so stocks in the autumn of 1946, and eventually stocks and supplies in the crucial first three months of the year, when they always reach a low point, in 1947.'[2] Despite Jay's warnings, the government was extremely slow to act. From June 1946 onwards, Attlee himself sent a number of minutes about coal stocks to ministers concerned, including the minister of labour and the Chancellor of the Exchequer. But the main stumbling block was Shinwell, who simply refused to accept that a fuel crisis was looming.

In June 1946, the Prime Minister called a meeting with Shinwell at No. 10. Jay, who attended, had prepared a paper for Attlee in which he underlined in red ink his prediction that coal stocks would sink to 4 million tons, one week's supply, by March 1947, an 'impossibly low stock level'. He pointed out that this 'easily predictable and avoidable disaster is likely to occur at exactly the moment when the National Coal Board takes over the first great nationalised industry in this country'.[3] At the meeting with Shinwell, Attlee put his finger on Jay's figure of 4 million tons and asked the minister of fuel and power whether he disputed the estimate for March 1947 and what he proposed to do about it. According to Jay, Shinwell looked out of the Cabinet Room window and replied: 'Prime Minister, you should not let yourself be led up the garden path by the statistics. You should look at the imponderables,' and continued with a twenty-minute harangue which 'had no relation to fact'.[4] When Jay heard Shinwell's response, he concluded that, unless Attlee immediately sacked Shinwell, Britain would be certain to face a fuel crisis in early 1947.

But Attlee did not dismiss Shinwell. Instead, he tried to put pressure on him to increase recruitment into the coal mines. This pressure came partly through Hugh Gaitskell, who had been appointed parliamentary secretary at the Ministry of Fuel and Power in April 1946, but mainly through the Cabinet itself. In late 1946, the Prime Minister set up a Fuel and Power Committee, with Dalton as chairman, to prod Shinwell, and then, in January 1947, when the fuel shortages intensified, he put Cripps in charge of an emergency plan to deal with the crisis.[5] The 'Cripps plan', announced to the Commons on 14 January, gave priority to power stations and halved the quota of solid fuel for industry but it was out of date before it was drawn up, as it was based on Shinwell's overoptimistic estimate of coal stocks. When the icy weather came on 20 January, Cripps's emergency measures were quickly shown to be inadequate. At Cripps's and Dalton's insistence, Shinwell was instructed by Attlee to reveal in his 7 February statement to the Commons the full gravity of the situation.

In late March the exceptionally cold weather ceased, to be followed by floods. The strain on fuel supplies eased, unemployment fell and the government's morale improved. However, as Dalton noted, though the fuel crisis may not have been 'the end of the world', it was 'the first really heavy blow to confidence in the government and in our post-war plans'.[6]

Shinwell's reputation as minister of fuel and power was shattered and he was belatedly replaced by Gaitskell in October. The Cabinet, including all its leading figures, had been implicated in Shinwell's fiasco, because it had failed to come to grips with the crisis. Above all, the Prime Minister, who had been repeatedly warned by Jay of the strong probability of a fuel crisis, allowed Shinwell to continue in his post, despite the minister's boneheaded refusal to face up to the facts. Attlee's defenders have argued that, at the beginning of 1947, the Prime Minister was beset by a whole range of problems, including the decision to send out Viscount Mountbatten of Burma as the last viceroy of India with a firm date (June 1948) for British withdrawal. But Attlee's blunder came earlier, in June 1946. He then allowed his fear of the trouble that Shinwell could cause on the back benches, especially among miners' MPs, to override the crucial need to tackle the fuel issue. By failing to sack Shinwell then, Attlee made the fuel crisis inevitable. More fundamentally, Labour planning was exposed as a hollow sham.

Meanwhile an even greater crisis was brewing. As Dalton wrote in his memoirs, 'all through this year the Battle of the Balance of Payments faced me day by day'.[7] Under the terms of the 1945 Anglo-American Loan Agreement, sterling would become fully convertible on 15 July 1947. In other words, on that date, sterling holders would be able to convert their pounds directly into dollars. The only way to prevent British gold and dollar reserves being speedily depleted was to strengthen the UK balance of payments and persuade sterling holders to retain their confidence in the British economy. Even if their objectives were achieved, to make sterling convertible when all the other European currencies were not was in effect to shift the dollar shortage of other countries onto British shoulders. In the circumstances of 1947, an irresistible run on the pound and a humiliating reversal of convertibility were almost inevitable.

What actually happened was that a grave situation was made worse by a deteriorating balance of payments. The disruption of production caused by the fuel crisis alone cost £200 million in exports, while the price of dollar imports had risen by 40 per cent since 1945. Meanwhile the gold and dollar deficit, which for most of 1946 had amounted to a little over $50 million a month, rose in February to more than $200 million a month and by July had increased to over $500 million monthly. At that rate, the Anglo-American loan, which had been intended to last at least three years, would be exhausted in a year and a half.[8]

On 16 January 1947 Dalton, desperate to cut external spending and to encourage more manpower into the export industries, made an unsuccessful attempt to get the Cabinet to agree to a substantial cut in armed services manpower. The Cabinet minutes were blandly written but the Chancellor described the meeting as 'a very bad and rowdy Cabinet in which a substantial group ganged up against Cripps and myself in opposition to all our proposals'. Morrison was away ill with thrombosis, while Ernest Bevin was also absent sick. According to Dalton, most of the others displayed 'easy-going, muddle-headed irresponsibility'. He was especially annoyed with the Prime Minister, who said that the manpower gap was only $2\frac{1}{2}$ per cent of the total labour force and could easily be closed by 'greater productivity'.[9]

On 20 January Dalton wrote a furious minute to Attlee from his Wiltshire country retreat, West Leaze, entitled 'Note on a Difference of Opinion'. In it, he upbraided the Prime Minister for his talk about greater productivity. 'Vague hopes of increased productivity later don't help now. What we want now is more labour in the export trades, and in the trades which serve the export trades.' In biblical terms, he asked: 'What shall it profit Britain to have even 1,500,000 men in the Forces and Supply, and to be spending nearly £1,000 millions a year on them, if we come an economic and financial cropper ten years hence?' In fact, the 'cropper' was no more than six months away. His note contained a threat of resignation: 'I must warn my colleagues that I could not carry on indefinitely, if my views on such important matters were to continue to be brushed aside as of no account.'[10]

The Chancellor was clearly right. A Britain living on US (and Canadian) credit and faced with convertibility simply could not afford to maintain its level of military force or overseas commitments. To some extent Attlee was sympathetic to the case for retrenchment. Only a few days before, he had sent Bevin a long memorandum expressing his doubts about plans for a substantial British presence in the Middle East. But he had been outgunned by an alliance between Bevin and the chiefs of staff. Faced with this new threat from Dalton, he temporised. Instead of the 10 per cent cut which Dalton demanded, the Prime Minister persuaded the defence minister to offer a paltry 5 per cent. Somewhat weakly, given the ferocity of his memorandum to Attlee, Dalton accepted this.

Though neither Dalton nor Attlee then knew it, a major shift in US policy not only towards Britain but towards western Europe as a whole was about to take place. This change was precipitated by two British notes in late February to the US secretary of state, George Marshall, informing him that after 31 March Britain could not continue to be responsible for aid to Greece and Turkey. Bevin had given in to pressure from the Treasury for an end to this expenditure. Added to the prospect of other British withdrawals (from

India, Burma and Palestine), these notes confronted the United States with the big decision of whether or not to take over from the British the world role which they could no longer uphold alone.

On 12 March, President Harry S. Truman, concerned about the spread of Soviet power in Europe and the Mediterranean, announced to an initially sceptical Congress the 'Truman doctrine', whereby the United States would stand ready 'to support free peoples who are resisting attempted subjugation by armed minorities or by outside pressures', primarily by providing economic and financial aid, 'essential to economic stability and orderly political processes'.[11] Three months later, on 5 June, Marshall followed up Truman's historic announcement by his celebrated 'Marshall plan' speech at Harvard. US policy makers were increasingly worried about the dangers of economic and political collapse across Europe, especially in France and in Italy, but even in Britain. Hence the case for American support for a European recovery programme, with the initiative, according to Marshall, to come from Europe.

The story goes that Bevin, listening on his small bedside radio, first heard of Marshall's speech in a BBC American commentary. He reacted immediately. Indeed his biographer has argued that his prompt action was his most decisive personal contribution as Foreign Secretary.[12] In an astonishing burst of creative energy, especially for a man in his late sixties suffering from heart disease, Bevin spent the next three months master-minding Europe's response to Marshall's life line. The consequences were far-reaching and, for western European countries, highly beneficial. The Soviet Union and its allies refused to participate, but the Marshall plan underwrote the remarkable post-war economic and political renaissance of western Europe.

The Marshall plan did not come into effect until July 1948, too late to rescue the British government and its Chancellor from the financial crisis created by the convertibility of the pound. As 15 July 1947, the day of convertibility, drew nearer, the pressure on Dalton grew to an almost unbearable level. He wrote later:

> Very often, during these months, I lay awake at night doing mental arithmetic. We have so many dollars; last month we spent so many: if we spend the same

next month, we shall have only so many left. But we mustn't let our dollar reserves fall below so much, or we shall be sunk.[13]

Dalton began to resort to sleeping pills at night and to Benzedrine to keep going during the day. One sign of the stress which he was under was that he came out in boils. His private secretary at the Treasury, Burke Trend, said: 'His body and his mind had turned in on themselves.'[14]

At the end of March, Dalton warned his Cabinet colleagues that the US credits were running out fast and were likely to be exhausted by February 1948. He repeated the warning to the Commons in his April Budget, but, though he increased tobacco duty and hinted at future action to restrain dollar imports, he had little else concrete to say on how to reduce the balance of payments deficit quickly. In May he tried to persuade his colleagues to cut dollar imports by £200 million but he was forced to settle for £100 million. Dalton was tempted to ask the United States to defer the date of convertibility but both the Treasury and the Bank of England advised against this, primarily because there was no certainty that Congress would agree and raising the issue would in itself be damaging to confidence.

In public, Dalton assumed a Canute-like posture, assuring the House of Commons that 'in large measure, 15 July has already been discounted and the additional burden of assuming these new obligations . . . will be noticeably less than many people may suppose'.[15] His advisers, especially from the Bank of England, apparently believed this absurdly optimistic assessment. It is doubtful whether the Chancellor, with his nightly mental arithmetic, was taken in. In the real world, Britain's dollar and gold reserves were draining away – and neither the Chancellor nor the Cabinet seemed to have much idea of what to do about it.

The following extract from Dalton's diary for 30 July displays the confusion of the Labour government during the financial crisis:

> Big Five meeting at 10 p.m. with Bridges [Sir Edward Bridges, permanent secretary to the Treasury] and Eady [Sir Wilfrid Eady, Treasury official for overseas finance]. A most shocking performance. I put before them my draft of the paper for tomorrow's Cabinet proposing a variety of actions. Bevin, who had obviously had a very good dinner, . . . was at his worst. Morrison, after an

hour of this, left the room in indignation, declaring . . . that he had had enough of this drunken monologue. The PM, Cripps and I – and of course, both the eminent officials – showed infinite patience and good manners. Very late in the proceedings we got to the most important parts but discussion was, I thought, most inconclusive. Attlee showed no power of gripping or guiding the talk. We adjourn at half an hour past midnight, Bevin enquiring as he lurched towards the door . . . 'Where do we sleep tonight – in 'ere?'

Dalton concluded: 'This is not the way to ride the storm or even to conduct a serious government at any time.'[16]

That night the Chancellor was so angry that he almost screwed himself up to resign, unless he could persuade the Cabinet to make substantial cuts in food imports from hard currency countries, to stop paying dollars for the British share of German civil supplies in the merged British and American occupied zone, and to agree to big cuts in overseas military expenditure and manpower. When, next day, he saw Attlee to tell him how he felt, the Prime Minister seemed surprised. He appeared to think that a lot of progress had been made and that they had reached agreement on most things. As Cabinet minutes show, after a series of meetings and pushed by an alliance between Dalton and Cripps, the Cabinet decided on an immediate package including a reduction in food imports paid for in dollars of £12 million a month, an extra half day in the pits, an expansion of steel production and defence cuts, including the release of 80,000 men from the forces.[17] Action on these lines had been advocated by Dalton for at least a year and, if introduced earlier, might possibly have made a difference. Now it was too little, too late.

In an effort to calm both the Labour Party and the currency markets, Attlee led for the government in a two-day debate on the state of the nation. In his speech, the Prime Minister announced the measures agreed earlier in Cabinet and said that 'we are engaged in another Battle of Britain'.[18] Dalton commented that, though the manner of Attlee's speech had been disappointing, it had much substance in it; but 'how painfully it had to be built up from a multitude of confused, ambiguous and imprecise Cabinet decisions'.[19] He described his own speech the following day as being 'terribly dull and uninspiring in spite of being sustained by Benzedrine . . . It was an old, old desperate story, lit by no new light or hope.'[20] The one big success

157

of the debate on the government side was Cripps, who wound up on the second day. He skilfully combined a grasp of long-term trends with a mastery of detail. Above all, he displayed the leadership which the Labour back-benchers had been demanding. Cripps's moving peroration gripped the Commons:

> The struggle of production, the battle of the balance of payments, is as tough a proposition as any that this country has faced, and there is no easy way out . . . It is by our faith in ourselves in our country, in the free democratic traditions for which the people of this country have for centuries fought and battled . . . it is by our faith in the deep spiritual values that we acknowledge in our Christian faith, that we shall be enabled and inspired to move the present mountains of our difficulties.[21]

However, the Commons debate and the government package failed to halt the drain of dollar reserves. In August, it increased to over $600 million a month (or an annual rate of about $7.5 billion). The drawings in the five days up to 15 August amounted to $175.9 million. On Friday 15 August (the day that India became independent), Bridges and Trend drove down to West Leaze, where the Chancellor was recuperating in the sunshine, to tell him that the game was up and convertibility would have to be suspended. Eady was belatedly sent to Washington to tell the Americans about the crisis situation, while Morrison, who had remained in charge in London, rang Attlee, who was holidaying in north Wales, to arrange an emergency Cabinet for Sunday 17 August. By car, train and plane, ministers returned hurriedly to London.

The Cabinet minutes show that Dalton's proposal to admit failure and suspend the convertibility of sterling met with little opposition.[22] Bevin wanted it made clear to the United States that it was not Britain's intention to repudiate the terms of the loan agreement but that we were compelled by *force majeure* to take emergency action. Aneurin Bevan said that it should be brought home to the US government that, unless the British government took steps now to protect the residual sterling position, world trade would break down completely within a short period, with results which would cause serious harm to the US economy. Morrison, with an eye to the political fallout from suspending convertibility, feared that the government would be criticised for having failed to take drastic measures earlier, certainly before Parliament adjourned for the summer recess.

At 9 p.m. on 20 August, Dalton was able, after tough negotiations in Washington, to announce in an exchange of notes with his US counterpart, John Snyder, the suspension of convertibility. Dalton wrote later: 'This seemed to me at the time a personal humiliation and a bad set-back to the government. But, on a rational view, it should have been obvious for some while that this retreat would be inevitable.'[23]

The Chancellor's reputation never recovered from the August crisis. In his autobiography, Morrison blamed Dalton and the Treasury: 'The 1947 economic crisis was at root largely due to the faulty administration at the Treasury for which Dalton must be held responsible as head of the department.'[24] It is certainly true that neither the Treasury nor the Bank of England anticipated the run on sterling in July and August, and both gave Dalton the misleading advice that convertibility had already been discounted. However, the roots of the convertibility crisis go back earlier.

Edmund Dell, in his study of post-war Chancellors, argued that the decisive moment in Dalton's chancellorship was not the convertibility crisis itself but his decision in December 1945 to recommend acceptance of the loan on US terms. If so, it was a decision which was backed by the whole Cabinet, even Bevan and Shinwell, on the grounds that there was no alternative; and, even though the convertibility condition proved impossible to sustain, the loan bought the government nearly two years during which it managed to implement key parts of its programme.

The most serious charge against Dalton was that he failed to persuade his Cabinet colleagues to take the action necessary to improve the balance of payments, and to maintain convertibility by protecting the UK's dollar reserves. After all, he was not asking the Cabinet to break Labour's election promises or slash social spending, as in 1931. He was merely arguing that it was essential to cut back on the armed forces and expensive overseas commitments and to reduce dollar imports substantially, especially of food and tobacco. However, his fellow Cabinet ministers refused to listen until it was too late. Dalton's biographer wrote: 'It is the job of a politician not only to know what needs doing but to carry it through.'[25] And it was here that he failed. In the financial crisis of 1947, Dalton, so buoyant and self-confident in 1945 and 1946, was revealed as politically weak.

But Dalton's failure does not excuse the rest of his colleagues. Cripps alone gave him consistent support. Morrison, who had been seriously ill with thrombosis earlier in the year, and in any case was out of his depth on economic issues, contributed little, even though he was meant to be in charge of economic planning. Bevin, who was almost entirely wrapped up in fashioning the European response to the Marshall plan, actively opposed Dalton's attempts to cut back the armed forces (supported by A. V. Alexander, the minister of defence). Above all, Attlee, who might have been expected to back his Chancellor, gave him little help. In part, this was because of his ignorance of economics and finance. Perhaps more important was his extreme reluctance to oppose Bevin, who was his main political ally. Attlee's performance throughout the summer was almost entirely passive. He seemed content merely to act as a chairman without giving the lead that the Cabinet and the party so desperately needed.

The summer crisis over convertibility, following so closely on the winter fuel crisis, inevitably raised questions about the leadership. Dalton wrote later: 'Some doubted whether Attlee had the personality, or the strength of popular appeal, to be the leader in these increasingly critical months.'[26] In the move against Attlee, Cripps took the initiative. Throughout 1947 his reputation was on the rise. Increasingly he was seen not only as the most dynamic figure in the government, but also as the only Cabinet minister who could be trusted to tell the truth about the grave situation which the country faced.

The day after Dalton presented his April 1947 Budget, Cripps approached him about possible changes to the government. Cripps's idea was that Bevin should be brought back to the home front and take charge of planning and publicity. Cripps believed that Bevin was the only minister 'who can really talk to the trade unions like an uncle'.[27] Cripps was also convinced that Morrison was incapable of understanding planning. Dalton, who had designs on the Foreign Office if Bevin moved, spoke to Attlee about these possible changes. The Prime Minister made a cautious response. He buttered up Dalton by telling him that he was so much in the top of everything at the Treasury that it would be a serious loss if he were moved.

He also reiterated his view that it would be unwise to have Bevin and Morrison together on the home front. A few days later, on Dalton's return from a rest in the country, Bevin made it clear to the Chancellor that he had no wish to leave the Foreign Office. The Foreign Secretary had come back from a meeting in Moscow both much recovered in health and hopeful about the new phase in US foreign policy. He added that his wife, Florence, much liked the official residence, 1 Carlton Gardens, recently allocated to the Foreign Secretary.

In July backbench Labour MPs, tied to Westminster by late night sittings and worried by the deepening financial crisis, feverishly discussed a change in leadership. Many favoured swapping Attlee for Bevin. Organisers of the revolt included Morrison's parliamentary private secretary (PPS), Patrick Gordon Walker, and Dalton's PPS, George Brown. Naively they believed that, if they circulated a resolution demanding a change, they would get so many signatures that Attlee would have to resign. Dalton, under increasing pressure and fed up with the Prime Minister's lack of support, advised Brown to tell the malcontents to raise the issue at the parliamentary party meeting – 'let them come and talk freely and kick up a row', the Chancellor said.[28]

On 26 July Bevin, Morrison and Dalton all made speeches at the Durham Miners' Gala. Bevin and Dalton shared a car back to London. The Chancellor took the opportunity of sounding the Foreign Secretary out. Bevin complained about Attlee's weakness as a leader and failure to make up his mind, reiterated that Morrison was a sick man and described Cripps as 'more than halfway to Moscow'. But when Dalton passed on Brown's report that a large number of members wanted Bevin to become Prime Minister, the Foreign Secretary, while agreeing that his own PPS had said the same thing, replied he did not want to do anyone out of a job. He did not respond to Dalton's comment that his ability to speak favourably to trade unionists made it natural in 'the crisis of our fate' for many in the party to think of him as 'our predestined leader'. As the car turned into Downing Street, Dalton urged him 'not to put out of his mind the possibility of becoming PM'.[29]

Bevin's private secretary, Pierson Dixon, was also in the car. Both he and Dalton thought that the Foreign Secretary had not entirely rejected the idea of becoming Prime Minister. But by the following week Bevin was parading his loyalty to Attlee and criticising Dalton for trying to tempt him into betraying the Prime Minister. He instructed his PPS to tell Labour members that he was standing by Attlee – 'he is a great little chap'.[30] He also gave Brown, a former full-time official of the Transport and General Workers' Union, a ticking off for 'acting as an office boy for that bastard Dalton';[31] and he made sure, through Attlee's PPS, that the Prime Minister was made aware of Dalton's approach to him and what the Chancellor had said about Attlee.

Until the House broke up for the summer recess, the Parliamentary Labour Party remained in turmoil. In addition to the financial crisis, a row broke out over steel nationalisation. During the summer, Morrison, at Attlee's instigation, had been asked by the Cabinet to pursue a compromise scheme with the leaders of the steel industry. However, at Cabinet on 31 July Aneurin Bevan threatened to resign if the government did not proceed with full nationalisation. After lengthy discussion, the Cabinet agreed on 7 August to reject Morrison's scheme, reaffirming the government's intention to introduce a full nationalisation bill during the parliament, but not necessarily in the next session. All this stirred up Labour MPs, especially on the left, and at a party meeting on 11 August a damaging vote was only just avoided. Meanwhile, the July backbench move to depose Attlee petered out, as such summer revolts usually do. Dalton noted: 'It is one of the ever recurrent parliamentary miracles how great waves of opinion make no final impact, but disperse themselves in broken spray.'[32]

*

The attempted September coup, initiated by Cripps, was a far more serious affair. It came from within the Cabinet itself, with three members of the 'big five' – Cripps, Dalton and Morrison – agreeing on the need to topple Attlee, a potentially decisive group if they could act together.

On 5 September, at 9.45 a.m., Cripps came to see Dalton with a scheme to depose Attlee and make Bevin Prime Minister and minister of production. Cripps would be his chief of staff as Lord President, in charge of economic planning, which Morrison, who was out of his depth in the job, would be persuaded to give up, though he would remain as deputy Prime Minister. Attlee would move to the Exchequer: 'To move from one official home to another next door would not be too hard a fate,' said Cripps. Dalton would take Bevin's place as Foreign Secretary. 'No one else could do it,' said Cripps; Dalton would, if need be, 'shout at Molotov and bang the table' in a way that Attlee could not. Cripps proposed that he, Dalton and Morrison should go to Attlee and tell him that he should resign in favour of Bevin.[33]

Dalton doubted whether Morrison would support a scheme from which he would gain little. He therefore told Cripps that he would go to see Attlee only if Morrison went as well. Cripps dined alone with Morrison that evening. As Dalton had expected, the Lord President rejected the Cripps plan. Morrison wanted Attlee to be deposed but thought that he and not Bevin should take his place. And if there was to be a change of leadership, then it should be done openly. There must not be a *fait accompli* in favour of Bevin, whom Morrison had long distrusted.

At noon the following day Dalton found Morrison in a depressed mood. His old resentment of Attlee came out into the open. According to Morrison, Attlee had never 'led' the party and he did not know how to say 'thank you' to those (i.e. Morrison) who did their best to help him. He attacked Bevin, describing him as 'a strange mixture of genius and stupidity'.[34] If Bevin became leader, Morrison feared being knifed. Morrison believed that he could do the job of Prime Minister better than anyone else and was hurt that neither Dalton nor Cripps, both of whom had supported him as a potential leader in the past, no longer did so. It was Morrison's failure as an economic minister that lay behind these shifts in attitude.

On 8 September Cripps told Dalton that, with Morrison now out of the picture, he had decided to see Attlee alone. At first, he was going to threaten to resign if Attlee did not step down. But when the Cabinet accepted his export plan on the morning of 9 September, resignation no longer seemed appropriate. However, Cripps went ahead with the meeting with Attlee, hoping, with his habitual self-confidence, to persuade the Prime Minister to go.

The Cripps–Attlee meeting took place at 10 Downing Street after dinner on 9 September. If the winter's fuel crisis and the summer's financial crisis had demonstrated Attlee's weakness as a Prime Minister, his exchanges with Cripps revealed that he remained a master, as one historian of the Labour Party has put it, of the *'coup de repos'*.[35] According to Dalton's account of Cripps's talk with Attlee (relayed by Cripps to Dalton later that evening),

Cripps had begun by setting out his plan. Attlee was to be replaced by Bevin, who would also become minister of production, while Dalton was to go to the Foreign Office and Attlee to the Treasury. Calmly Attlee replied that he had no head for financial matters, Bevin did not want to leave the Foreign Office, the party would not want him as leader, and he and Morrison would never get on in such close proximity.[36]

Attlee's own version of the meeting adds a detail. After Cripps had finished speaking, the Prime Minister picked up the scrambler and asked for Bevin. When Bevin came on the phone, Attlee said: 'Stafford's here; he says you want to change your job.' Bevin replied that he had no intention of leaving the Foreign Office.[37]

Both versions agree on Attlee's 'killer' response. Unmoved by Cripps's scheme to depose him and taking at face value his argument that a co-ordinated assault should be made on the country's economy, Attlee asked Cripps: 'Why shouldn't you take the job and become minister of production?' In addition, the Prime Minister proposed a small economic committee of senior Cabinet ministers – the 'big five' plus Viscount Addison. In effect, Cripps was being offered Morrison's responsibilities as economic co-ordinator. It was an offer which Cripps, after all he had said about the need for economic planning, could not easily refuse. Dalton noted: 'Within the government, the movement, begun by Cripps, with my support, to put Bevin in Attlee's place, has now turned into a movement to put Cripps in Morrison's place, or at least in the most important part of it.'[38] Attlee thus disposed of the challenge to his leadership, first by buying Cripps off with a job which he coveted, and then by persuading Morrison to give up, without losing too much face, a job which had brought him little but trouble. Ironically, it was the refusal of Morrison, who despised Attlee, to join Cripps and Dalton in replacing the Prime Minister which gave Attlee the initiative and scuppered the coup.

So the tortoise survived, having surmounted the greatest political crisis of his premiership. Bevin remarked to Arthur Moyle, Attlee's PPS: 'He plucked victory from defeat. I love the little man.'[39] Of the rest of the 'big five', Morrison, though remaining Attlee's deputy and, following the sacking of Arthur Greenwood, taking over his duties, including the chairmanship of the Services Committee, was in effect demoted. Dalton continued for the time being as Chancellor, but with a reputation much damaged by the convertibility crisis. Bevin's position, already immensely powerful, became even stronger. He was Attlee's rock. If the Foreign Secretary had wavered during the crisis, then it is doubtful if Attlee could have survived.

However, a new strong man had emerged: Cripps. When Attlee announced the reshuffle, Cripps stood out as the economic supremo, with the title of minister of economic affairs and in charge of the Central Economic Planning Staff, the Economic Information Unit, the Economic Section of the Cabinet Secretariat, and overseas economic and trade policy. He had an empire stretching across Whitehall. Three new ministers were appointed to key economic posts: Harold Wilson at the Board of Trade, George Strauss at the Ministry of Supply and Hugh Gaitskell, who succeeded Emanuel Shinwell at Fuel and Power. Gaitskell noted in his diary: 'Cripps wants to run the thing with HW [Wilson], RS [Strauss] and myself as his lieutenants.'[40] Dalton welcomed the new arrangements, especially the appointment of younger ministers, such as Gaitskell and Wilson. Generously he continued to regard Cripps as a natural ally, even though Treasury officials saw Cripps's new empire as a dangerous competitor. Six weeks later, however, Cripps took over the Chancellorship as well, thus combining economic and financial management as well as planning under his control.

The downfall of Dalton was part tragedy, part farce. He and Cripps between them had decided that the urgent need to bring the balance of payments under control required an additional deflationary budget to supplement the cut in the import bill already announced to the Commons on 23 October. On 12 November, Dalton delivered his fourth and last Budget speech. It was a tough Budget, which turned out to be even tougher than he estimated. According to Dalton, his tax increases would bring in £208 million in a full year, while there would be a budget surplus of £318 million. In fact, the budget surplus in 1947/8 turned out at £635 million. Dalton had done most of Cripps's dirty work for him. As the economic historian J. C. R. Dow commented, 'the autumn budget of 1947 set the pattern for the next three years; and it is unjust to Dr Dalton that so little of the credit properly given to his successor has been meted out to him'.[41]

But, as Dalton walked into the chamber to deliver his Budget, he was accosted by a journalist friend, John Carvel, lobby correspondent of the *Star*, a London evening paper. Carvel asked him what was in the Budget. Instead of politely brushing him off, Dalton foolishly replied in a single, fatal sentence – no more on tobacco, a penny on beer, something on dogs and pools but not on houses, an increase in purchase tax but only on articles now taxable, profit tax doubled. Carvel hurriedly telephoned his scoop through to his paper in time for it to be published just before Dalton announced his tax proposals. The Conservatives were informed of the leak by the *Star*'s rival newspapers and, the following day, a Tory MP put down a Private Notice Question (a procedure for answering urgent issues).

Dalton immediately offered the Prime Minister his resignation. That afternoon, in a short meeting at No. 10, Attlee accepted Dalton's offer on the grounds that, though no damage had been done, the principle of the inviolability of the Budget was of the highest importance and the discretion of the Chancellor of the Exchequer must be beyond question.[42] (Apparently, the Prime Minster's first reaction had been 'Why on earth did he want to talk to the press?'[43] and there is no doubt that Attlee was always a stickler for conventions.) Dalton's resignation came at a convenient time for Labour. The government's economic policy badly needed a new beginning and the replacement of Dalton by Cripps provided it.

*

The year 1947 had been a terrible one for the Labour government. The Tories went ahead in the public opinion polls for the first time and also made many gains in the November local elections. Yet Attlee always looked back on 1947 with pleasure.[44] The reason was Indian independence.

In a way that he seldom was as Prime Minister, Attlee was in the driving seat over India. Following his membership of the Simon commission in the late 1920s (see p. 70), Attlee retained a deep interest in the subcontinent. After the 1945 election victory, he was determined on a speedy progress towards Indian independence. He chaired the Cabinet's India Committee and, by appointing a peer, the elderly Lord Pethick-Lawrence, as secretary of state, he ensured that effective power was in his own hands. All the main decisions on India were made by Attlee.

After the failure of the second Cripps mission in the summer of 1946 and the outbreak of communal violence between Hindus and Muslims, especially in Calcutta, Attlee decided on a change of policy. The only way, he believed, to bring the Congress Party and the Muslim League to their senses was to 'give them a deadline, and tell them on that date we go out. So you'd better get together right away.'[45] To implement the new policy, he decided to change viceroys, sacking Viscount Wavell, who was a distinguished soldier but not a master of politics, and appointing in his place the glamorous royal Lord Mountbatten of Burma, with instructions to hand over power by June 1948. On 1 January 1947 Bevin wrote Attlee a letter of protest against what he, like Churchill, saw as an unseemly scuttle. Attlee, for once, faced him down: 'If you disagree with what is proposed, you must offer a practical alternative. I fail to find one in your letter.'[46]

Events now speeded up dramatically. Within a few days of his arrival in India, Mountbatten reported back to London: 'The only conclusion that I have been able to come to is that unless I act quickly I may well find the real beginnings of a civil war on my hands.'[47] After one last attempt to reach an agreement on a united India, the new viceroy proceeded with a plan for partition into two states – India and a Muslim Pakistan. Fearing further disintegration, he also drastically brought forward the date for independence from June 1948 to 15 August 1947, a decision which Attlee endorsed. In his unusually eloquent speech on the unopposed Commons third reading of the Indian independence legislation, Attlee said: 'In parting with this bill from this House, I do it not with a feeling of elation, but with a feeling of responsibility, some feelings of anxiety, but also with an unquenchable hope that these things will work out for the good of all the people of India.'[48]

Attlee was right to feel anxious. India's national politicians broadly accepted the boundaries of the two new countries, recommended by the British administrator and lawyer Sir Cyril Radcliffe and announced after 15 August, but in the Punjab partition led to mass migration as 5.5 million Hindus and Sikhs fled to India and 5.8 million Muslims fled to Pakistan. During this two-way exodus, which lasted from August to November, between 200,000 and one million people were slaughtered. Could a less precipitate transfer of power have reduced the bloodshed? According to the assistant policy commissioner in Lahore, who was a Muslim, 'a few British battalions could have saved the Punjab'.[49] Attlee defended his policy later: 'Whether we could have stopped it [the violence] then if we'd still been in control I don't know – it's very doubtful . . . I can only say the death toll would have been far higher if we hadn't come out – if we'd tried to hold India.'[50]

The key issue is whether Attlee was right to send Mountbatten to India as viceroy with increased powers and a firm date for independence. Mountbatten exaggeratedly claimed that he demanded plenipotentiary powers in an interview with Attlee and Cripps and that Attlee replied that he had got the powers and the job. Of course, there was never any question of Mountbatten being given plenipotentiary powers. It was Attlee and the Cabinet who were in charge. Attlee described the viceroy's role to Mountbatten in a cricketing analogy: 'I put you in to bat on a very sticky wicket to pull the game out of the fire.'[51]

Once a date for independence had been set (and, as Attlee and Mountbatten agreed, there was a strong case for so doing), Mountbatten, who as a successful war leader and a member of the royal family, was in many ways an inspired choice to be the viceroy to hand over power, had to be given some latitude. It was Mountbatten's opinion that, unless he brought forward the date of independence, there would be civil war. Attlee had either to accept his judgement or get himself another viceroy. When Mountbatten announced 15 August as the day when power would be transferred, Attlee minuted: 'Accept Viceroy's proposal.'

This decision led to appalling carnage in the Punjab. But against that, the Labour government's achievement in leaving the subcontinent on good terms with the two new states, which subsequently became members of the Commonwealth, has also to be weighed in the balance. Here Attlee deserves much of the credit. His biographer concluded: 'For what happened in India in 1947 and in the aftermath he must take the praise or bear the blame.'[52]

10

1948–9: The two giants

At the end of January 1948, the chargé d'affaires at the US embassy in London sent back to Washington the following report on the situation in Britain: 'Government has staged strong comeback since August/October when it appeared to be tottering and there was much speculation Attlee would resign, government would not last more than a few months, there would be early general election or possibly a coalition government. This speculation has now completely died out.'[1]

Labour's recovery, on both the political and the economic fronts, continued throughout 1948 and into 1949. Paradoxically, despite his weak performance in the fuel and financial crises, the Prime Minister had come through 1947 with an enhanced reputation for shrewdness and nerve. For the first time since he became leader of the party in the 1930s, his position at the top was unchallenged. Alongside him, however, there were now two immensely powerful figures, Stafford Cripps and Ernest Bevin, who, more than Clement Attlee, gave the government in the period from 1948 to the general election of 1950 its authority.

The 'big five' became the 'big three'. After his resignation, Hugh Dalton had a mental and physical breakdown. He stayed the first night after leaving 11 Downing Street in the flat of his friends Nicholas and Olga Davenport. During the night they heard a loud crash. They found Dalton lying unconscious on the bathroom floor and dragged him back to bed, where he recovered consciousness. Dalton then proceeded to pour out his heart to Olga Davenport. Nicholas Davenport wrote later: 'The frustrations and anxieties of his office had been a slow torture and now that the tension had been broken and he felt released he cried his heart out.'[2] Dalton then retreated for the next few months to West Leaze, where he made a slow recovery. Davenport remarked that Dalton's wife, Ruth, seemed incapable of looking after the former Chancellor, as she was quite unable to cook or make a home. However, the Daltons continued to live together, both at West Leaze and in a small flat off Victoria Street, 'not so much a marriage, more two people choosing to grow old together'.[3]

On 1 June 1948, Dalton returned to the Cabinet as chancellor of the Duchy of Lancaster. The chancellor of the Duchy is a non-departmental minister, available for any special duties which the Prime Minister may require. Attlee had brought him back because there was some sympathy in the party for his unfortunate downfall. Attlee may also have feared that Dalton could cause trouble on the backbenches. Dalton was given fifth place in the Cabinet's official pecking order, after Attlee, Bevin, Morrison and Cripps, but in reality his political importance was over. His biographer elegantly summed up the change: 'Before, he had been a history-maker, driven by ambition and a vision of the future. Afterwards, he was a politician, exerting influence, living the Westminster life.'[4]

As leader of the House of Commons and deputy Prime Minister, Herbert Morrison continued to play a vital role in the government, and the nearer the election drew, the more crucial that role became. But with Cripps taking over economic affairs and the chancellorship, Morrison was no longer the dominant figure on the home front that he had been from 1945 to 1947. Maurice Webb, the chairman of the Parliamentary Labour Party and a close friend of Morrison's, expressed party feeling in a letter: 'I fear the terms of the announcement will be commonly interpreted as notice of your withdrawal from the highest places . . . I suppose this means the end of Morrison is a typical comment made to me.'[5] It was not the end, but it was a severe setback from which Morrison never completely recovered.

It was Cripps, with the possible exception of Neville Chamberlain the most powerful Chancellor since David Lloyd George, who now provided the government's momentum. Immensely able, exceptionally hardworking, and with the moral authority that came both from his approach to his work and from his religious convictions, Cripps towered over his colleagues. Hugh Gaitskell, who as minister of fuel and power worked closely with Cripps, wrote revealingly in his diary entry for 16 February 1948: 'The more I see the more impressed I am. He has really the most amazingly keen intelligence . . . The second great quality he has is courage which is closely combined in his case with superb self-confidence.'[6] Gaitskell then quoted Edwin Plowden, a prominent industrialist and Cripps's chief planning officer, who said: 'When he has made up his mind he is absolutely certain he is right and therefore completely indifferent to any criticisms or objections or arguments.'

At the same time, he was extremely kind and charming to those with whom he worked, writing warm personal notes at Christmas to his ministers and civil servants. Robert Hall, head of the Economic Secretariat, wrote that 'he commanded a most uncritical respect among civil servants, which is very unusual in my experience. He was a wonderful man to work for especially if he respected you.'[7]

Cripps's working hours were legendary. He got up at 4 a.m. and worked on his papers until 7 a.m., when he went for a half-hour walk in St James's Park with his wife Isobel. Then followed a cold bath, and a frugal breakfast of yogurt, fruit, toast and marmalade, after which Cripps left his flat at 11 Downing Street for his nearby office at the Treasury to give himself an hour of work before his first meeting. The Chancellor continued this ferocious pace throughout the day.[8] Attlee used to tell the story of how a caller arrived at 5 a.m. at No. 10, claiming to have a meeting with the Chancellor. The policeman looked puzzled until the visitor explained that he had an appointment with Sir Stafford Cripps. The policeman at once replied: 'Oh, him, please come in.'[9]

Every weekday morning at 9.30 Cripps held a morning meeting or 'prayers' with Treasury ministers and his top civil servants and advisers. He had wished to start at 9.00 but agreed to a compromise of 9.30 (10.00 on Mondays). Edward Bridges, permanent secretary to the Treasury and head of the civil service, lived in Epsom and this top Whitehall mandarin was sometimes seen running down Great George Street in order to reach the Chancellor's room by 9.30. Once when Hilary Marquand, the paymaster general, arrived half a minute late, Cripps icily said: 'Good afternoon!'[10] At this short meeting, anyone could briefly raise any point or ask any question. Though formal decisions were never taken, initiatives were often launched. Douglas Jay, economic secretary at the Treasury, commented that the 9.30 meetings gave him a daily chance to find out what was happening and certainly saved time in circulation of memos.

Another means devised by Cripps for keeping in touch was the fortnightly private dinner at the House of Commons, paid for by Cripps and taking place on Thursdays, of hand-picked economic ministers. Apart from the Chancellor himself, regular diners included Aneurin Bevan, minister of health, John Strachey, minister of food, Harold Wilson, president of the Board of Trade, George Strauss, minister of supply, Gaitskell, Marquand and Jay.

At these dinners talk ranged freely from general discussions on economic policy to detailed analysis of vital issues such as the world cereal market. In his diary for 23 April 1948, Gaitskell noted: 'At our dinner with the Chancellor last night Aneurin Bevan was also present and appears to have joined the group. I must say Stafford is showing much more political acumen than I expected. He is obviously anxious to have Bevan as an ally.'[11] The close relationship between Cripps and Bevan went back to the 1930s, when they were both left-wing rebels. Bevan, always a great talker, dominated dinner conversation with a series of mischievous jibes about his colleagues, including Bevin, of whom Bevan said: 'He does at least have the courage of his own bad grammar.'[12] But Bevan would always shut up when Cripps, putting a hand on his arm, would tell him to be quiet as serious economic debate was about to begin. Gaitskell was impressed not only by the eminence of the group but also by Cripps's authority over them. 'I could not help feeling that Stafford was surveying his future Cabinet,' Gaitskell remarked.[13]

At the Treasury, Cripps was backed up by a brilliant group of civil servants and economists. Jay described it as by far the ablest group with whom he ever had the chance to work. It included Bridges, Plowden, who shared Cripps's religious beliefs, and Hall, who was formerly an economist at Trinity College, Oxford and who, during the war, worked at the Ministry of Supply. On the overseas side, where Hugh Dalton's Treasury had so clearly failed, the group included Otto Clarke, a brilliant economist and statistician, and Leslie Rowan, a tough Whitehall operator.

Cripps's team was completed by a very determined 'irregular' – his wife. Isobel Cripps had shared the ups and downs of her husband's career – left-wing rebellion in the 1930s, Moscow and London during the war, and Cabinet life under the Labour government. Now she became the source of persistent leaks from Attlee's Cabinet (but remained unidentified). Devoted to advancing her husband's career, she took tea every Friday afternoon with Hugh Massingham, columnist of the *Observer*. Briefed by her husband on what had happened in Thursday's Cabinet, she passed on to Massingham what the leading ministers, such as Attlee, Bevin, Cripps, Morrison and Bevan, had said. So accurate were Massingham's accounts that they could almost have been written directly from the Cabinet minutes. Government security and intelligence experts were called in but they were quite unable to track the source of the leak.[14]

After the confusion and muddle of 1947, Cripps gave the government new impetus and purpose. While protecting the welfare advances of the Labour government, he squeezed resources out of consumption and into exports and investment. In a speech early in 1949 at Workington, Cumberland, Cripps described his strategy of austerity as follows:

> You will see, then, that as long as we are in this impoverished state, the result of our tremendous efforts in two world wars, our own consumption requirements have to be last in the list of priorities. First are exports . . . second is capital investment in industry; and last are the needs, comforts and amenities of the family.[15]

Cripps had a number of weapons in his economic armoury. These included a voluntary wages freeze (negotiated, with Bevin's help, with the TUC); import controls; rationing, especially of food and petrol, to save dollars; and more generally what the Chancellor called 'democratic planning', symbolised by the publication of annual economic surveys and the long-term economic programme produced as part of the Marshall plan. Under Cripps, the annual Budget became increasingly important, so much so that he has been called the first modern Chancellor.[16]

In his first Budget of April 1948, Cripps laid out its expanding role: 'The new task of the Chancellor of the Exchequer is not merely to balance the Budget: it is a much wider one – to match our resources against our needs so that the main features of our economy may be worked out for the benefit of the community as a whole.'[17] Building on Dalton's tough November 1947 Budget, Cripps planned for and achieved substantial budget surpluses. Their purpose was Keynesian – to contain inflationary pressure and, by restraining demand, to act directly on the balance of payments. In his April 1948 Budget, he predicted a surplus of £789 million (the out-turn was actually £831 million).[18] He also introduced a one-off capital levy, justified on social grounds: 'It is undoubtedly right', said the Chancellor, a man with a large fortune, 'that those who possess large capital assets should make some contribution to help the country in this emergency.'[19]

Cripps's style was completely different from his predecessor's. Whereas Dalton was wily, controversial and often boisterous, Cripps was measured and straight, telling it as he saw it. Hall's diary entry for 8 April noted: 'The Chancellor spoke very clearly but with hardly a gesture and little change of tone. The House did not seem to appreciate the main points and only cheered the obvious ones.'[20]

But Cripps's performance earned growing appreciation. In March, Hall reflected Whitehall opinion when he said that Cripps had saved the country from a complete *débâcle*.[21] In November, a Tory provincial paper wrote that Cripps was attracting more attention than any other leader not only 'because his duties touch every one of us more intimately; it is also because he is trusted better'.[22] It was not just the British who admired him. In February 1949 the well-known American columnist Joseph Alsop said: 'There is only one way to describe it. In the last year the British people have accomplished a miracle.' He pointed not only to the encouraging economic statistics but also to the effect of Cripps, 'the strange, coolly intelligent, ruthlessly determined leader'.[23]

The economic statistics for 1948 were genuinely encouraging. Production rose rapidly, full employment was maintained. Most important of all was the spectacular rise in exports, bringing about a dramatic turnaround, year on year, in the balance of payments. The deficit on the current payments balance, which had been £630 million in 1947, fell to only £30 million in 1948, and in both 1949 and 1950 the UK was in balance. Greatly assisted by the flow of Marshall aid, which came on stream in July 1948, the 'dollar gap' was substantially reduced.

Cripps's 1949 Budget was a 'no change' one. His speech was notable, however, for a warning to his own party about the cost of the new social services introduced by the Labour government. No one wanted to cut them, for 'we all know their immense value'. But he argued that redistributive taxation had reached its limit, so that any extension of social services would therefore only come about if national income increased.[24] This was quite different from Attlee's cost-free approach in 1946, when he said: 'The question is asked – can we afford it . . . I cannot believe that our national productivity is so slow, that our willingness to work is so feeble or that we can submit to the world that the masses of our people must be condemned to penury.'[25] According to Hall, Cripps's realism was not well received on the Labour side; 'clearly the government leaders disliked the very plain statements that we had to pay for our social services, which the opposition applauded'.[26]

The concentration on exports, the downgrading of resources going to consumption and the extensive system of rationing undoubtedly helped turn the economy round. But Cripps's 'austerity' strategy had social and political shortcomings. Every subject was issued with a ration book from which coupons had to be cut to authorise purchases: the weekly ration per person was 13 ounces of meat, 1½ ounces of cheese, 6 ounces of butter and margarine, 1 ounce of cooking fat, 8 ounces of sugar, 2 pints of milk and one egg.[27] These restrictions lasted until Labour lost power in 1951.

Although the majority of the population experienced higher standards of nutrition and health than ever before, middle-class and Tory-backed organisations such as the British Housewives' League were critical of the Chancellor and the government. On the whole, Cripps was respected for his high-mindedness and honesty, though his occasional remarks about such issues as women's clothes laid him open to ridicule, especially when, on one occasion, he went so far as to criticise Christian Dior's New Look skirt length. The chairman of the Conservative Party, Lord Woolton, sent a shrewd political message to the middle classes when he said: 'Sir Stafford Cripps believes in austerity. He practises it himself almost as though it was a religious cult. That might be good for him, but it is of no use to us.'[28] It was a warning to Labour that the alliance between the working classes and the middle classes which had brought the party to power in 1945 could be broken apart.

The other great figure of this time was the Foreign Secretary, Ernest Bevin. The historian of the Attlee governments has written: 'The period between [US secretary of state George] Marshall's Harvard speech on 5

June 1947 and the coming into being of NATO in April 1949 is a period of sustained creativity such as few, if any, British Foreign Secretaries have produced since the time of the Elder Pitt.'[29]

When Bevin became Foreign Secretary in 1945, he assumed that it was in Britain's interest to seek a satisfactory peace settlement not only with the United States but also with its other great wartime ally, the Soviet Union. He also believed that, if at all possible, the division of Europe into rival blocs should be avoided. As late as February 1947 he was still seeking a fifty-year treaty of friendship with Moscow. It was his experience of Soviet intervention in Greece, Turkey, northern Iran, eastern Europe, and above all in Germany, combined with obstructive behaviour at the Council of Foreign Ministers (CFM) and the United Nations, which made Bevin turn to a new idea: the creation of a new grouping which would unite Britain not only with its western European allies but also with the United States in a defensive alliance against the Soviet Union.

For the first eighteen months after the end of the war, US leaders remained aloof from the United Kingdom, which they saw as a bankrupt imperialistic power. In December 1945 Bevin's fear was that the Americans might do a deal with the Soviets over his head. But, as we have seen, following the UK decision to withdraw from Greece and Turkey, US policy shifted, with the announcement of the Truman doctrine in March and Marshall's speech at Harvard in June 1947 proposing massive aid to the beleaguered countries of Europe. Bevin's prompt response to Marshall's offer led to the creation of the European Recovery Programme or Marshall plan, which helped save the economies of western Europe.

The Soviet refusal to discuss Marshall's proposals represented a turning point in the relations between the Soviet Union and the West. The subsequent breakdown of the CFM talks in London on the future of Germany marked the beginning of the Cold War. After the failure of the London conference, Bevin judged that it was essential to rally opinion in the UK, Europe and the United States, and to stand firm against the bullying tactics of the Soviet Union. So, on 22 January 1948, the British Foreign Secretary made a big speech to the House of Commons, calling for a Western Union.

Outlining the ruthless methods which the Soviet Union was using to eliminate opposition in eastern Europe, he said that 'the free nations of western Europe must now draw together' and that 'the time is ripe for a consolidation'. Bevin spoke movingly of the political, economic and spiritual unity of western Europe and concluded with these words: 'We shall not be diverted, by tyrants, propaganda or fifth-column methods, from our aim of uniting by trade, social, cultural and all other contacts of these nations of Europe and the world who are ready and able to co-operate.'[30]

Although the British Foreign Secretary had intentionally avoided mentioning what kind of relationship the new European grouping might have with the United States, Bevin's 'Western Union' speech was the start of the process which led to the setting up of NATO the following year. In a favourable analysis of his speech, the *Times* commented: 'What Mr Bevin has done is to strike the dominant chord. Just as he was swift to seize the initiative offered by Mr Marshall last June, so he has now been quick to offer an initiative himself.'[31] It was essential to show the United States that Europe meant business. Following his speech, Bevin set in train talks in the western European capitals which resulted in the treaty of Brussels, by which the UK, France, Belgium, the Netherlands and Luxembourg agreed to set up the Western European Union, a military alliance for mutual defence which was to last fifty years.

Meanwhile, events moved rapidly. When Bevin sent Pierson Dixon to Prague as ambassador in January 1948, he wrote to him that he had a great fear about what was about to happen in Czechoslovakia. He was right. In late February, the non-Communist ministers were forced to resign and, in a well-planned coup, the Communists speedily took over. Dixon reported back to Bevin: 'The whole character of the state had been changed in less than a hundred hours.'[32]

The Communist coup in Prague had an electrifying effect on the West. In a meeting with the US ambassador, Lewis Douglas, Bevin called for the forging of a joint military and civil strategy with the United States. In a record of the conversation, Bevin told the ambassador that he had 'no fear of the future provided we got through the next six or eight weeks. But I was really anxious lest the period immediately before us should turn out to be the last chance of saving the West.'[33]

Other ominous signs alarmed Bevin. These included reports that the

Soviet delegation on the four-power body in charge of Berlin was behaving in a disruptive manner and that there was pressure on Norway to sign a pact of so-called friendship and military alliance with the Soviet Union, and rumours that the Communist Party in Italy would stage a Prague-type coup at or before the next Italian elections. Bevin did not believe that the Soviet Union was about to go to war. But he felt that the West (including the United States) had to act on the assumption that it was facing a calculated challenge from the Soviets and had, therefore, to show it had the will and unity to resist. On 11 March 1948, Bevin sent Marshall a powerful message in which he urged the need for the British and US governments to consult without delay on the establishment of an Atlantic security system, the first mention of what was to become NATO. Marshall immediately replied. After consulting the US President, he wrote a 'Top Secret' letter the next day to the British ambassador: 'Please inform Mr Bevin that in accordance with your aide memoire of 11 March, we are prepared to proceed at once in the joint discussions on the establishment of an Atlantic security system.'[34] Talks began at an official level but the idea of a North Atlantic pact could not make any decisive progress until after the US presidential election in November.

Meanwhile, the West faced a new danger when the Soviets blockaded Berlin. Once again, Bevin, at a time when France was without a government, acted with firmness and resolution on behalf of western Europe. On the surface, the crisis arose over the Western allies' decision on 18 June to introduce a new currency in the three western zones of Germany. The Soviet response was to bring in their own currency in the Soviet zone, including the whole of Berlin. The underlying issue, however, was the Soviet attempt to stop the Western allies setting up a West German state by exerting pressure on Berlin.

The Soviets cut all road, rail and canal links between Berlin (which was situated in the Soviet zone) and the western zones, as well as ending the supply of electricity to the western sectors from the east. Bevin made clear to the Americans that it would be a disaster for the Western allies to abandon Berlin. With the support of the Cabinet committee on Germany, he agreed to the stationing of American B-29 bombers in East Anglia, as well as their deployment in Germany. Above all, he gave his backing to the bold idea of supplying the western sectors of Berlin by airlift and persuaded the

Americans, with British help, to do it. It was an astonishing success, with up to 7,000 tons of food and fuel being flown in daily by US and British planes. For 323 days, the two million of inhabitants of western Berlin were supplied with food and fuel by air.

In November 1948, the re-election of Harry S. Truman as President gave the green light for serious negotiations on the North Atlantic pact. Bevin's biographer wrote that the signing on 4 April 1949 of the treaty setting up NATO was 'not only the climax of his career as Foreign Minister but with a German settlement at last secured and the prospect of the Berlin blockade being lifted – the greatest ten days of his life'.[35] As he signed the treaty in Washington on behalf of the United Kingdom, Bevin knew that he had succeeded in his primary aims of constructing a defensive alliance against the Soviets and of locking the Americans into Europe. This is not what Bevin had had in mind in 1945, but his experience of the Soviet Union snuffing out any prospect of democracy in eastern Europe, above all in Czechoslovakia, and the blockade of Berlin convinced him of the need for a powerful consolidation of the West, above all in the form of a North Atlantic alliance, to limit Soviet gains in Europe and to allow western Europe to prosper in freedom, greatly assisted by the Marshall plan.

The establishment of NATO in 1949, following the implementation of the Marshall plan in the summer of 1948, represented a phenomenal achievement for a man in his late sixties who was also in ill health. Like Stafford Cripps, Bevin gathered around him a strong team. It included the ambassador to Washington, Sir Oliver Franks, brought in from Oxford to negotiate the creation of the Organisation for European Economic Co-Operation (the group of European nations which helped implement the Marshall plan) and NATO; Gladwyn Jebb, later UK permanent representative to the UN; Ivone Kirkpatrick, head of the German Section of the Foreign Office; and Edmund Hall-Patch, seconded to the Foreign Office from the Treasury and the UK representative to the Organisation for European Economic Co-Operation. Bevin called them all by their Christian names, treating them 'as a benevolent uncle might treat some promising nephew who had talent but still a good deal to learn about the ways of the world'.[36] But, though he respected his officials, it was Bevin who took the decisions.

He read not only his Foreign Office papers but other Cabinet papers thoroughly and speedily, getting up at 5 a.m. with a cup of tea to give him three hours of reading. He seldom wrote anything down, apart from 'speak', 'see me', 'yes' or 'no', preferring to conduct business orally. He liked to summon his officials to his office and hear their views, including the more junior ones. Kirkpatrick remember him saying: 'Are none of you going to argue with me?'[37]

Bevin had little formal education. As he told the King, he gathered his knowledge from the ''edgerows of experience'. But it was a wide experience, first as the UK's leading trade unionist, then as Winston Churchill's minister of labour and member of the War Cabinet. He had not only a retentive memory but also a creative mind which continuously turned over problems. Very often, he would come into the office on a Monday and say: 'I've been thinking.' Quick to grasp a point, he disliked being hurried into coming to a conclusion. But once he had made up his mind and a decision had been taken, he stuck firmly to it. His young trade union colleague George Brown described him as 'a man with little or no taught advantages, who relied wholly upon his own brain, his own imagination and his capacity for envisaging things and people. In this capacity he was not surpassed and I think not even matched by anyone else I have ever met.'[38]

He had little or no private life, apart from visits to old friends and an occasional trip with his wife, Florence, to the seaside. The idea of spending a weekend with a Cabinet colleague was deeply unattractive to him. Even an invitation to Chequers from Clement Attlee, of whom he was very fond, filled him with gloom: 'They don't give you enough to eat. They give you sherry in glasses the size of thimbles and the only warm room in the house is the lavatory.'[39] He and his wife liked living in the second-floor flat of the Foreign Secretary's official residence at 1 Carlton Gardens. Towards Florence he showed great patience, allowing her to interrupt him at work with domestic problems. On one occasion his private secretary heard him on the telephone saying: 'You want to beat it and then put olive oil on it.' He explained: 'Mrs Bevin's got a tough bit of steak.'[40]

*

Attlee may have been overshadowed by Bevin and Cripps, but, even so, his reputation stood high. At the beginning of 1949, a profile in the *Observer* described him as the complete master of his Cabinet and said that 'his prestige with the public has also risen steadily, and stands ahead of that of his government as a whole'.[41] One of Attlee's secrets was his lack of vanity. He knew that Bevin and Cripps were bigger men than he. But he did not resent their greater abilities. Instead he supported them both in Cabinet and extolled their virtues in public speeches, because he knew that Labour's continued success in government depended upon them.

Nineteen forty-eight was a good year for the Prime Minister. On 28 June he made an exceptionally effective broadcast during an unofficial London dock strike, justifying the calling of a state of national emergency and appealing to the dockers to go back to work. So persuasive were his words that they complied in forty-eight hours. On 4 July he was able to deliver another well-received broadcast, saying that the following day a comprehensive system of social security would come into effect which would include national insurance, industrial injuries, national assistance and the National Health Service. Characteristically, and shrewdly, he paid tribute to all political parties for their contribution to the growth of British welfare services.

Much to Attlee's annoyance, on the same day Aneurin Bevan, the architect of the NHS, made a speech to a Labour rally in Manchester. He claimed that 'the eyes of the world are turning to Britain', adding: 'We now have the moral leadership of the world.' He also put the case for further nationalisation, including that of steel, in the next session of Parliament. At one point in his speech, when contrasting Labour's social advances with the Conservative means test of the 1930s, he foolishly referred to the Tories as 'lower than vermin' – a phrase which was, of course, immediately picked up by the press. Attlee was furious, sending Bevan a personal letter in which he called Bevan's remark 'singularly ill timed', because it diverted attention not only from Attlee's non-polemical broadcast but, more importantly, also from Labour's popular welfare reforms, including the NHS itself.[42]

Attlee's handling of the Belcher affair in October 1948 showed him at his most punctilious. Hearing of allegations that a junior minister at the Board of Trade, John Belcher, had taken bribes to get a prosecution against a football pools firm dropped, Attlee immediately sent for the Lord

Chancellor, Lord Jowitt, and instructed him to investigate the allegations. Jowitt concluded that there was not sufficient evidence to warrant criminal proceedings. However, he did not believe that his report would allay public suspicions. He therefore advised Attlee to set up a tribunal of inquiry, which the Prime Minister immediately did. He felt that transparency was essential; justice should not only be done but be seen to be done.

The tribunal, under a high court judge, Mr Justice Lynskey, assisted by two senior barristers, began work in November. Newspapers were allowed to report its proceedings (thus ensuring transparency) but without comment, as its findings might lead to prosecutions, which must not be prejudiced. Its report found that Belcher had been indiscreet and that a Labour trade unionist, George Gibson, had promised to add his influence as a Bank of England director to help one of the central figures in the affair, Sidney Stanley. But the tribunal dismissed other accusations, including one that Hugh Dalton had intervened to help one of his constituents get a licence to extend a house. Attlee acted swiftly. Belcher left his post and resigned his seat, while Gibson resigned from the Bank of England. The Labour government emerged from the scandal unscathed, thanks mainly to Attlee's reputation for Victorian rectitude.

The period from the autumn of 1947 to the spring of 1949 was a good time for the Labour government under the guidance of the 'big three', with the economy recovering and security buttressed by the NATO alliance. But this relatively calm period was about to be disturbed by the Chancellor's growing ill health and a devaluation crisis.

11

1949–50: Devaluation and a pyrrhic victory

The period from spring 1949 until the February election of 1950 was a difficult time for Labour. Stafford Cripps's growing ill health was a major factor in the slow and uncertain response of the government to the devaluation crisis, although the emergence of younger men, especially Hugh Gaitskell, eventually provided an effective solution. In its turn, the impact of devaluation on Cripps's morale led to the general election of 1950 coming earlier than it need have, with the result that Labour only just scraped back with a majority of five.

By 1949 the strain of office was affecting the health of Labour's top ministers. In September 1948 Hugh Dalton recorded a lunchtime conversation with Ernest Bevin which was almost entirely confined to health problems. Bevin was alarmist about Clement Attlee: 'His mind's gone. It isn't eczema he's got, it's shingles.' Apparently Bevin's doctor, who accompanied him to most of his foreign conferences, had said to him: 'Has the PM got a good doctor? I've been watching him tonight. His nerves aren't right.'

Dalton then spoke about his own health problems when he was Chancellor – insomnia, constipation and boils – which had disappeared almost overnight after he had resigned. For his part, Bevin replied, he had not had a real holiday that year. The night before he had been woken up every three hours by telegrams from the United States, which had needed quick answers. The Foreign Secretary then referred to his heart problems. He had nearly 'pegged out' in Moscow in April. His detective had apparently said afterwards: 'I thought you were due for a little box that day,' and he had had a heart attack at the US embassy in March.[1]

Attlee, after a short holiday in Ireland at the beginning of August 1948, had gone into hospital suffering from eczema and was there diagnosed with a duodenal ulcer; afterwards he had to take things easy for three months. Cripps told Dalton, in their first tête-à-tête since Dalton had returned to the Cabinet, that Attlee was in poor health and it would be 'a disaster if he led us' in the next election.[2]

However, it was Cripps's health which gave most cause for alarm. His private secretary, Burke Trend, wrote to him in February 1949:

> Bluntly, the way in which you've been living and working, for the last year at least, is lunacy . . . The concern that you are overloading yourself is very great, and the desire to help lighten the burden is very genuine . . . we can make a plan to reduce the strain; but we must know that, if we work it, you will be content![3]

Cripps's tendency to overwork and then fall sick, usually from acute colitis, was nothing new. It had happened in 1916, in the summer of 1943 and in India in 1946. By February 1949 he had made himself ill again. In May, after his second Budget, the Crippses had two weeks' holiday in Italy, which gave the Chancellor some respite, but by July he was in such a bad way again that he was forced to go for six weeks' rest and treatment to the Bircher-Benner clinic in Zurich, a sanatorium which specialised in a raw food diet. Cripps's ill health was to be a factor in the devaluation crisis which dominated the summer and early autumn of 1949.

After a good 1948, in which exports rose spectacularly and the balance of payments seemed to be coming into surplus, the tide turned once more against the UK and the sterling area in the spring of 1949. A recession in the United States hit UK exports, while imports from the US rose, moving the UK balance of payments on current account into deficit. Between the first and second quarter, the drain of scarce dollars rose from £82 million to £157 million and the reserves fell to just over £400 million, even taking into account Marshall aid.

Against this background, speculative pressure against sterling increased, in the expectation that it would be devalued. It was known that the US authorities favoured sterling devaluation. In February John Snyder, the

US Treasury secretary, giving evidence to a congressional committee, said that devaluation should be 'explored' with countries receiving Marshall aid.[4] In April the International Monetary Fund agreed to begin an inquiry into European exchange rates. Many economists had also come to the view that devaluation would be advantageous: in May a report for the Economic Commission for Europe concluded that 'European currencies in general are over-valued in relation to the dollar'.[5] For a lasting equilibrium, it was necessary to make the soft currencies harder and the hard currencies softer and that could only be done through the devaluation of sterling against the dollar.[6]

Cripps was strongly against devaluation, which he saw as more a moral than an economic question, in effect as a form of financial manipulation. He also felt it would be letting down the holders of sterling. In May, he used a visit to Italy to issue a categorical denial that the UK was about to devalue and in July he repeated the denial to the Commons: 'The government have not the slightest intention of devaluing the pound.'[7] That same month, he also assured the Commonwealth Economic Conference that the UK would not devalue.

Cripps told the Economic Policy Committee on 17 June the gloomy news that many items in the dollar balance sheet were all going wrong at once: 'Our exports to the US [were] very low in April and recession will keep them low; colonial dollar surplus has vanished, US no longer buying Malayan rubber and tin: Commonwealth countries spending too much, especially Australia and South Africa: forestalling, postponement of orders, etc. on devaluation talk.'[8] Cripps also warned the committee that 'within twelve months all our resources will be gone' and that there might well be a 'complete collapse of sterling'. Apparently Attlee turned to Dalton as they left the meeting and said: '1931 all over again,' to which Dalton replied: 'It reminds me awfully of 1947.'[9]

For the Economic Policy Committee on 1 July, Cripps circulated a memorandum showing the decline in reserves and reviewing the policy options: (1) the current policy of improving competitive power through higher productivity; (2) severe deflation; (3) devaluation. He ruled out the second option as being against Labour policy and dismissed devaluation except as 'part of some great new and imaginative scheme to solve the world's dollar problems'. He was supported in his opposition to devaluation both by Aneurin Bevan, who saw it as a step in the direction of deflation, and Bevin, who wanted 'a wholly new approach' to bringing the sterling and dollar areas into equilibrium with each other. Only Herbert Morrison argued that 'it might be better to devalue sterling as an act of deliberate policy than be forced to do so by outside pressure'.[10]

Cripps's main proposal was for dollar economies by both the UK and the Commonwealth, cutting sterling area imports from the United States by 25 per cent. He continued to oppose devaluation. Attlee offered little leadership, in part because he found exchange rate issues difficult to comprehend; he dismissed them as 'nineteenth-century economics'. But, according to Hugh Gaitskell, the real reason why few decisive conclusions were reached by the Economic Policy Committee which met in July was the Chancellor's state of health. Gaitskell noted in his diary: 'It was quite clear from his vacillations that he was not really capable of thinking the problems out for himself.'[11]

On 18 July Attlee announced to the Commons that Cripps's doctors had advised that the Chancellor's digestive ailment necessitated special treatment at a clinic in Zurich and that he, the Prime Minister, had decided that the necessary foreign exchange should be provided to ensure that the Chancellor made a speedy recovery. Attlee told the House that, during Cripps's absence, he would be in charge of the Treasury and would be assisted by the president of the Board of Trade (Harold Wilson), the minister of fuel and power (Gaitskell) and the economic and financial secretaries to the Treasury (Douglas Jay and W. G. Hall). In effect, with Cripps absent, the chancellorship had been put into commission, with three younger men, Wilson, Gaitskell and Jay, all economists, now in the driving seat.[12] This was an inspired move and over the next four weeks helped provide a solution to the crisis.

The day before, Jay, while on his usual Sunday walk round Hampstead Heath, made up his mind that the UK would have to devalue. On his own Hampstead Heath walk and at about the same time, Gaitskell reached the same conclusion. Official opinion was also moving in the same direction. Two senior civil servants, Robert Hall and Edwin Plowden, had been in favour of devaluing since spring. Crucially, Edward Bridges, permanent secretary to the Treasury, who previously had agreed with Cripps that devaluation was an almost immoral act, came round to the view that there was now no alternative, though he argued that devaluation should be accompanied by other measures, including cuts in government spending (to make way for exports), tighter monetary policy and a stronger incomes policy.

On 21 July, with the gold and dollar reserves falling below £400 million, Gaitskell and Jay met Wilson and they agreed to recommend devaluation to the Prime Minister. On the same date, Gaitskell and Jay persuaded ministerial colleagues at Cripps's dining club in the Commons of the need to switch policy. Gaitskell, who was emerging as the leader of the group in favour of devaluation, wrote in his diary: 'Nye was won over without great difficulty.'[13]

On 25 July Gaitskell, Wilson and Jay had a meeting with Attlee. Gaitskell and Jay forcefully put the case for devaluation. According to Jay, 'Wilson took refuge in ambiguity.'[14] Attlee was impressed by Gaitskell's and Jay's arguments. He already thought highly of Jay, who had been right about the coal shortages when Emanuel Shinwell had been wrong, and he also had a good opinion of Gaitskell's performance at the Ministry of Fuel and Power. Gaitskell's decisiveness over devaluation made him, in Attlee's eyes, the obvious choice to succeed Cripps if ill health forced the Chancellor to resign.

The Cabinet, which met on 29 July, agreed in principle that the pound should be devalued and gave the Prime Minister authority to take whatever action was necessary during August. A few days later Attlee sent a letter to Cripps in Switzerland, drafted mainly by Jay and delivered personally by Wilson, who was holidaying nearby. The key sentence reads:

> All of us are now agreed, including the responsible officials, that this [devaluation] is a necessary step (though not of course the only step) if we are to stop the present dollar drain before our reserves fall to a level so dangerous as to impair the government's ability to handle the situation.[15]

The reasons given for the change of policy were that the universal expectation of devaluation was holding back purchases of British exports and discouraging the holding of sterling and that UK reserves were falling to crisis level. As to the timing of the devaluation, Attlee favoured a date before talks being held in Washington in mid-September between the US, the UK and Canada, so that it did not appear as if the UK was trading an offer of devaluation for concessions from the United States.

According to Wilson, Cripps's reaction focused on the timing rather than the principle. He favoured announcing the decision on 18 September, after he returned from the Washington talks. When the Chancellor returned to England, he was still not sleeping without the aid of drugs. At a meeting on 19 August at Chequers, at which Attlee, Cripps, Bevin, Wilson and Gaitskell were present, Gaitskell was dismayed to see Cripps handing back to Bridges all the papers which had been prepared for him and saying: 'I am not going to do any work for a week, I must go home and sleep.'[16]

According to Gaitskell, the meeting was a depressing, rambling occasion, lasting for about two and a half hours. Characteristically, the Prime Minister did not intervene at all but sat at his desk 'doodling and listening to the argument'. Cripps was 'quite out of touch'. Bevin swayed this way and that, 'and every now and then we were treated to a long monologue on some event in recent history, such as how he had handled the flour millers in 1924, and what he had said to Ramsay MacDonald in 1931, etc.'. Eventually the Foreign Secretary made it plain that he supported devaluation at some time and, despite some scepticism from Cripps, that settled the issue. However, it also became clear that the Chancellor was totally against an early date. Finally the Prime Minister summed up: 'The Chancellor does not want to do it before Washington. Therefore we cannot do it before Washington.'[17]

A Cabinet meeting at 10 Downing Street on Monday 29 August confirmed the conclusions of the Chequers meeting. Attlee began by saying that opinion had hardened in favour of devaluation. He recommended that the Foreign Secretary and the Chancellor should be authorised to discuss devaluation with the US authorities and 'to form a view, in the light of those discussions, on the amount and the timing of this measure'.[18] The Chancellor said that it was impossible to show arithmetically that devaluation would prove advantageous but conceded that an atmosphere had been created in which the pound could not reach stability without it. Ministers voiced general support for devaluation, leaving it to Cripps and Bevin to determine its date and level.

The same day, the two great men, together with Florence Bevin, Edwin Plowden, Roger Makins of the Foreign Office and two private secretaries, boarded the RMS *Mauretania* for the United States. The rest of the delegation went ahead by air. Both Cripps and Bevin were in poor health: Bevin could not travel by air because of his heart and stayed in bed resting, while Cripps used the boat journey to prolong his convalescence. Curiously the two ministers did not actually meet for the first three or four days. Cripps rose at 4 a.m., often pacing the deck till dawn, and retired to bed early at around 4 or 5 p.m. Meanwhile Bevin did not rise until late afternoon. It was not until well into the voyage, when Cripps agreed to stay up a little later, that Plowden and Makins had the opportunity to brief the two statesmen together.[19]

They did not decide on the new rate for the pound until the British delegation reached Washington. The consensus among the officials was that it was better to set the rate low rather than go too high and risk another devaluation. The final choice lay between $2.80 to £1 (a 30 per cent devaluation from the then current level of $4.00) or $3.00 (a 25 per cent devaluation). On 12 September the officials put the alternatives to Cripps and Bevin in Bevin's sitting room at the British embassy in Washington. Cripps had to be dissuaded from asking the Americans and the Canadians what rate they would suggest. Finally Cripps turned to Bevin, who was still dressed in his pyjamas and dressing gown, and asked his opinion. Bevin's first reaction was to ask Plowden: 'What effect will a rate of $2.80 have on the price of the standard loaf of bread?'[20] Once reassured, the Foreign Secretary went for the rate of $2.80 to £1. In this almost casual way, the new rate, which was to last until the Wilson government devalued again in November 1967, was decided.

The Washington talks began in a somewhat frosty atmosphere but warmed up once Bevin and Cripps had informed the US ministers of the devaluation decision and its extent and timing. The Americans promised lower tariffs and a simpler customs procedure, as well as agreeing to the use of Marshall aid dollars to buy Canadian wheat. It was also agreed that the US, the UK and Canada should set up a permanent economic council to continue discussion on stabilising sterling and achieving equilibrium between the sterling and dollar areas.

On Saturday 17 September, following Cripps's return from the United States, the Cabinet met at 10 Downing Street to discuss the broadcast in which the Chancellor would announce the decision to devalue. Robert Hall and Plowden had prepared a draft which started by admitting that devaluation was a defeat for his previous policy. Cripps rejected this, saying that Bevin had told him never to apologise for his actions as a minister. Clem Leslie, responsible for press relations at the Treasury, believed that Cripps's failure to apologise damaged his reputation, 'as people thought he was trying to brazen it out, something the public thought was unlike him'.[21] After devaluation, Cripps lost public support: in the spring of 1949 Gallup recorded a net approval rating for the Chancellor of 33 per cent; after devaluation this margin had been cut to 11 per cent.[22]

Cripps was troubled by the charge that, over devaluation, he had deceived the public and should therefore have resigned. On the afternoon before he announced the decision, he invited Winston Churchill as leader of the opposition to a confidential briefing on the contents of his coming broadcast. Churchill apparently spent little time discussing devaluation but instead referred back, in a mood of tearful nostalgia, to the wartime coalition, 'when all good and patriotic men had worked together for the common cause'.[23] However, when devaluation was debated in the Commons, Churchill reverted to the party political slapstick of his youth and accused the Chancellor of deceiving the nation. Cripps was deeply offended and refused to attend a ceremony at Bristol University at which he was to receive an honorary degree from Churchill, who was chancellor of the university.

Concern about his honour led Cripps to insist that there should be a general election before the Budget. He held the view that any Budget introduced before an election would be an 'electioneering' Budget and, therefore, immoral. At a meeting of ministers on 7 December he argued for a general election early in the New Year. Herbert Morrison preferred May or June, because he felt that the winter weather would depress the turnout of Labour voters. He was supported by Douglas Jay and Hugh Gaitskell, who believed that by the summer the beneficial effects of devaluation would have worked through and the economy would be seen to be on the upswing. Bevin, who was recuperating in Eastbourne, sent a note saying that, as he was 'no politician', he would accept their decision. After consulting his colleagues, Attlee announced that the election would be held on 23 February, the first winter general election since 1906. The Prime Minister would almost certainly have preferred a later date but he knew that Cripps would have resigned if the election had been delayed, which would have been a shattering blow to the government. At about this time, Attlee remarked to Jay about Cripps: 'He's no judge of politics.'[24] Nonetheless his presence, as Attlee well understood, remained essential to the survival of the government.

Labour went to the country, having carried out the programme on which it had been elected in 1945 and without having lost a single by-election. Most ministers, therefore, expected a clear Labour victory, though Jay thought that the result would be close. Public opinion polls, not then a big feature of general elections, suggested that Jay was nearer the mark. In November, a few weeks after devaluation, a Gallup poll showed the Tories ten points in the lead but by 30 January Labour had edged ahead.[25]

Inevitably, the general election of February 1950 was lower key than that of 1945. Churchill called it 'demure'.[26] He was holidaying in Madeira when the election was called and came back to England by flying boat. The Conservative campaign, however, was less dominated by Churchill than it had been in 1945, with Anthony Eden, R. A. Butler and Harold Macmillan all playing prominent parts. On the Labour side, the surprise star was the Prime Minister himself. Driven by his wife, Vi, in a pre-war Humber saloon, he made thirty-four speeches, mostly in marginal constituencies, averaging seven public meetings a day. Whenever they had a spare moment, Clement would do the crossword and Vi would catch up on her knitting – the very picture of middle-class respectability. As usual his speeches, delivered without notes, were sober and dignified. It was significant that Cripps, usually so critical of Attlee as a performer, suggested that the Prime Minister deliver the final election broadcast on 17 February instead of Morrison. Gaitskell wrote in his diary:

> One result of the election has been the increase in stature of the PM. He certainly displayed his remarkable political instinct and gifts at their very best. He always found the exact words to counter Churchill, and it is generally agreed that his broadcast was outstanding. When one considers that he

191

normally is thought of as a poor broadcaster and a man with no gift for leadership, this is rather extraordinary.[27]

The tortoise had come into his own.

As in 1945, Morrison played a key role. Not only was he chairman of the National Executive Committee's special campaign subcommittee, but he spoke at about eighty meetings up and down the country. His biographers called him 'Labour's election handyman'.[28] At an eve-of-poll press conference he made an appeal to Liberal and middle-class voters, stressing that they were a valuable element in society. Bevin's poor health prevented him playing an active part in the election, though he was persuaded to speak for Morrison in his Lewisham constituency. 'I'll come for you, Mabel,' he told Morrison's agent, Mabel Raison, 'but not for that so-and-so candidate of yours.'[29] The Lewisham meeting went well, though Bevin had to have treatment for his heart before he could go home. Meanwhile Cripps, despite his ill health, was one of the stars of Labour's campaign. In his broadcast at the beginning of the campaign, he said: 'If you still want full employment, fair shares and decent standards, stick to the policies and the party which have so far given them to you.'[30] This set the tone of Labour's campaign: moderate and responsible, and stressing economic recovery, welfare and full employment, rather than the 'shopping list' of industries and services to be nationalised, as set out in the party's manifesto. Aneurin Bevan, with his propensity to alarm floating voters, was kept out of the limelight and off the air.

The weather was fine for most of polling day, though it started to rain heavily in the evening. The turnout was a record 84 per cent. Labour substantially increased its poll compared with 1945 and finished over three quarters of a million ahead of the Tories: it won 13,266,176 votes and gained 46.1 per cent of the poll, compared with 12,492,404 and 43.5 per cent for the Conservatives and their allies. The first returns went well for Labour, with the party polling heavily in its safe urban seats. It looked as though Labour might be returned with a comfortable majority. But the next day, the Conservatives made substantial gains in rural seats and in the suburbs, especially around London, with the result that Labour's comfortable lead in terms of votes cast gave the party a precarious overall majority of only five, a minuscule lead in seats compared with its 146 in the 1945 parliament.

The first explanation for Labour's wafer-thin majority was the redistribution of parliamentary constituencies, which probably lost Labour as many as forty seats. Secondly, the Labour majority would almost certainly have been greater if, as Morrison had urged, the election had been delayed until the summer of 1950. Thirdly, Cripps's 'austerity' strategy of putting exports and investment ahead of raising living standards led to substantial middle-class disaffection. But though Cripps may have been marginally a net vote loser, from 1947 onwards he had given the government a new sense of purpose which enabled it to regroup. Above all, he had laid the basis for economic recovery.

12

1950–51: Running out of steam

The second Attlee government, which was in office from February 1950 to October 1951, had few legislative achievements to its credit. However, it presided over an impressive economic recovery and, until the Korean War started in June 1950, it looked as if it might pull through to better times. However, the impact of the war and the subsequent rearmament programme overburdened the economy and led indirectly to a disastrous split in the Cabinet over health charges, which brought about the resignation of Aneurin Bevan. At the October 1951 election, though Labour won more votes than the Tories, it finished twenty-six seats behind. The six years of Labour government were over.

On the day after the 1950 election, the Cabinet met. When he was asked outside 10 Downing Street what it had decided, Clement Attlee replied: 'The result of the meeting? Oh. We're carrying on. That's all.'[1] However, when the Cabinet met again the following day, it was agreed that 'there could be no question of attempting to carry through any of the controversial legislation which had been promised in the party's election manifesto'.[2] That meant dropping the 'shopping list' of public ownership commitments, such as the nationalisation of cement, water, sugar refining and meat distribution, and the mutual ownership of industrial assurance, though the government went ahead with the iron and steel nationalisation that had been started in the previous parliament.

Most political commentators predicted another general election within a few months. But, in fact, the government was in a stronger position that at first sight it seemed to be. The economic news was uniformly encouraging. Partly due to devaluation, the current account in 1949 had shown a small surplus and in the first two quarters of 1950 the balance of payments moved into substantial surplus. Gold and dollars flowed into the reserves, so much so that at the end of the year the Chancellor (by that time Hugh Gaitskell) was able to announce that the UK would not require any further assistance from Marshall aid. Production moved ahead strongly, while unemployment stayed under 2 per cent. Inflation was stable. As the economic situation improved, the government felt able to abolish petrol and clothes rationing.

Public opinion, influenced by the better economic news, was favourable. By-elections in two marginal seats, West Dunbartonshire and Brighouse & Spenborough, which if lost would have all but removed the administration's majority, were safely held. Morale among Labour MPs remained high. Labour won all the votes on the crucial Finance Bill. It became increasingly clear that, so long as the government held together, it could continue in office.

But there was also an underlying weakness. After five years in power, Labour was running out of steam. Now that the 1945 programme had been implemented, the government was unsure what to do next. Most of the leading ministers were getting old: Attlee and Ernest Bevin were nearing seventy, while Stafford Cripps, Hugh Dalton and Herbert Morrison were all over sixty. After a decade in office they were worn out; Bevin and Cripps especially were in very poor health. At the end of May, Gaitskell wrote in his diary: 'The Foreign Secretary seems to be very much iller than he was six months ago . . . He still has a remarkable power of recovery. One morning he will be very poorly, hardly capable of coherent speech and the next day he will be shrewd, sensible, imaginative – all his old, best qualities.'[3] Cripps had intended to resign after the election but, with Labour's majority so small, felt he had to continue in his post. Not enough younger ministers had been promoted, though Attlee appointed Gaitskell minister of state for economic affairs, a kind of deputy Chancellor, to take some of the Treasury load off Cripps, especially for planning and overseas finance.

As in 1949, the 1950 Budget was in most respects a 'standstill' one. The Chancellor reduced income tax on lower incomes but increased tax on petrol. Once again, he planned for a substantial surplus of £700 million a year, to dampen down inflation. This time the policy of running big surpluses was challenged in Cabinet by the leader of the House of Lords, Viscount Addison, with the support of the Prime Minister. Attlee wrote to Cripps: 'I am not highly skilled in these matters and some of my colleagues are in like case. I think that we should welcome an exploration of this subject in Cabinet before the main lines of the Budget are settled.'[4] Attlee's intervention led to an explicit declaration of Keynesian economic policy, which was circulated to the Cabinet. According to the Chancellor, the purpose of economic policy was to manage demand and offset cyclical fluctuations in the economy, without leading either to inflation or to unemployment.

The 1950 Budget concealed a political bombshell. Cripps and his team of Treasury ministers were increasingly concerned about the rising cost of the National Health Service. Gaitskell in particular had pressed Cripps to secure a ceiling on NHS expenditure. In his Budget speech, the Chancellor made it clear that 'it is not possible in existing circumstances to permit any overall increase in expenditure on the health services'. He added that 'it is not proposed to impose any charge immediately in connection with prescriptions', but there was a sting in the tail: 'The power to charge [introduced in December 1949] will, of course, remain so that it can be used later if needed.'[5]

Cripps's relatively bland words masked a ferocious Cabinet argument. Bevan, reappointed by Attlee as minister of health, fiercely opposed any attempt to introduce NHS charges. He declared that the 'government's abandonment of the principle of a free and comprehensive health service would be a shock to their supporters and a grave disappointment to socialist opinion throughout the world'. For his part, Cripps refused to introduce any further supplementary NHS estimates (as he had been forced to do in March) and said that the only alternatives were either imposing charges or curtailing services. Attlee intervened on Cripps's side to express his concern about the rising costs of the NHS.[6]

A compromise was reached. A ceiling was imposed on health expenditure; charges were postponed; and a new Cabinet committee, chaired by Attlee, was set up to monitor NHS costs. For the moment a crisis was averted, but Bevan wrote to Cripps to say that he would no longer attend the Chancellor's Thursday dinners. When Cripps asked why, Bevan replied: 'I am not such a hypocrite that I can pretend to have amiable discourses with people who are entirely indifferent to my most strongly held opinions.'[7] Bevan's bitter complaint was directed not only at his old friend, Cripps, but also at a fellow diner, Gaitskell, who by his own admission had served in the recently set-up Cabinet committee on health costs as 'Treasury prosecutor against the minister of health'.[8] Clearly trouble lay ahead, especially with Cripps's health failing.

In May Labour's National Executive Committee met senior Cabinet ministers and trade unionists to discuss the future direction of the party, following its narrow election victory. On the surface, it was a constructive and harmonious meeting. Morrison introduced the debate. He stressed Labour's losses in the south, especially in outer London, and its marginal seats in the south-east – an example of the party's perennial 'Southern Discomfort' problem.[9] Morrison noted middle-class concerns about taxation, housing and above all nationalisation, especially the 'shopping list' approach. He also said that 'it was more important to pay attention to making effective existing socialisation rather than to proceed with a further nationalisation programme'.[10]

Morrison was opposed by Bevan, who insisted on the importance of retaining the commitment to nationalisation and won the support of Sam Watson, the miners' leader from Durham and that year's party chairman, and Morgan Phillips, now the party's general secretary. Typically, Attlee listened to the arguments without coming down on either side. Morrison had grasped that voters were sceptical about further nationalisation and that Labour needed to rethink its strategies and policies now that its programme had been completed. But he lacked the intellectual energy and grasp to go beyond 'consolidation' – hardly a ringing cry for a centre-left party. Genuine revisionism had to wait for younger figures such as Crosland, Gaitskell, Healey and Jenkins in the later 1950s.

After the election, Hugh Dalton became minister of town and country planning, though he still retained his Cabinet ranking as fifth in the pecking order. His relatively minor post gave him plenty of time to devote to encouraging promising younger politicians, including George Brown, James Callaghan, Barbara Castle and Denis Healey. His favourite was Anthony Crosland, the dashing economist from Trinity College, Oxford.

The financial journalist Nicholas Davenport described how, during the convertibility crisis of 1947, he and his wife, Olga, invited Dalton to spend his sixtieth birthday with them. Crosland came over to dinner from Oxford 'in his bright red sports car, wearing the red beret of the Parachute Regiment. We had an entertaining evening of drink and talk . . . As he drove away, I could see in Hugh's eyes the rekindling of his romantic love for gallant and handsome young men.'[11] Dalton took Crosland under his wing, helping him to win selection for South Gloucestershire and then encouraging his protégé's career in Parliament. Roy Jenkins, another of Dalton's young men, described the relationship between Dalton and Crosland as a form of sadomasochism: 'Tony was cruel to him, calling him an old windbag to his face. Hugh would take it and come back for more.'[12]

Dalton was also a keen supporter of Gaitskell, urging Attlee to appoint him minister of state for economic affairs and eager that he should be the successor to Cripps as Chancellor. Jenkins said that 'Dalton's promotion of Gaitskell in the nasty, backbiting world of high politics was one of the most selfless things I have ever seen'.[13]

Attlee was now the government's indispensable man. The *Manchester Guardian* commented on 4 July 1950 that an Attlee-must-go movement, conceivable in 1945 (and also in 1947), was no longer imaginable: 'It is hardly too much to say that he is the party's greatest asset in the popular mind.'[14] A Gallup poll at the end of May showed that his personal standing had risen since the general election, with 50 per cent approving of him as Prime Minister and only 39 per cent disapproving.

Even after five years in office, Attlee remained an intensely private man. He claimed that he saw more of his family than he had ever done before becoming Prime Minister. Clement and Vi converted the top floor at No. 10 into a flat for them and their children, Janet, who was working in Bristol, Felicity, who was employed in a nursery school in Bermondsey, Martin, a cadet in the Merchant Navy, and Alison, who was at boarding school. One of Attlee's biographers, Kenneth Harris, described Vi as a difficult and neurotic woman. Sir David Hunt, who was Attlee's private secretary from 1950 to 1951, saw it differently. She was, in his opinion, 'a good-natured woman at heart' who was fiercely devoted to her husband and resented what she saw as a barrier of protocol which the civil servants tried to create around him.[15]

Attlee tried to arrange his work so that he could spend the maximum amount of time with Vi, walking with their Welsh terrier in St James's Park after breakfast, and going up to the flat for lunch and tea if possible. At weekends, they went as a family to Chequers in the Buckinghamshire countryside, which they all loved. In the summer, if there were no official guests, the family played energetic tennis, with Attlee sometimes getting through as many as half a dozen sets, even though he was in his sixties. They enjoyed Christmas at Chequers and on Boxing Day usually gave a large children's party. Alan Gordon Walker, son of Patrick Gordon Walker, Attlee's last Commonwealth secretary, remembers receiving a present from the Prime Minister dressed up as Father Christmas.

According to one senior civil servant, Attlee was 'orderly, regular, efficient and methodical to a degree that put him in a different class from any of the Prime Ministers who followed him'.[16] Sitting in the Cabinet Room, he would rapidly read and dispose of the papers brought to him by his private office. At the bottom of a memorandum, he would write Yes or No, sometimes adding a short sentence. If he put his initials, CRA, at the end of a document, it meant that the document was approved. If he wrote 'Agreed – CRA' it was warmly approved.

One criticism of Attlee was his remoteness. Though a good listener, he did not like to exchange views with others. Colleagues were expected to have done their thinking before they saw him. Harold Wilson said: 'You'd think twice before you asked to see him.' He would go to the members' tea room to listen but not to talk. His parliamentary private secretary, Arthur Moyle, described meetings at No. 10 with MPs: 'As they came through his door into the [Cabinet] room Attlee would put down his pen, raise his head with his nose pointing to the sky and take a long sniff, like a fox terrier about to bark. Then he'd stare at the visitor, and say nothing.'[17]

Attlee often said that choosing and sacking ministers was one of his most difficult tasks. He wrote to his brother, Tom, on 24 March 1950, after the formation of his second administration: 'The distasteful business of reconstructing the government is now through. It always means relegating some good friends to the back benches.'[18] His remoteness was an advantage when it came to getting rid of colleagues. When one of his departing ministers queried the decision to sack him, the Prime Minister simply replied: 'Not up to the job.' He can, however, be criticised for being too slow to promote younger MPs.

Attlee himself said about his conduct of Cabinet: 'You must stop people talking – unnecessary talk, unnecessary approval of things already agreed, pleasant by ways that may be interesting but not strictly relevant. And you shouldn't talk too much yourself, however good you are at it.'[19] Douglas Jay once said about him: 'He would never use one syllable where none would do.'[20] His terseness was a formidable political weapon. As a chairman, it enabled him to get business speedily through Cabinet without exposing his own views. Normally, it worked well. But in the economic crises of 1947 and 1949, it was less than adequate. And, crucially, Attlee's style of leadership depended on more dynamic colleagues to give impetus and flair to his government.

By 1950, the chemistry of the Cabinet was changing. The old stars, Bevin and Cripps, were operating at half speed. Morrison and Bevan had become the dominant voices, soon to be joined, following Cripps's resignation in October, by Gaitskell. Given the risk of conflict between Bevan and the other two leading figures, it was a potentially combustible situation.

Then in mid-summer, Attlee and his government were faced with two momentous events. The first was the announcement on 9 May of the Schuman plan (named after the French foreign minister, Robert Schuman), a revolutionary proposal to pool the coal and steel resources of France and West Germany under a common higher authority. The new organisation would also be open to the participation of other European countries, including Britain.

The plan was the brainchild of Jean Monnet, a dedicated European who was then head of the French Planning Commission. He has been described as 'having done more to unite Europe on a permanent basis than all the emperors, kings, generals and dictators since the fall of the Roman Empire'.[21] In April 1949 Monnet had had discussions at his country home near Paris with Edwin Plowden, head of the UK Central Economic Planning Staff, and Robert Hall, Head of the Economic Section of the Cabinet Office, about strengthening Franco-British economic co-operation, including a scheme to tackle the countries' shortages of coal and food by a system of mutual exchange. Only after Bevin and the Foreign Office had rebuffed these ideas on the grounds that they could threaten national sovereignty did Monnet turn away from the British and look instead to the newly elected West German government, under its Chancellor, Konrad Adenauer. Monnet's idea was that joint control of the two countries' coal and steel industries would not only guarantee peace between France and Germany but would also become the nucleus of European unity.

It would be wrong to describe Bevin as being simply anti-European. He had played a leading role in three developments which had a dramatic impact on the shaping of post-war Europe. It was his prompt reply to George Marshall's historic June 1947 speech which led to the setting up of the Organisation for European Economic Co-Operation (OEEC) and the successful implementation of the Marshall plan. Responding to the Communist coup in Czechoslovakia in February 1948, Bevin was the architect of the treaty of Brussels, which united Britain with France and the three Benelux countries in a defensive alliance. Above all, he was at least in part responsible for the creation in April 1949 of NATO, through which the United States had become directly involved in the defence of western Europe. As he told the Commons in January 1948, 'Britain cannot stand outside of Europe and regard her problems as quite separate from those of her European neighbours'.[22]

But if Bevin and the British government considered it a vital British interest to preserve the security and to promote the recovery of western Europe, including the rehabilitation of West Germany, they wished to do it on the basis of co-operation between nation states. They rejected any idea of UK participation in European institutions in which there was a prospect of pooling sovereignty. For example, in March 1948, Bevin insisted that the OEEC should work through inter-government agreement rather than through the integration advocated by the United States and the other Europeans. Similarly, he and the British Labour Cabinet were very sceptical about setting up a council of Europe and a European assembly, for which Winston Churchill had spoken so eloquently at The Hague in 1948, in the conference that set up the European Movement. 'If you open that Pandora's box, you never know what Trojan 'orses will jump out' was Bevin's celebrated comment.[23]

By 1950 Bevin's foreign policy priorities could be described in terms of three relationships: with the United States, with the Commonwealth and the colonial territories, and with continental Europe. Of these three, the link with Europe came third. For Bevin, too close an involvement with plans for greater European unity was likely to be at the expense of Britain's special relationship with the United States (even though the Americans were continually urging the British to play a more active role in Europe) and its world role as leader of the Commonwealth and the colonies and manager of the sterling area.

The Foreign Secretary remained convinced that the countries of mainland Europe were politically unstable and economically shaky; in his view, they were quite unready to embark on ambitious plans for European integration. Certainly a grouping of Britain with the countries of western Europe was not strong enough to stand alone in the Cold War world. Bevin's underlying concern was that, if the UK committed itself too closely to Europe, the United States might be tempted to return to its pre-war isolationism. Grand talk about European unity was just that – talk and possibly dangerous talk as well. Monnet shrewdly summed up the difference between the British and the continental attitudes towards European integration in the following terms: 'With the exception of the UK and the neutrals every country in western Europe has been defeated in war and every country has been occupied by an enemy army of occupation. So we are disillusioned with our institutions and are ready for change and a new approach.' Presciently, he added: 'You are not, but when you see that it works you will want to join.'[24]

When Bevin heard about the Schuman plan from the French ambassador in London on 9 May 1950, his first reaction was fury that Schuman had presented him with a *fait accompli*. Schuman had failed to consult him before announcing his proposals to the French Chamber of Deputies. Bevin also suspected that Dean Acheson, the US secretary of state, had been involved in the deception. Acheson, who had been in Paris for a day or so on his way to talks with Bevin in London before the meeting of the NATO Council, had to admit that he had been informed by Schuman and Monnet about the plan on 6 May but had been sworn to secrecy. Subsequently, it took all Acheson's diplomatic skills to stop Bevin denouncing what he believed to be a Franco-American plot.

The French initiative presented the British government with an acute dilemma. On the one hand, it would have been churlish to oppose such a bold and imaginative attempt to end the long-lasting enmity between France and Germany which had cost so many lives. In a holding statement to the Commons on 11 May, Attlee made it clear that, while it was necessary to seek further information about the proposals, the government formally welcomed the Schuman plan as 'a notable contribution' to the rehabilitation of Germany and to the unity of Europe.[25] On the other hand, both in the Cabinet and across Whitehall the idea of 'pooling' coal and steel resources and of a common higher authority was thought likely to lead to an unacceptable loss of sovereignty. The question was whether to reject the idea of British participation at the outset or to become involved in negotiations to try and influence the shape of the plan.

On 14 May Monnet arrived in London to explain the French proposals. Cripps asked Monnet whether France would go ahead with Germany, even without the UK. Monnet replied: 'I hope with all my heart that you will join in this from the start. But if you don't, we shall go ahead without you.'[26]

To the surprise and alarm of his officials, Cripps told Monnet that, in his view, the United Kingdom should negotiate on the basis proposed by the French, subject to certain provisos, including the rejection of a capitalist cartel and of American participation. He said that he did not believe that 'the United Kingdom would ever be able to come in later on a scheme which had been worked out by France, Germany and Benelux, and he thought, therefore, that we should collaborate from the outset'.[27] Edwin Plowden told Monnet that these were Cripps's personal views, which had not been discussed by his colleagues; after the meeting, Plowden and Roger Makins from the Foreign Office made sure that Bevin and Attlee were briefed on what Cripps had said. Cripps, who was in such poor health that he tended to be influenced by the last person who had talked to him, was speedily brought back into line by the Economic Policy Committee, which authorised officials to take part in discussions of a detailed scheme 'on the understanding that their association with this work would not commit the United Kingdom to adopting . . . the scheme evolved'.[28]

There followed a period of what Edmund Dell called 'diplomacy by telegram',[29] during which the French and the British probed each other's position. Then on 1 June Schuman brought matters to a head by handing the British ambassador in Paris an ultimatum: either the British accepted in principle the pooling of coal and steel production and the institution of a new high authority or it would be excluded from the negotiations. Bevin responded by proposing conversations between France and West Germany in which the UK would also participate. As the West German Chancellor had already agreed two days before to engage in negotiations with the French, Bevin's memorandum seemed like either an arrogant Foreign Office bid to teach the French how to 'suck eggs' or an attempt to wreck the plan before it got off the ground. It was a far cry from the Bevin who responded so imaginatively and promptly to George Marshall's Harvard speech, or who worked so resourcefully and creatively to help create NATO.

Bevin was a sick man. He was in hospital between 10 and 14 March for injections to relieve his heart complaint, and then had to go back into hospital from 11 April to 4 May for an operation on his haemorrhoids. Acheson saw him at the US embassy in London, and was shocked by the deterioration in the Foreign Secretary's physical condition: 'I found Ernest Bevin in distressing shape . . . He had recently undergone a painful operation and was taking sedative drugs that made him doze off quite soundly during the discussion.'[30] Bevin's deputy, Kenneth Younger, agreed, writing in his diary: 'At the talks themselves he has been in far from his best form. He said himself he is only half alive.'[31] On 30 May, two days before the French ultimatum, Bevin entered the London Clinic for another operation, this time for a fistula. He was to remain in hospital for another month. He had to give his reaction to the new situation from his hospital bed.

The ultimatum from Paris came as a shock to the ministers and officials who were left in London during the Whitsun break. Ironically, Attlee and Cripps were both in France on holiday. Younger, who was in charge of the Foreign Office while Bevin was in hospital, telephoned Plowden, who suggested that they should see Herbert Morrison, who was running the government in Attlee's absence. Tracked down to the Ivy restaurant, where he was having supper after the theatre, Morrison listened to the two men in a passage at the back of the building. Pausing for a moment, he said: 'It's no good. We can't do it: the Durham miners wouldn't like it.'[32] In Younger's account, it was 'the Durham miners won't wear it'. In other words, Morrison believed that the miners, having recently achieved the nationalisation of the coal industry, would not agree to putting British pits under the control of a

European authority. In fact, Sir William Lawther, president of the National Union of Mineworkers, was subtler. He said: 'The best way to have the details the way you want them is to be on the inside working them out.'[33]

Morrison and Younger went to see Bevin in the London Clinic. Like Lawther, Younger argued the case for British involvement in the negotiations because 'while we might be able to join in the plan before it reached finality, we should, by failing to participate at the start, greatly reduce our chance of getting a scheme worked out on lines proposed by ourselves'.[34] Bevin heaved a sigh and said dismissively: 'Splash about, young man, you'll learn to swim in time.'[35] He then turned to Morrison, 'Now, 'Erbert', and told him that the ultimatum should be rejected. He suggested that there should be a face-to-face meeting of the countries involved at which the question of procedure should be first decided. The exchange of notes had, in Bevin's view, simply 'led to misunderstanding and delay'.[36] Bevin's proposal might possibly have been a runner in early May. Now it was far too late.

The Cabinet met in the afternoon of 2 June, under Morrison's chairmanship. It was a 'skeleton' Cabinet, with most of its leading figures absent, though its conclusions would probably not have been any different if they had been there. It rejected the French ultimatum and lamely took up Bevin's proposal of a meeting of ministers of the countries at which 'the question of the most effective and expeditious method of discussing the problems at issue could be examined and settled'.[37] But with all the other participants (the Benelux countries and Italy as well as France and West Germany) prepared to go ahead with the negotiations, the French government understandably refused to agree to such an unfocused meeting.

What made things worse was that the government's attempt to wrap up its rejection of the Schuman plan in the warm words of a White Paper was undermined by the publication, the day before its release, of a Labour Party policy statement, *European Unity*. The document's first draft was written by Denis Healey, secretary of the party's International Department, but it was toughened up by Hugh Dalton, chairman of Labour's Industrial Committee, who was ferociously anti-German. Dalton took the press conference on 12 June in his most bombastic manner; according to Younger, 'he was so rude to all the foreign journalists that they went away determined to make trouble for him'.[38]

The press picked out two passages in particular. The first appeared to imply that a Labour government would co-operate only with other socialist governments. The second passage ran as follows:

> Britain . . . is the nerve centre of a world wide Commonwealth which extends into every continent. In every respect except distance we in Britain are closer to our kinsmen in Australia and New Zealand on the far side of the world, than we are to Europe. We are closer in language and in origins, in social habits and institutions, in political outlook and in economic interest.[39]

Even if Dalton's press conference was unfortunate in its tone and timing, Attlee and his other senior colleagues agreed with the Labour statement's analysis that the UK's world-wide role precluded too close a relationship with the European continent, especially when its leaders, such as Konrad Adenauer, Robert Schuman and Alcide De Gasperi of Italy, were Catholic right-wingers.

In the two-day Commons debate on the Schuman plan at the end of June, the government was very much on the defensive. The Conservatives, led by Eden and Churchill, persuasively argued that the government should have entered the negotiations on the same basis as the Dutch government. In a skilful opening speech, Anthony Eden, a former Foreign Secretary, pointed out that the Dutch had reserved the right to withdraw from the negotiations 'if the discussions show the plan not to be practicable'.[40] He also said that the UK ought to have been better prepared for the French initiative and indeed ready with its own proposals, given the importance of the rehabilitation of West Germany and of good Franco-German relations. Attlee complacently wrote to his brother: 'I think WSC [Churchill] made a fool of himself over the Schuman Plan . . . It is generally thought we had the better of the debate.'[41]

Dean Acheson wrote that the UK's failure to join the Schuman plan, which was the first step towards the creation of the European Union, was the UK's great mistake of the post-war period: 'It was not the last clear chance for Britain to enter Europe, but it was the first wrong choice.'[42] Sir Oliver Franks, UK ambassador to the United States at the time and perhaps the most able public servant of his generation, said that 'the decision [not to join the Schuman Plan] cost us the leadership of Europe which we had enjoyed from the end of the war until May 1950'.[43]

Plowden agreed that the UK would have done well to join the European Coal and Steel Community (ECSC) from the outset. But he also argued that there was no possibility of 'persuading the British people or any British government at that time to enter into the Coal and Steel Community on the terms laid down by the French'.[44] Churchill and Eden made good debating points when they said that the government should have adopted the conditional position taken up by the Dutch. But once in government themselves after October 1951, the Tories failed to join the ECSC and, even more damaging for UK interests, refused to enter the European Economic Community when it was set up in March 1957. So it is doubtful whether their response to the Schuman plan would in practice have been much different from Labour's. In one of his first Cabinet papers as Prime Minister in November 1951, Churchill set out his policy towards European integration: 'We help, we dedicate, we play a part, but we are not merged and do not forget our insular or Commonwealth-wide character.'[45]

Some hold that the Labour government's position would have been altered if Cripps and Bevin had been in better health. It is true that the Chancellor's initial reaction to Jean Monnet's proposals was that the UK should join the negotiations. But, when it came to a decision, he would not have opposed the Foreign Secretary. Even a fit Bevin would not have backed British participation in the Schuman plan. His first priority would have remained the strengthening of NATO.

The attitudes of the three other members of the 'big five' were much the same. Morrison's off-the-cuff remark 'The Durham miners won't wear it' summed up his opinion of the sovereignty issue. Dalton was the most hostile of the five and never changed his sceptical view of European integration. The Prime Minister was sympathetic to the French but, as he explained to the French ambassador, René Massigli, 'it was quite impossible for us to sign a blank cheque'.[46] He did not consider the Schuman plan important enough to mention in his autobiography.

By contrast, Attlee's response to the second unexpected event that summer, the communist North Korea's invasion of South Korea across the 38th parallel on 24 June, was firm and immediate. The following day Britain voted with the United States in the United Nations Security Council, calling for an immediate cease-fire and North Korean withdrawal to the 38th parallel. The resolution was carried by nine votes to nil, with Yugoslavia abstaining and the Soviet representative absent because the Soviet Union was boycotting the Security Council. On 26 June Attlee and Younger went to see Bevin in hospital; they agreed that Britain should give full support to the United States.

On 27 June the Cabinet agreed, without dissent, that Britain should support the US representative in the Security Council in calling on members of the UN to come to the aid of the South Koreans (though the majority of the Cabinet were against the US resolution making reference to communist encroachment in other parts of Asia). Dalton summed up the Cabinet discussion as follows: 'It is felt they [the Americans] are our friends, they are calling the Russian bluff now and we must keep in line with them.'[47] The resolution, which gave UN authority to US action, was this time carried in the Security Council by seven votes to one, with Yugoslavia opposing, India and Egypt abstaining, and the Soviet representative still absent. The prompt action of the UN received strong support in Britain and throughout the non-communist world. However, the Korean War was to strain relations with the United States, put an enormous burden on the British economy, and lead to conflict within and resignations from the Labour Cabinet.

On 15 July Sir Oliver Franks, taking advantage of his position, wrote a powerful memorandum to Attlee, urging the Cabinet to send troops to Korea on the grounds that such an action would keep Britain separate from 'the queue of European nations and demonstrate to the Americans that we were one of the two world powers outside Russia'.[48] The Prime Minister used Franks's letter as a successful argument for sending land forces to Korea, as 'a valuable contribution to Anglo-American solidarity'.[49] The small British contingent included the 'Glorious Gloucesters', whose courage later in the year in holding back the Chinese north of Seoul for several days won admiration on both sides of the Atlantic.

In September, the nature of the conflict changed. From being a desperate defence of a small perimeter in South Korea, the war became, following a bold landing behind enemy lines, an onslaught by the UN troops, led by the American general Douglas MacArthur, on North Korea. The headstrong

MacArthur, who appeared to wish to widen the war to mainland China, pursued North Korean forces north of the 38th parallel up to the river Yalu on the Manchurian border. This ill-judged offensive drew in the Chinese, whose troops attacked MacArthur in substantial numbers, forcing him back across the parallel.

With the US commander threatening to bomb China and an off-the-cuff remark at a press conference from President Truman suggesting that the United States was considering using the atomic bomb, Labour backbenchers called for the Prime Minister to fly out at once to Washington. Aneurin Bevan and Dalton both put pressure on Attlee and, following an emergency Cabinet meeting, the Prime Minister was able to announce to the Commons that he was flying to see the US President. He was not accompanied by Bevin, who was not fit enough to face the long journey by air.

On one level, this was one of Attlee's finest hours. He held talks with Truman and Dean Acheson daily from 4 to 8 December. Acheson described him as a 'Job's Comforter' and his thought 'as a long withdrawing melancholy sigh'.[50] All the same, Truman and Attlee got on well, Truman giving the assurance that he had never seriously considered the use of the bomb and had no intention of allowing the war to spread beyond Korea (though MacArthur, whom he later sacked, certainly had). However, the Americans remained firm in refusing to recognise Communist China or to back its admission to the UN. They also insisted that the British should expand their defence programme.

Attlee returned home to be hailed as a peacemaker. But the reality was that he had agreed to consider a massive increase in defence spending which would impose a heavy load on the British economy. In August 1950 the Cabinet had decided on an increase of £800 million, making a total of £3.4 billion over the three financial years beginning in April 1951. On 8 September, as the situation in Korea became more desperate, the total was increased to £3.6 billion. Now, on his return from Washington, Attlee told the Cabinet that he supported a further acceleration in the defence programme.

On 25 January 1951, Hugh Gaitskell, who, following the resignation through ill health of Stafford Cripps in October 1950, had been appointed Chancellor of Exchequer, successfully presented a paper to Cabinet calling for £4.7 billion, even though rearmament on this scale (double the pre-Korean level of defence expenditure and 14 per cent of national income) would, because of the increased demands on the metal and textile industries, threaten exports and investment, as well as leading to a weakening of the balance of payments. In arguing for this level of defence expenditure, Gaitskell was acting more like a minister of defence than a Chancellor. The hike in defence spending, the third in sixth months, was the prelude to a major Cabinet battle between Gaitskell and Bevan over National Health Service charges. Writing thirty years later, the historian of the Attlee governments concluded: 'This destructive and bitter conflict between the two most gifted and eloquent of the younger socialists of the day has many of the overtones of a tragedy.'[51]

When Cripps resigned, there had been a number of possible candidates for the chancellorship. Dalton had the experience but was ruled out as being 'past it'. In any case, he supported Gaitskell for the job. Morrison had the weight but neither the aptitude nor the inclination. When asked by Edwin Plowden if he would accept the post, Morrison replied: 'When I listen to Stafford in Cabinet explaining all those figures I just know I couldn't do it.'[52] Bevan was a charismatic figure, with fervent support among the grassroots of the party. But neither Cripps nor Attlee thought that he would be suitable for the Treasury. By contrast, Gaitskell was well equipped for the job and had the backing of Morrison, Cripps and Dalton. In Attlee's view, the appointment of Gaitskell would cause least trouble.[53]

The Prime Minister was reckoning without Bevan, who was furious when he heard the news about Gaitskell's promotion. According to his biographer, Michael Foot, Bevan's objection to Gaitskell was more sociological than personal: Gaitskell, in Bevan's estimation, represented nothing, 'unless it was the civil service-cum-middle class which was already vastly overrepresented at Westminster'.[54] Yet, as Kenneth O. Morgan has perceptively pointed out, Bevan's friends were almost invariably middle class too. But they were a different kind of middle class: whereas Gaitskell's intimates tended to be economists and administrators, Bevan's were politicians, journalists (including newspaper proprietors such as Lord Beaverbrook and Brendan Bracken), writers and artists.[55]

Arguably, the differences between them were personal and temperamental,

25. Londoners queue to buy coke during the fuel crisis of February 1947.
It was a year of crises which nearly brought the Labour government to its knees.
(Topical Press Agency/Getty Images)

26. Cripps, who became Chancellor
following Dalton's resignation, leaves
Downing Street to present the 1948
Budget. After the confusion of 1947,
Cripps brought a sense of strategy
and moral authority.
(Topham Picturepoint)

27. Aneurin Bevan, the left-wing
rebel whom Attlee appointed as
minister of health, introduces the
National Health Service, 5 July
1948. (Popperfoto/Getty Images)

28. Bevin, watched by Cripps (*on Bevin's right*) and Harold Wilson, president of the Board of Trade (*behind Cripps*), signs the Marshall plan. The British Foreign Secretary's swift reaction to the idea of US economic and financial aid to Europe was a key factor in the plan's successful implementation. (Hulton-Deutsch Collection/Corbis)

29. Viscount and Viscountess Mountbatten, the last viceroy and vicereine of India. All the main decisions on Indian independence were made by Attlee. (Fox Photos)

30. The 1949 devaluation crisis: Cripps and Bevin arrive in the United States to begin discussions with the US government. They decided on sterling's rate against the dollar in Bevin's bedroom at the British embassy in Washington. (Keystone/Getty Images)

31. Cripps and Wilson walk across Downing Street to attend Cabinet following devaluation. The Chancellor's gloomy face illustrates his belief that both he and his government had suffered a moral defeat. (Topham/AP)

32. Attlee speaks at a meeting during the winter election of 1950, which Labour narrowly won. Concerned to protect his personal integrity following devaluation, Cripps had insisted on an early election. (Hulton-Deutsch Collection/Corbis)

33. All smiles as Bevin meets the US secretary of state, Dean Acheson (*left*), and the French foreign minister, Robert Schuman, in May 1950. In fact, Bevin was furious because he felt that the French with US support had bounced the plan for a European coal and steel authority on the UK. Britain's refusal to join cost it the leadership of Europe. (Fred Ramage/Getty Images)

34. Attlee is welcomed to the United States by the President, Harry S. Truman, during the Korean War. During talks, the British Prime Minister received assurances that the US had no intention of using an atomic bomb against China but was forced to agree to massive increases in UK defence spending. (Bettmann/Corbis)

35. Bevin, very ill, in December 1950. He died four months later with the key to his dispatch box in his hand. Cripps had been forced to retire through ill health in October 1950; Attlee's two giants had gone. (Walter Sanders/Time & Life Pictures/Getty Images)

36. Bevan attends a memorial service for Bevin at Westminster Abbey. That month, April 1951, Bevan resigned from the government over the imposition of health charges. This blow was the beginning of the end for the Labour government. (Brian Seed/Time & Life Pictures/Getty Images)

37. Attlee listens, apparently sceptically, as Morrison, who succeeded Bevin as Foreign Secretary, defends his bellicose handling of the Iran crisis. Attlee said later that putting Morrison in charge of the Foreign Office was the worst appointment he ever made. (Cornell Capa/Time Life Pictures/Getty Images)

38. Dalton talks to miners in his Bishop Auckland constituency during the 1951 general election campaign. Despite winning more votes than any party had done before, Labour narrowly lost the election and was out of office for the next thirteen years. (Hulton-Deutsch Collection/Corbis)

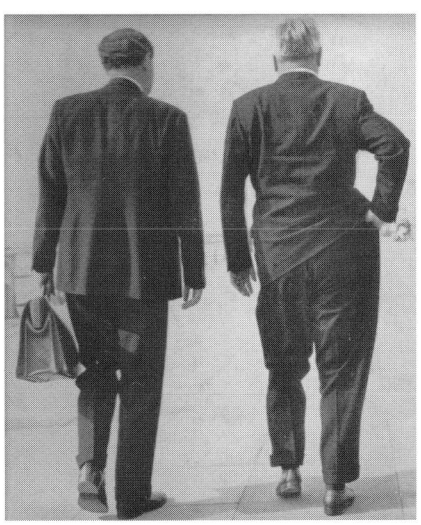

39. Morrison congratulates Hugh Gaitskell on becoming party treasurer. Morrison underestimated the strength of Gaitskell's support, which on Attlee's retirement in December 1955 gave Gaitskell the leadership on the first ballot by a substantial majority.
(Reg Birkett/Keystone/Getty Images)

40. Gaitskell and Bevan together in opposition. The historian of the Attlee governments wrote: 'This destructive and bitter conflict between the two most gifted and eloquent of the younger socialists of the day has many of the outcomes of a tragedy.'

41. Morrison and Attlee puff at their pipes at the 1955 party conference. Attlee was determined that neither Morrison, whom he thought too right wing, nor Bevan, whom he thought too temperamental, should succeed him.
(PA Photos)

42. A frail Attlee, sitting on a chair, acts as a pallbearer at
Winston Churchill's funeral in January 1965.
A few months later he told the author that he was 'a museum piece'.
He died in October 1967. (TopFoto)

as the following anecdotes imply. Earlier, as relations between the two men deteriorated over the issue of health charges, John Strachey asked Bevan why he was going out of his way to quarrel with Gaitskell, 'one of the really considerable men of the government'. 'Considerable?' Bevan replied. 'But he is nothing, nothing, nothing.'[56] Douglas Jay recounted meeting Bevan in the Commons shortly after Gaitskell had become Chancellor to be greeted with 'a torrent of vitriolic abuse on the head of Attlee for daring to make such an appointment'.[57] In a vehement letter to the Prime Minister, Bevan wrote: 'I think the appointment of Gaitskell to be a great mistake.'[58]

Gaitskell admired Bevan's brilliance. He noted in his diary on 21 March 1950 that Bevan 'is so much the best debater; so much the most effective speaker on the front bench, indeed in the House, that he can always raise his prestige by a performance of this kind'.[59] However, he was determined to bring health service costs under control and thought that Attlee had made a big mistake after the 1950 election in keeping Bevan as minister of health. Certainly, after his success in creating the NHS, Bevan thoroughly deserved promotion. In January 1951 the Prime Minister did manage to shift Bevan sideways to the Ministry of Labour, apparently on the condition that there would be no new attack on the social services.[60]

On 9 March 1951 Ernest Bevin resigned from the Foreign Office. He had been in poor health for months, with most of his routine work being done by his minister of state, Kenneth Younger. Attlee himself often acted as unofficial Foreign Secretary. Bevin had been finding it increasingly difficult to speak in public and his continuance in office was coming under attack from the opposition. Attlee decided to move him out of the Foreign Office by making him Lord Privy Seal. Bevin is said to have complained that he was neither a lord, nor a privy, nor a seal. Bevin heard the news from Attlee over the phone while he was attending a party for his seventieth birthday thrown by his Foreign Office staff. Pat Kinna, who worked in his private office, witnessed Bevin's reaction: 'I think', he said, 'he is the only person I have seen with a broken heart.'[61]

Attlee appointed Morrison to succeed Bevin, mainly because he was a big figure in the Cabinet; later, Attlee admitted that it was a bad mistake – the 'worst appointment I ever made'.[62] Morrison was in two minds about accepting the Foreign Office. In the end, 'he felt that if he turned down the

211

number two position in the government he would disqualify himself from the leadership succession'.[63] He also was determined to keep Bevan from getting the post.

Dalton believed that Bevan would have liked to take over the Foreign Office and that this second disappointment in five months was the main cause of his subsequent resignation from the government.[64] However, there is no direct evidence that Bevan wanted the Foreign Office. Attlee wrote in the *Observer* on 21 October 1962: 'Among others I asked Bevan whom [*sic*] he thought would make a good Foreign Secretary. I can't remember what he said, but he certainly did not ask for the job himself.'[65] Foot in his biography of Bevan gives Bevin's resignation only a passing mention. On the other hand, Bevan made, at his own request, a much applauded wind-up speech in the foreign affairs debate on 15 February 1951, which suggests not only that he might have made an authoritative spokesman on foreign affairs but also that he may have had his eye on the post. Younger thought that Bevan would have been 'a rather right-wing and very solidly anti-communist Foreign Secretary',[66] while, two days after his resignation, Bevin told Francis Williams: 'I'd sooner have had Nye than 'Erbert. He might have turned out quite good.'[67] Attlee, however, was not prepared to risk promoting Bevan to such a crucial position. It was to prove a costly error of judgement.

Twelve days after Bevin's resignation the Prime Minister was admitted to St Mary's Hospital, Paddington, with a suspected duodenal ulcer. As Attlee wrote later with characteristic understatement, 'it was unfortunate that I was ill just then'.[68] The fateful clash between Gaitskell and Bevan was about to come to a climax and the 'hands on' guidance of the Prime Minister was badly needed if the government was to avoid one or possibly more resignations, which were bound to be highly damaging.

The battle ground was the new Chancellor's first Budget on 10 April and the issue was the long-running conflict between the two men over health charges. Gaitskell's Budget was dominated by the need to finance the rearmament programme, which, according to the *Economic Survey for 1951*, had become 'the first objective' of economic policy.[69] Inevitably, he had to put up taxes: he raised income tax by sixpence in the pound and increased profits tax, petrol tax and purchase tax on major consumption items. He was also determined to constrain (though not cut) social expenditure, above all on the National Health Service. Health expenditure was to keep within a £400 million upper limit; to pay for rising hospital costs, Gaitskell proposed to charge directly for half the cost of false teeth and spectacles, raising £23 million in a full year. Initially, he also argued for prescription charges.

It was the charges for false teeth and spectacles which became the *casus belli*. The day after Attlee went to hospital and with Morrison in the chair, the first Cabinet clash took place. The ailing Bevin, now Lord Privy Seal, put forward a compromise: a ceiling of £400 million would be agreed for the NHS in return for dropping prescription charges. He said that the public would accept charges for false teeth and spectacles, as 'there was a widespread impression that some abuses had occurred in this part of the health service'. Bevan hit back ferociously: 'He thought it deplorable that for the sake of £23 million in a very large budget the principle of a free health service should be abandoned.' He also linked the charges to the size of the increased defence programme, which he had already criticised at previous Cabinets, adding that shortages of raw materials would mean that the sum allocated for defence could not be spent. Why not take £23 million off the defence budget instead? Bevan and the president of the Board of Trade, Harold Wilson, recorded their dissent, but the Cabinet backed Gaitskell and the NHS charges.[70] Bevan threatened to resign if NHS charges were imposed, Gaitskell if the Cabinet went back on its decision.

Attlee said later: 'It oughtn't to have gone so far, but both sides dug their feet in and took up positions and wouldn't budge.'[71] Though an accurate summary of what happened, it was an odd comment to come from the Prime Minister. After all, it was his job to persuade the two men to compromise. Early on, before the dispute had come to Cabinet, it might have been possible to nip it in the bud by persuading Gaitskell to give way on the health charges, perhaps adopting the formula already used for prescription charges of accepting the principle without setting a date for implementation. Instead the Prime Minister, despite being chairman of the Health Service Expenditure Committee, sat on the fence, allowing the row to drag on. Once he had the support of Cabinet, Gaitskell stood firm, showing 'the will like a driving spear' which was to be one of the characteristics of his subsequent political career. His friend and fellow Treasury minister Douglas Jay told him that, though he agreed on the merit of the health charges, he did not think the money raised (£23 million in a full year) was worth the trouble it would cause. Gaitskell refused to listen.[72]

On the night of 3 April at a meeting in Bermondsey, Bevan went public with his threat of resignation, saying, in answer to an interruption: 'I will never be a member of a government which makes charges on the National Health Service.'[73] Dalton, alarmed by the political impact of Bevan's departure and delighted to play the role of elder statesman, had meetings with both Bevan and Gaitskell. Bevan accused Gaitskell of behaving like a second Snowden in his efforts to please the Treasury, and Gaitskell insisted on the Cabinet standing up to what he saw as Bevan's blackmail. Dalton urged Bevan not to resign and told Gaitskell that he, Gaitskell, thought too little of the party and too much of the voters.

On 9 April the Cabinet, under Morrison's chairmanship, twice discussed Gaitskell's Budget, inevitably focusing on the health charges. The morning Cabinet adjourned to give Morrison time to see Attlee in hospital. Morrison returned with a message supporting the Chancellor. Gaitskell told this later meeting that, having had a Cabinet decision in favour of his position before Easter, it would be impossible for him 'to have it refused at the last minute. I said that if I resigned I would make no trouble whatever and would always support the party.'[74] When the votes were taken at 9.00 p.m., the Cabinet reaffirmed its majority support of Gaitskell, with Bevan and Wilson against and the education minister, George Tomlinson, arguing for accepting the ceiling of £400 million but dropping any mention of health charges.

On 10 April, Budget day, Attlee made a last-ditch attempt from his hospital bed to reach a compromise, seeing Bevan and Wilson at 10.30 a.m. and Gaitskell at 11.15. Gaitskell refused to accept the formula proposed the previous day by Tomlinson and now put forward by Attlee, because he believed that, if the charges were not part of the Budget, they would not be implemented. The Chancellor offered his resignation to Attlee several times and, for one moment, thought that the Prime Minister had muttered: 'Very well, you will have to go.' What he had actually said was: 'I am afraid they will have to go.'[75] Gaitskell, however, put out one minor olive branch. He was prepared to leave out of his Budget speech any mention of when the charges would come into force. This concession opened the way for a continuing dialogue with the rebel ministers, who did not resign immediately.

Gaitskell's Budget speech was warmly received. Bevin, who died in his Carlton Gardens flat four days later with the key to his red box still clutched in his hand, sat next to Gaitskell through the 2¼-hour speech and, when Gaitskell sat down, murmured: 'That was a great speech.' At a Parliamentary Labour Party meeting Bevan said, amid applause, that he had decided not to take 'a certain course'.[76] Attempts were made to appease him and Wilson, including making a statement that the charges would not necessarily be permanent; but Bevan insisted on resigning on 21 April, followed by Wilson and John Freeman, a junior minister at the Ministry of Supply. Although Bevan's resignation speech was a flop and his shrill, bad-tempered contribution at the PLP shocked most Labour MPs, the departure of such a charismatic figure from office opened up a disastrous split in the party which not only harmed Labour's election chances but was to damage it throughout much of the 1950s.

On the actual issues, Bevan had a strong case, particularly over the increases in defence spending. By the end of 1951 it had already become clear that, because of shortages of labour, materials, components and machine tools, the original defence programme could not be completed within three years. The incoming Tory government quickly scaled down the huge Labour rearmament plan. With respect to health charges, these were not essential to Gaitskell's budget. Bevan was right to see them as a symbol, in Gaitskell's case of his determination to bring health spending under control, in Bevan's case of the principle of a free National Health Service.

Bevan's tactics, however, were deplorable. His public threat in Bermondsey united the Cabinet against him. Until then, ministers had been only reluctantly behind Gaitskell. Subsequently Bevan's behaviour in Cabinet as well as a savage personal attack on Gaitskell in the left-wing *Tribune* newspaper infuriated his colleagues. Dalton wrote: 'He showed . . . unbearable conceit, crass obstinacy and a totalitarian streak.'[77] Gaitskell appeared much more reasonable and courteous in argument. He was, however, equally obstinate. He noted in his diary: 'In a situation of this kind it is impossible not to feel . . . that perhaps after all you were really being too stubborn, that you had got the thing out of perspective, and that you were really risking too much not for yourself, but for the government.'[78] Nine years later, he summed up the struggle between himself and Bevan: 'It was a battle between us for power – he knew it and so did I.'[79]

Could this personal battle for power have been avoided or at least postponed? Attlee blamed Morrison, as acting Prime Minister, for the resignations.[80] Certainly, Bevan believed that Morrison and Gaitskell ganged up against him. There is no evidence that Morrison ever approached Bevan directly to persuade him to compromise, although on 9 April he put pressure on Gaitskell to urge him to make concessions. But the main responsibility lay with Attlee. Clearly, his illness did not help, reinforcing his passive style of leadership, but his earlier intervention might have made Gaitskell compromise. With respect to Bevan, Attlee delayed until the very last moment before trying vainly to persuade him to accept the decision of the Cabinet majority. It is possible that Bevan was always determined on resignation, though his eleven-day hesitation after Gaitskell's Budget speech before resigning suggests otherwise. It is difficult not to conclude that, with the possibility of an early general election, Attlee could and should have done more to prevent the conflict between these two exceptionally able men leading to Bevan's resignation.

In the six months between Bevan's resignation and the announcement of a general election on 19 September 1951, the Labour government was very much on the defensive, 'protecting', as its historian vividly wrote, 'its redoubts like the British army at Quatre Bras and Waterloo, but incapable of advancing to occupy any new ground, and with no potential Blücher on the horizon'.[81] The 'big five' no longer existed. Bevin, Attlee's right-hand man and legendary Foreign Secretary, was dead. Cripps, outstanding Chancellor, had resigned in October 1950 and was to die of cancer in April 1952. Dalton had created a role for himself as elder statesman but was no longer a front-line player. Morrison, so able as party manager and as leader of the House, was now failing to fill Bevin's shoes at the Foreign Office. What is more, Attlee, who, to give his best, always needed the support of colleagues more dynamic and creative than himself, had mishandled the process of bringing on the next generation. Not only had he allowed Bevan, the 'big beast', to resign but he had also let Wilson, apart from Gaitskell the ablest of the party's economists, go with him. Nor had he done enough to bring younger politicians into senior positions. The government really was running out of steam.

Morrison had the bad luck to face an immediate crisis in his new job at the Foreign Office. The Iranian Prime Minister, the nationalist Dr Mohammed Mossadeq, nationalised a major British asset, the Anglo-Iranian Oil Company. Mossadeq, whose habit of wearing pyjamas in public was derided by the British press, proved a formidable opponent. Morrison tried to nego-tiate an agreed solution but talks broke down. The new Foreign Secretary often sounded as though he was determined to use force. He was indeed becoming something of a jingo. The story goes that within twenty-four hours of taking office he asked for a life of Palmerston.[82] But in the post-war world of rising nationalism and declining British power, 'sending a gunboat' in the Palmerston mode was no longer an option, especially when the United States was against military intervention. At a Cabinet meeting in September, with Attlee strongly in favour of referring the dispute to the UN, the military option was finally ruled out. In October, the *Observer* commented that 'our fault was not excessive weakness but empty bullying . . . Mr Morrison is rightly blamed for his disastrous mishandling of the Persian oil crisis.'[83]

From his first parliamentary day as Foreign Secretary, the Conservative opposition were critical of Morrison, especially when he left Foreign Office questions to his junior minister, while answering questions himself about the Festival of Britain. Although the festival, which opened in May, was widely judged to have been a success, it was easy for the Tories to say that Morrison was more interested in it than in his Foreign Office duties. The crisis over Iran was followed in June by the defections to the Soviet Union of two Foreign Office diplomats, Guy Burgess and Donald Maclean, a scandal for which Morrison was unfairly blamed. After a poor winding-up speech in a foreign affairs debate at the end of June, his reputation never recovered.

More crucial for the Labour Party's electoral prospects was another balance-of-payments crisis in the summer. A healthy surplus of £300 million in 1950 became a deficit of more than £400 million in 1951. A key factor was the rise in import prices, induced by the increase in world-wide demand for raw materials following US rearmament. Exports were also hit by the UK rearmament programme. Home consumers were faced by higher taxes following the Budget, as well as by cuts in the rations of butter, bacon and cheese. On 4 September Gaitskell was forced to fly across the Atlantic for urgent talks in Washington and Ottawa.

While his two chief lieutenants, Gaitskell and Morrison, were in Canada, Attlee announced the dissolution of Parliament and the calling of a general election for 25 October. Attlee had long planned holding an election in the autumn, mainly because the King was to make a six-month tour of Australia and New Zealand early in 1952. (In fact, after the election was announced, the King fell ill and cancelled the tour. He died a few months later.) Gaitskell and Morrison were both aware of Attlee's intentions, but they were understandably surprised not to be consulted. Gaitskell's private secretary recalled: 'To Hugh, it came as a thunderclap. He was very, very upset by it.'[84] The timing was hardly ideal, hot on the heels of bad news about the balance of payments, the impact of Bevan's resignation and the Iran crisis. If the government had been able to keep going through the winter, conditions were likely to have been more favourable. From mid-1952 onwards, the British economy experienced steady growth. But it was the new Tory government, not Labour, which derived the benefit.

According to the *Manchester Guardian*, the October election of 1951 was as decorous and restrained as that of 1950.

> That it is so is due in no small measure to the Prime Minister . . . He has never cheapened himself or his argument to gain applause. He has just been his quiet, assured self . . . There is astonishingly little in his speeches about what his government will do if re-elected . . . Yet it is an admirable exhibition of one of the supreme arts of politics, the enhancement of personal respect.[85]

As in 1950, once again driven by his wife, he toured through England, travelling 2,000 miles and addressing nearly seventy meetings. As in 1950, he made the final election broadcast in which he described Labour's achievements, above all in raising the standard of living of the mass of the people. The Nuffield College election survey said of his broadcast: 'Moderation, reasonableness, and dignity were all implied in a broadcast which was certainly among the more successful of the campaign.'[86]

The temperature was raised in the last days of the campaign when Morrison claimed in his election broadcast that Tory hysteria was a menace to world peace. This theme was taken up on the eve of the poll by the *Daily Mirror* with the slogan 'Whose Finger on the Trigger?'. Churchill later sued the paper for libel and the action was settled out of court after the *Daily Mirror* issued an apology.

As in 1950, Labour won more votes than the Conservatives, almost fourteen million in total. It was the largest vote ever won by a political party. But, largely due to a reduced number of Liberal candidates, there was a small shift of opinion against the government compared with 1950. The Conservatives won twenty-one seats from Labour, eleven of which were in London and the south-east, and had an overall majority of seventeen, with 321 seats against 295 for Labour. Though it was a 'close-run thing', Labour was out.

13

1952–5: A divided and rudderless opposition

Hugh Dalton wrote in his diary after Labour's 1951 defeat: 'The election results are wonderful. We are out just at the right moment, and our casualties are wonderfully light.'[1] His assumption, and that of other senior Labour figures, including Clement Attlee, was that the party would soon be back in power. In fact, the Conservative Party, accepting most of what Labour had done and more in tune with post-war affluence, won three successive general elections with increasing majorities: in 1951 under Winston Churchill, in 1955 under Anthony Eden and in 1959 under Harold Macmillan. It was a depressing decade in opposition for the Labour Party. It spent too much of the 1950s in fratricidal conflict and too little in adapting itself to the economic and social changes which its own government of 1945–51 had done so much to bring about.

Despite the 1951 election defeat, Attlee continued as leader of the party. Vi wanted Clement to retire to Cherry Cottage, a house near Chequers in the Buckinghamshire countryside which they had bought. But Attlee stayed on. His health was good and his prestige in Parliament and the party remained high. Dalton noted: 'Attlee very strong in the Party; can do what he likes for the moment. His OM [he had been awarded the Order of Merit by the King] well deserved, and everyone praises him.'[2] The narrowness of the Tory election victory was an argument for Attlee remaining; at the first meeting of the Parliamentary Labour Party after the election, he received a standing ovation and was unanimously re-elected as leader. For the time being, his age (Attlee was sixty-eight) was not an issue, especially as Churchill, the incoming Prime Minister, was seventy-seven.

A further consideration must have been in Attlee's mind. If he had resigned, his successor would almost certainly have been Herbert Morrison, who was five years his junior. Attlee did not trust Morrison, nor did he think that he would make a good leader of the Labour Party. His misgivings had been strengthened by Morrison's failure at the Foreign Office, as well as what Attlee perceived as his mishandling of the row over health charges which had led to the resignation of Aneurin Bevan. He considered that a Morrison leadership, backed by the right inside the PLP and the trade unions, would exacerbate the left–right split in the party. For his part, Morrison thought that Attlee ought to have resigned following the 1951 election, which would have opened the way for him. Morrison wrote in his autobiography that a number of influential Labour MPs who had approached Attlee to persuade him to step down thought that he was receptive to their view. Morrison commented wryly: 'They were presumably misled into believing taciturnity meant agreement.'[3] They should have realised there was never any chance of Attlee doing Morrison a favour.

Attlee's attitude to Bevan was different. He liked Bevan personally and greatly admired his intelligence and oratorical skills. In many ways Attlee saw him as the Labour Party's natural leader, except for one thing: his lack of judgement and self-control. From his 'vermin' speech in 1948 to his resignation in 1951, he had shown a fatal tendency to kick over the traces at the wrong moment. Attlee was also unhappy about the impact on him of his friends like Richard Crossman, Ian Mikardo and Michael Foot, who tended to encourage the rebellious side of Bevan's character. Attlee also considered that Bevan's wife, Jennie Lee, who was herself a left-wing Labour MP, was a bad influence on her husband, saying of their relationship: 'He needed a sedative. He got an irritant.'[4]

From March 1952 through to March 1955, Labour politics was dominated by the Bevanite revolt, and the bitter quarrel between left and right which split the party. Hugh Gaitskell described Bevanism as 'only a conspiracy to seize the leadership for Aneurin Bevan'.[5] It is certainly true that the loose alliance of semi-Marxists, left-wingers, pacifists and assorted malcontents in the Keep Left group, which had been an annoyance to Ernest Bevin in the 1940s, was transformed by Bevan's resignation from the government into a serious challenge to the leadership. But was it, as Gaitskell claimed, a challenge *for* the leadership?

As Foot justly argues in his biography, Bevan 'had every right and title to consider himself a candidate for the office'.[6] He had been a Cabinet minister since 1945; he was the architect of the National Health Service; and he was, as Gaitskell himself acknowledged, the best debater on the Labour side in Parliament. In his book *In Place of Fear*, published in 1952, Bevan had began to put forward the tentative beginning of a revisionist approach for the Labour Party:

> The philosophy of democratic socialism is essentially cool in temper . . . a child of modern society and so of relativist philosophy. It seeks the truth in any given situation, knowing all the time that if this be pushed too far it falls into error . . . Its chief enemy is vacillation, for it must achieve passion in action in pursuit of qualified judgements.[7]

Surely this was the principled yet flexible post-Attlee leader around whom many in the party, not those solely on the left, could unite.

One difficulty with Gaitskell's assertion was that, if Bevanism was 'a conspiracy', Bevan himself was an extremely reluctant conspirator. Crossman, himself a Bevanite, wrote in successive diary entries:

> So far from being a great strategist and organiser of cabals, Nye is an individualist . . . He dominates its discussions simply because he is fertile in ideas. But leadership and organisation are things he instinctively shrinks from. (17 December 1951)
>
> Nye made a final appeal that we should not separate ourselves off from the party in any way. By this time I think some people there felt that Nye didn't want to be a Bevanite at all. (28 January 1952)
>
> A special meeting of the Bevanite group. Nye . . . indicated that he thought that the group should cease to be exclusive. (10 April 1952)

Bevan could certainly inspire his supporters, but he also had a remarkable propensity to offend his political opponents and, according to the right of the party, to turn off the voters in droves. A group of powerful right-wing trade union leaders, including Arthur Deakin, Bevin's successor as general secretary of the Transport and General Workers' Union, Tom Williamson of the National Union of General and Municipal Workers, and William Lawther of the National Union of Mineworkers, were determined to stop him from becoming leader. Bevan's behaviour repeatedly played into their hands.

The defence debate on 5 March 1952 was the occasion of the first open display of Bevanite defiance against the Labour leadership. The shadow Cabinet, concerned not to repeat the pre-war error of voting against the defence estimates, proposed to table an amendment supporting the government's defence White Paper but also declaring somewhat absurdly that the opposition had 'no confidence in the capacity of His Majesty's present advisers to carry it out'. The party meeting rejected the Bevanite alternative, moved by Crossman, which restated the original case against the £4.7 billion rearmament programme; and a letter, signed by Attlee, Morrison and the chief whip, William Whiteley, was sent to all Labour MPs, requesting them to back the shadow Cabinet amendment and abstain on the White Paper. Bevan and fifty-six other left-wing Labour MPs, defying the party whip, refused to support the official opposition amendment and voted against the White Paper.

Rebellion on this scale against a three-line whip was unprecedented. So the leadership called a party meeting for the following week, at which Attlee quietly moved a resolution in a packed Grand Committee Room deploring the conduct of the rebels, bringing back the PLP's standing orders, which had been in suspense since 1945, and requiring that all members should stand by majority PLP decisions. However, the so-called 'Keep Calm' group, led by George Strauss, John Strachey and Kenneth Younger, introduced a milder motion which omitted all reference to the rebels; this was carried easily. Attlee's original resolution was then defeated, leaving the Bevanites the victors. Although standing orders had been reintroduced, a blind eye had been turned to the rebellion of nearly a fifth of the PLP.

The trade union leaders were furious at what they saw as the weakness of the parliamentary leadership. Attlee's view was that the reintroduction of standing orders was the furthest he could go without bringing about a wounding split in the party. The Bevanite revolt also convinced Attlee that he was right to stay on as leader. He thought that if he had stood down, Morrison, with the backing of the unions, would have driven the Bevanites out of the party. The problem was the lack of direction. Gaitskell's official biographer wrote of Attlee's leadership at this time: 'His style had always been that of a chairman reflecting majority views; and in opposition, faced with a bitter internal feud, he preserved his own position and the party's unity by giving no lead at all.'[8]

The September 1952 party conference was held at Morecambe in appalling weather. Michael Foot described it as 'rowdy, convulsive, vulgar, splenetic; threatening at moments to collapse into an irretrievable brawl'.[9] With the exception of Jim Griffiths, Bevanites won all the constituency-elected seats on the National Executive Committee. Bevan came top – he, Barbara Castle, Tom Driberg and Ian Mikardo all increased their votes. Harold Wilson and Richard Crossman replaced two of Labour's old leaders, Morrison and Dalton. Dalton, who expected to lose, noted: 'The figures show a tremendous concentration of the Bevanite vote; half vague emotion, half Mikardo's cunning organisation.'[10] Morrison took his defeat on the chin. Winding up for the executive in the afternoon, he was greeted with thunderous applause from the start. He struck the right note, reassuring delegates that he would 'allow no bitterness to poison my soul'.[11] He also received a great ovation at the end of his speech. Attlee wrote to his brother Tom: 'Morrison had a very fine comeback . . . in particular his speech showed generosity, a quality which is generally rather lacking.'[12] But he expressed no public support or sympathy for his deputy. Indeed, despite the dramatic happenings at Morecambe, he gave little sign of life at all, apart from one low-key speech on the Tuesday.

Reaction was left to others. Morrison's supporters deeply resented the tone of the Bevanite onslaught, especially the noise from the galleries. Crossman wrote about 'really nice people telling you how unfair the demagogy was'.[13] Trade union leaders were furious at Morrison's defeat, with reminders to delegates of where the party's money came from and even talk about removing Attlee for his weak leadership. A Gallup poll showed that 40 per cent of Labour voters were sorry at Morrison's defeat and only 11 per cent pleased.[14]

The strongest response came from Gaitskell, who had run unsuccessfully for the executive, in a powerful and emotional weekend speech at Stalybridge in Cheshire. He began by condemning the 'gross political ingratitude' and 'blind stupidity' of rejecting Morrison. He then referred to what he alleged was communist influence at the conference, reporting that he had been told that 'about a sixth of the constituency Party delegates appeared to be communists or communist controlled'. He attacked the left-wing press for 'a stream of grossly misleading propaganda with poisonous innuendos on Attlee, Morrison and the rest of us' and concluded:

> Let no one say that in exercising the right to reply to Bevanites we are endangering the unity of the party. For there will be no unity on the terms dictated by *Tribune* . . . It is time to end the attempt at mob rule by a group of frustrated journalists and restore the authority and leadership of the solid and sensible majority of the movement.[15]

Though Gaitskell did not regret having made the Stalybridge speech (it was much appreciated by the trade union leaders), he privately accepted that it was probably a mistake to have made the allegations about communist infiltration and that it was going too far to talk about 'frustrated journalists' and 'mob rule'. Foot's comment was that it was 'a strange riposte to the situation from a performer normally so cool and meticulous'. He also claimed that 'Stalybridge scotched the prospect of any post-Morecambe accommodation'.[16] Here, Foot (one of the journalists to whom Gaitskell was referring) was wrong.

After conference, Attlee at last moved decisively to impose an uneasy peace on the party. On 11 October he attacked the Bevanites at a party meeting: 'What is quite intolerable is the existence of a party within a party with a separate leadership, separate meetings, supported by its own press . . . Drop it, stop this sectionalism. Work with the team. Turn your guns on the enemy, not on your friends.'[17] At the PLP meeting on 24 October he forced through a resolution calling for 'the immediate abandonment of all group organisations within the party other than those officially recognised'. Bevan and his allies accepted the decision; Bevan himself stood for the shadow Cabinet and was elected in twelfth and last place. By 3 December Crossman, himself a Bevanite, was writing in his diary: 'Mysteriously, and with quite astonishing rapidity, the mood of the parliamentary party has changed. The Bevanite and anti-Bevanite feuding has melted away and everyone is rather shamefacedly aware that both sides are on the same side after all.'[18] Attlee had, at least for the time being, brought the party to its senses.

For the next fourteen months, Labour was more united and therefore more effective as an opposition. Attlee celebrated his seventieth birthday in January 1953. Though he had his appendix out in April, it was clear that he had no intention of retiring. Indeed, in his view, the truce between left and right strengthened the case for him staying on to keep the peace. In the House, he made statesmanlike speeches, especially on foreign affairs. He left the 'nitty-gritty' to Morrison, who led the opposition to the Tory legislation denationalising transport with energy and skill. However, at the conference, Morrison's last-minute decision not to run for party treasurer against the ailing Arthur Greenwood greatly disappointed the right-wing trade union leaders, who felt that Morrison had let them down. (Morrison, however, got on to the executive ex officio as deputy leader of the PLP.) Arthur Deakin told a journalist that the deputy leader was 'yellow'. Increasingly the unions began to look to Gaitskell, whom they supported for the treasurership following Greenwood's death in 1954, thus ensuring him victory.

Gaitskell's rise to the leadership of the Labour Party was even more meteoric than Tony Blair's forty years later. Elected to Parliament in 1945, he became Chancellor of the Exchequer in 1950 and leader only five years later. Gaitskell's explanation was as follows: 'The leadership came my way so early because Bevan threw it at me by his behaviour'.[19] If Bevan had continued to conduct himself in the responsible manner which he had shown during 1953, he would have become once again a serious contender for the leadership. Instead he proceeded to shoot himself in the foot.

Early in 1954, the debate over German rearmament heightened the temperature inside the PLP. An amendment moved by Harold Wilson refused to give support for it in existing circumstances. It was defeated by only two votes. Then, a week after Attlee had made 'what everyone agreed was one of the most impressive speeches of his life'[20] on the defence White Paper about the dangers of the hydrogen bomb, Bevan issued what appeared to be an open challenge to Attlee's leadership. The Foreign Secretary, Anthony Eden, had announced to the House that the British and US governments had agreed to discuss with the countries of south-east Asia the possibility of establishing a collective defence system. Speaking for the opposition, Attlee mildly asked Eden whether the new organisation would be free for all countries in the area to join. Suddenly, Bevan, who, as a member of the shadow Cabinet, was sitting at the end of the front bench, pushed past a dozen pair of knees and almost trampled on his leader in his haste to get to the dispatch box. He said that the Foreign Secretary's statement would be resented by the majority of people in Great Britain and proceeded to ask a series of hostile questions which implied that Attlee could not be trusted to speak for Labour voters. At a meeting of the shadow Cabinet the next day, the Labour leader mildly rebuked Bevan, who flounced out, announcing that he was resigning. Then at the party meeting which followed, Bevan repeated his intention to resign, professing himself deeply shocked by Attlee's response to Eden's proposals, which would, according to Bevan, prejudice the hope of a negotiated settlement of the Indo-China War. Attlee was heard to remark: 'Just when we were beginning to win the match our inside left has scored against his own side.'[21] Bevan not only split his party; he even split the Bevanite group. For Wilson (with the support of Crossman) took Bevan's place in the shadow Cabinet.

Almost a year later, Bevan not only attacked Attlee and the Labour leadership in a speech on the floor of the House (in the debate on the White Paper) but also intemperately interrupted Attlee's wind-up speech: 'What we want to know is whether . . . the amendment associates us with the statement that we should use thermo-nuclear weapons, in circumstances of hostilities, although they are not used against us.' When Attlee replied that deterrents 'are the best way of preventing war', Bevan rudely said: 'That's no answer, that's no answer.'[22]

The shadow Cabinet voted to withdraw the whip from Bevan, a decision which was endorsed by the party meeting and then reported to the NEC. Only Attlee's direct intervention prevented Bevan from being expelled from the party. To save Bevan, Attlee proposed that he be asked to prepare a statement on which he would be questioned by an NEC subcommittee. This time Bevan responded by seeking a personal meeting with the Labour leader, at which they jointly prepared an apology for Bevan to make to the committee. The executive accepted this and the whip was restored to Bevan on 21 April, just after Eden, the new Prime Minister following Winston

Churchill's resignation, had called a general election. Attlee's official biographer concluded:

> It had been a near thing, but Attlee had got his way, and he got it in the nick of time. He had not yielded anything of his bipartisan commitment on foreign and defence policy, he had conceded nothing to the left which militated against the image of Labour as a responsible national party, he had brought Bevan back into the fold and he had reunited the party for the impending election.[23]

In a quiet election (described by Hugh Dalton in his diary as tedious, apathetic and uninteresting), the Conservatives, with a new leader and a reflationary economic policy, comfortably defeated Labour. The Labour Party, led by a seventy-year-old and campaigning mainly on its record in government, had little new to say. The Conservatives won 345 seats, Labour 277 and the Liberals 6. The question for the Labour Party was when Attlee would resign. At the first meeting of the shadow Cabinet after the election, he announced that he was ready to go at once or at an agreed date. He was immediately asked to stay, at least to the end of the session. He then told the PLP that he wanted to resign at once but that the shadow Cabinet had asked him to stay indefinitely. Dalton, who had published a letter urging all the older members of the shadow Cabinet, except Attlee, to retire in order to open the way for younger men, noted in his diary: 'This is almost certainly the end of Morrison.'[24]

Although Morrison was still the political pundits' favourite to succeed Attlee, and was initially backed by Gaitskell, who believed that Morrison deserved first turn, things began to move against him. The delay exposed his shortcomings. He was nearly sixty-nine and his parliamentary performances were not nearly as effective as they had been. There was a groundswell in favour of Gaitskell. Already in June, two of his younger supporters, Roy Jenkins and Anthony Crosland, were urging him to stand. In their view, Gaitskell was by far the best candidate; they also believed that a Morrison leadership would not only be a disaster but could leave the way open for Bevan. In September, just before the party conference, Attlee, who had had a slight stroke in August, put in the knife, telling Percy Cudlipp of the *News*

Chronicle: 'We must have at the top men brought up in the present age and not, as I was, in the Victorian age.' So much for Morrison. He then turned to Bevan: 'Nor do I think we can impress the nation by adopting a futile left-wingism.' Having eliminated two possible contenders, he said: 'I have had a long innings and I shall be glad when I can to hand over to a younger man.'[25] This was a clear indication that he would prefer someone of the next generation, of whom Gaitskell was the most prominent.

In October, Gaitskell spoke eloquently at the Margate party conference, explaining in revisionist terms that he had become a socialist not so much because of nationalisation but because of his belief in social justice and dislike of the class system. Later that month, he made a powerful attack on the Tory Chancellor, R. A. Butler, for his opportunistic management of the economy: 'He began in folly, he continued in deceit, and he has ended in reaction.'[26]

Labour MPs, including Harold Wilson, pressed Gaitskell to put his hat in the ring. By early November, he had been persuaded and he took Morrison out to lunch to tell him that he had decided to stand. Morrison, misreading the situation, told him to go ahead, though warning him: 'You'll be out on the first ballot.'[27] When on 7 December Attlee finally resigned (after telling the chief whip to inform Gaitskell), Morrison made an undignified attempt, with the connivance of Bevan, to get Gaitskell to stand down in his favour. Bevan said he was prepared to stand down if Gaitskell did. This manoeuvre was rejected by Gaitskell, who won the ballot of MPs easily, with 157 votes to Bevan's 70 and Morrison's 40.

Two verdicts may be passed on Attlee's decision to remain as leader after the 1951 election. The favourable one is that he prevented the split between left and right becoming worse, blocked Morrison and Bevan, and hung on until he was succeeded by the person from the new generation whom the majority of Labour MPs thought the most likely to lead the party to victory at the next election. The unfavourable one is that he did little to heal the split, totally failed to provide the new direction the party needed, and dished Morrison's chances in 1951, when he might have provided more decisive leadership than Attlee. On balance, the unfavourable verdict is the more persuasive. The tortoise probably should have retired soon after the 1951 defeat. It might have been better both for the party and for his own reputation.

14

The end of the race

The behaviour of top politicians in the twilight of their career tends to reflect their characters. Hugh Dalton was noisy and conspiratorial, Herbert Morrison resentful and withdrawn, Clement Attlee modest and dignified.

Dalton was delighted by Hugh Gaitskell's overwhelming victory in the 1955 leadership election and stayed in Parliament to cheer his protégé on. But his main interest was in the writing and publication of the second volume of his controversial memoirs, *The Fateful Years*, which came out in April 1957 to a largely favourable reception. Francis Williams described the book as, like its author, egotistical, noisy, rumbustious, conspiratorial and impolite, while John Freeman said that Dalton wrote as well as he talked: 'He is one of the best talkers in the world – shrewd, good tempered, indiscreet, generous (sometimes overgenerous) to his friends and not cruel to his enemies.'[1] He carefully planned his retirement from Parliament, hoping to hand over his seat to Brian Abel-Smith, a good-looking social policy expert from the London School of Economics. However, at the last moment, Abel-Smith pulled out of the selection conference, deciding that he did not want to be a politician after all and Dalton switched his support to James Boyden, a local adult education lecturer who was selected on the first ballot, beating the Bevanite candidate. To Dalton's delight, his close friend Anthony Crosland, out of Parliament since the previous election, was in February 1959 chosen for the Labour-held seat of Grimsby.

On 23 March 1959 Dalton suffered a stroke from which he never fully recovered. After dinner at the Commons, Richard Crossman noted in his diary: 'Suddenly, over dinner, we discovered that Dalton, mumbling about his memoirs, is now deaf and hardly articulate. Nye thought him drunk but he is only, quite suddenly, gaga.'[2] After Labour's defeat at the 1959 general election, Dalton asked Gaitskell if he could go to the Lords. He was given a life peerage in the 1960 New Year Honours list. However, like many former members of the House of Commons, Dalton refused to take the Upper House entirely seriously, calling it 'a placid sort of Life-After-Death' and 'my Elysian Dormitory'.[3] His remaining energy was concentrated on finishing the third and final volume of his memoirs, *High Tide and After*. He completed the book in March 1961, after which his health went rapidly downhill. His wife, Ruth, who for so long had lived a separate life, returned to nurse him.

Appropriately Dalton's last political act was to introduce the youthful William Rodgers, general secretary of the Fabian Society, to the retiring member for Stockton-on-Tees, George Chetwynd, Dalton's former parliamentary private secretary. With Chetwynd's support, Rodgers was selected as Labour candidate and went on to win the subsequent by-election. In January 1962 Dalton went into hospital and he died on 12 February. His ashes were scattered over the garden of his home at West Leaze.

Morrison was deeply hurt by his humiliating defeat in the 1955 leadership election and never completely recovered from it. He said at the time: 'I supposed what happened last week was the greatest dis-appointment of all because there was a melancholy finality about it.'[4] He deeply resented what he saw as betrayal by his friends and broke off relations with many of them. His solace was the support of his second wife, Edith. His first wife, Margaret, had died of stomach cancer in the summer of 1953. While holidaying in Switzerland a year later he had met Edith, a vivacious Lancastrian who played golf, and married her in January 1955. Edith provided the warmth and comfort which Morrison had missed in his first marriage.

In 1959 he retired from the Commons and was elevated to the Lords. He admitted to a farewell gathering of his constituents that he felt 'a bit of a humbug' accepting the offer of the Tory Prime Minister, Harold Macmillan, of a life peerage in the dissolution honours after saying 'no' so often.[5] He wanted to be Lord Morrison of London but the Garter King of Arms would not allow it. So he became Lord Morrison of Lambeth. He fitted well into the relaxed style of the Upper House, though he and Attlee never sat next to each other on the front bench. He took part in a number of campaigns, including supporting the Labour pro-Europeans at the time of Macmillan's 1961–2 attempt to join the Common Market. He also opposed the

Conservative government's proposal to abolish London County Council, telling the Lords that the government was mad.

In the autumn of 1964, the retina of his good eye became diseased and his sight began to fail. In 1960, he had been appointed president of the British Board of Film Censors, a job which he much enjoyed. Now, with his growing blindness, he could not see the films. The decision was made not to renew his appointment; Morrison took it badly, feeling that he had been sacked. In February 1965 he was taken to hospital for observation. His doctor was encouraged by his improvement there but Morrison said: 'What have I got to recover for? I cannot see. I've lost my job on the film censors' board. There is nothing for me in politics.' He died on 6 March, apparently of a cerebral haemorrhage. But his doctor's judgement was that he died 'because he saw no further point in living'.[6] His ashes were scattered from a boat in the Thames opposite County Hall, which he had had built. They were then swept under Westminster Bridge and past the Houses of Parliament, where he had been a member for so long.

Almost immediately after resigning the leadership in 1955, Attlee was made an earl. Quite unabashed by accepting an honour, he told his brother Tom that he had found the House of Lords a friendly place. Most mornings when the Lords was sitting, his wife drove him to Great Missenden station, where he boarded a train to Baker Street. Hardly anybody ever recognised the little old man with a battered brown case sitting by himself in a corner seat in a third-class compartment. Attlee then took the Underground to Westminster, where he proved a conscientious member of the Lords, speaking in the big debates (for example, in the Suez crisis in July 1956, warning the Prime Minister, Anthony Eden, not to commit an act of aggression), and usually staying on to vote if necessary.

In addition to his parliamentary duties, Attlee filled his time by writing reviews and articles for the *Observer*. He revealed a talent for the telling phrase or sentence. He remarked about Dalton's memoirs: 'We see his cheerful exuberance and his enjoyment of the political fight, mingled with certain insensitiveness to the feelings of other people.' Reviewing the second volume of Churchill's *A History of the English Speaking Peoples*, he concluded: 'This history is mainly important for the light which it throws on the author's reaction to the past. It might indeed be better called "Things in History

Which Have Interested Me".' He called Morrison's memoirs 'a fine work of fiction'.[7]

Attlee's earnings from his journalism and from extensive lecture tours of the United States supplemented his prime ministerial pension of £2,000 a year and his House of Lords attendance allowance of three guineas a day. He was determined to pay off the mortgage for the building of a new bungalow near Cherry Cottage, which had become too big for the Attlees. The idea was that his wife should live in the bungalow after his death; Attlee understandably assumed that Vi, who was thirteen years younger than him, would outlive him. But in June 1964 she collapsed from a cerebral haemorrhage while cooking Sunday lunch and died in hospital during the night. Attlee, who loved his wife dearly, was devastated.

However, showing typical fortitude, he pulled himself together, selling the bungalow (which was so much a projection of her personality) and moving into a four-room flat at 1 Kings Bench Walk in the Temple; he had been made an Honourable Bencher of the Inner Temple in 1946. At the age of eighty-one, he played a role in the 1964 election, which Labour won with a majority of four, speaking at a number of meetings and taking part, with the Labour leader, Harold Wilson, in the party's final election broadcast.

Attlee began to become increasingly frail. On 30 January 1965, despite feeling ill, he acted as a pallbearer at Churchill's state funeral and was photographed sitting alone, a small elderly figure, on the steps of St Paul's. In May 1965 he told the author, without a trace of self-pity, that he was a 'museum piece'. He was not well enough to take much part in the 1966 election, which Labour won easily with a majority of ninety-seven, but in a letter in February 1967 to Emanuel Shinwell, also a Labour peer, he gave public support to a campaign against Britain joining the Common Market; and in April he wrote a letter to the *Times* stressing the need to settle international disputes by peaceful means. In September he went into Westminster Hospital, where he developed pneumonia and died on 8 October. His ashes were buried in Westminster Abbey, near the flagstone commemorating his closest colleague, Ernest Bevin, and not far from the green slab inscribed with the name of his wartime Prime Minister, Winston Churchill.

Attlee's death, at the age of eighty-four, was the last of Labour's 'big five'.

The tortoise had outlived the hares. Bevin had died of heart failure aged seventy, while still in office, on 14 April 1951, while Cripps, aged only sixty-two, had followed, a victim of cancer, just over a year later, on 21 April 1952. Dalton had died nearly ten years after, aged seventy-four, while Morrison's death, at seventy-seven, took place over two years before Attlee's. If all the 'big five', with the exception of Cripps, lived what was then a normal life span, the two most able of the next generation of Labour leaders, Aneurin Bevan and Gaitskell, died tragically young. Bevan was sixty-two when he died of cancer in 1960, while Gaitskell was just fifty-six when he died of lupus erythematosus, a rare disease of the immune system, in 1963. Attlee remarked to Denis Healey as they walked together from the House of Commons to Westminster Abbey for Gaitskell's memorial service that he had expected that Gaitskell would go to his.[8]

Conclusion

The tortoise and the hares were of their time. Their attitudes were shaped by their Victorian and Edwardian upbringing. Their experiences in the First World War and in the 1920s (with the general strike) and the 1930s (with the 1931 crisis, unemployment and appeasement) had a marked effect on them all. Above all, the Second World War, which brought them into government and legitimised ideas of fairness, social protection, government intervention and the role of the unions, was a crucial turning point in their lives.

In 1945 they drew strength from the past. They were determined that, in contrast to what happened after the First World War, full employment would be maintained, a welfare state would be established to eradicate poverty, and new houses and schools would be built. A Labour government really would create a 'land fit for heroes'.

Despite all the difficulties, to a considerable extent they made their vision a reality. But they were also traditionalists, with conventional attitudes to institutions and to Britain's role in the world. Clement Attlee even used to draw up lists of how many Old Haileyburians there were in his government as compared to the Old Etonians. He was devoted to the monarchy and especially to the King, George VI, whom he got to know well. And, though Indian independence may be considered as one of his great achievements, he remained at heart a high-minded imperialist, as did Ernest Bevin and Herbert Morrison.

Once Labour's programme, based on the 1945 election manifesto, *Let Us Face the Future*, had been completed, the party leaders, already elderly, had little to say. Bevin and Stafford Cripps were dying, while Attlee was slow to bring in younger politicians into his government and had little enthusiasm for new ideas. Morrison knew that something more was needed but never got beyond 'consolidation'. Aneurin Bevan and Hugh Gaitskell might have been able to combine to create a fresh synthesis but were locked in fratricidal conflict. In 1951 Attlee's Labour Party could tell the world about its fine record but almost nothing about the future. It had run out of steam.

The 'big five' all considered themselves to be socialists, though each had a somewhat different emphasis. Attlee professed to be a 'Clause 4' socialist: as he wrote in *The Labour Party in Perspective*, published in 1937, the aim of the party was the establishment of the co-operative Commonwealth. In practice, he did not wish to see public ownership extending much beyond the initial nationalisations of 1945–51. The basis of his socialism was the drive to improve the conditions of the working classes, especially the people of the East End, whose hardship had brought him into politics. As he saw it, his governments, by introducing the welfare state and preserving full employment, had brought about a peaceful social revolution. Attlee could have said, with Morrison, 'Socialism is what the Labour government does.'[1]

When in 1960 the supporters of Gaitskell set up the Campaign for Democratic Socialism and issued a manifesto of principles, Morrison declined to join, saying: 'I find this manifesto a bit too much on the right in some respects. I've had a long left-wing life myself, getting things done and changing things.'[2] But it was Morrison above all who put the case for nationalisation not on ideological but practical grounds. He was a pragmatist who argued that the voters would not accept public ownership for its own sake and that the party should be prepared to adapt to the changing times.

Bevin was also a pragmatist, but one with great imagination and creative powers. He saw himself as a life-long socialist but his was a socialism dedicated to improving the lot of the British workers and building up their collective strength. Even as an exceptionally busy Foreign Secretary, he played an important role in discussing economic policy, preparing welfare legislation and involving the unions.

Dalton was a Fabian socialist. He was a supporter of the public ownership of basic industries but he also argued strongly for greater equality through taxation and the extension of social services. As Chancellor of the Exchequer, he deliberately maintained and to some extent extended the move towards income equality that had been made during the war.

Cripps's socialism was *sui generis*. In the 1930s he was a semi-Marxist. By the end of the war he had become fascinated by the application of managerial techniques and the improvement of productivity. He now believed in a constructive partnership between the public and private sector. One might call him a 'mixed economy' socialist. Pragmatic in politics, in his personal beliefs he was a life-long Christian, who was concerned to apply Christian principles to everyday life.

The Labour governments of 1945–51 were led by a group of politicians with great individual gifts. They brought varied qualities and experiences to the Cabinet table – Morrison's administrative flair, derived from local government; Bevin's creative power, which he had developed during his trade union career; Cripps's analytical and legal brilliance; and Dalton's academic and intellectual training. They needed Attlee to weld them into an effective team.

On the occasion of being enrolled as a knight of the Garter in June 1956, Attlee wrote one of his occasional verses:

> Few thought he was even a starter,
> There were many who thought themselves smarter.
> But he ended PM,
> CH and OM,
> An Earl and a Knight of the Garter.[3]

Apart from the amused satisfaction which the author shows in his own success, the limerick also reveals that Attlee was well aware not only of the part that luck had played in his becoming Prime Minister, but also of his own limitations. He had won the leadership almost by accident and remained as leader in 1935, in 1945 and in 1947, in part because his rivals could not agree on a successor. In time, he turned his shortcomings – his understatement, his shyness, his caution – into strengths; they became the hallmark of his premiership. In addition, his integrity, lack of vanity and skill in managing his Cabinet made him a leader whom his colleagues trusted and under whom they were prepared to serve. Attlee provided the framework within which his more brilliant and charismatic ministers could thrive.

If the big beasts of Labour's 1945–51 Cabinets needed Attlee as Prime Minister, he needed the ideas, inspiration and energy which they brought to the government. There was Bevin's genius, which led to the setting up of NATO and the implementation of the Marshall plan. There was Morrison's skill, which was so essential in getting Labour's programme through Parliament. There was Cripps's grasp, which rescued Labour from the crisis of 1947. There was Dalton's ebullience, which was so important in raising the party's morale in the first two years of the government. And, in the younger generation, there was Bevan's self-confidence, which was behind the creation of the National Health Service, and Gaitskell's will, which forced through the necessary decision to devalue in 1949.

Labour's Cabinet was one of mutual need. When Attlee and his leading colleagues were working at full blast, Labour was successful. When the health of key figures, such as Bevin and Cripps, began to give out, the government faltered. The tortoise and the hares both needed each other.

How successful were the Attlee administrations of 1945–51? Kenneth O. Morgan, summing up his history of the Attlee government (published in 1984, after one of Labour's greatest defeats), wrote: 'It was without doubt the most effective of all Labour governments, perhaps the most effective of any British government since the passage of the 1832 Reform Act.'[4] Certainly Attlee and his colleagues had great achievements to their credit, including the creation of the welfare state, the setting up of the NHS, the independence of India, Pakistan and Ceylon, the creation of NATO and the implementation of the Marshall plan. Moreover, these successes were achieved against a background of extreme difficulty, above all the sharp reduction in British power and resources (mostly to pay for the war), the need to re-equip industry, a succession of financial and balance-of-payments crises, the coming of the Cold War in 1948 and the outbreak of the Korean War in 1950.

The Attlee years undoubtedly had a big impact on what might be called 'the condition of Britain' question. With only a touch of hyperbole, Sam Watson, secretary of the Durham miners, told the Labour Party conference in 1950: 'Poverty has been abolished. Hunger is unknown. The sick are tended. The old folks are cherished; our children are growing up in a land of opportunity.'[5] Not all of this was due to the work of the Labour government. The wartime coalition, in which Labour played a crucial part, had introduced a number of important reforms, above all the 1944 Butler Education

Act, which established universal secondary education. But, if what happened during the war provided some of the impetus, Labour was entitled to argue that it was the governments of 1945–51 which established the welfare state on a lasting basis.

A key ingredient in the dramatic reduction in poverty compared with the 1930s was sustained full employment, always a top priority of the Attlee governments. Labour's leadership was strongly committed to the pledge of the 1944 employment policy White Paper of a high and sustained level of employment. Their record on unemployment was impressive, boosted by a vigorous regional policy which helped bring jobs to the pre-war high unemployment areas. Comparing the first six years after the Second World War with the first six years after the First World War shows that, whereas unemployment in 1921 had risen to 11 per cent and was still 7.1 per cent in 1924, in 1947 it was 1.3 per cent and by 1951 it had dropped to 1.1 per cent.[6] It is fair to add that the achievement of full employment in the post-1945 world was greatly assisted by the buoyancy of the American market and later by the impact of Marshall aid.[7] The British economy also benefited directly from financial assistance from the United States. Robert Hall, the head of the Cabinet Office's Economic Section, noted in his diary on 20 July 1951: 'We have had . . . an average of over a billion dollars a year one way and another since 1946 . . . In fact our whole economic life had been propped up in this way.'[8]

There is a school of thought which questions whether, in the dire economic circumstances in which the Labour government found itself in 1945, it ought to have proceeded so ambitiously and so quickly with its social programme. In a conversation with Peter Hennessy, the sociologist Ralf Dahrendorf said about the post-war Labour government: 'All that they did was wonderful but clearly wrong – right in social terms, wrong in economic terms . . . It was the right government at the wrong time.'[9] Dahrendorf's argument was that, instead of introducing the welfare state and redistributing income, the Attlee governments should, like the French planners and German social marketeers, have been preparing the ground for economic growth and reconstruction.

In this exaggerated form, the Dahrendorf thesis is unsustainable. It would have been unrealistic to expect a newly elected government to renege on the social commitments which had helped persuade the war-weary electors to vote it into office, especially when most of these policies, including a national health service, were also supported by the Conservatives. In any case, Labour did not believe that there was necessarily a conflict between welfare and growth. Their view was that healthy, secure and well-educated citizens would make a vital contribution to economic growth which, in its turn, would finance the welfare state.[10]

It was not as if the Labour Chancellors acted in a profligate way. Social expenditure increased three-fold in the first two years after the war but the increase was more than compensated for by a fall in defence spending from £4.4 billion to £850 million, overwhelmingly as a consequence of demobilisation. It was during Dalton's chancellorship that the budget swung into surplus, a trend which Cripps was able to maintain throughout his time at No. 11.

The available statistics on the share of public spending as a percentage of gross domestic product do not suggest that the increase in social spending overburdened the economy.[11] It is true that in 1938 (the last full year of peace), general government expenditure amounted to only 28.5 per cent of gross domestic product. During the war, however, government spending rose to 61.4 per cent of GDP. In 1947 Dalton brought it down to 38.8 per cent of GDP and by 1950 Cripps reduced it further to 33.7 per cent, a figure which Conservative governments could match only once during the 1950s and which was appreciably below Margaret Thatcher's lowest figure of 37.9 per cent in 1988.

Nor is it the case that Labour governments ignored the need to re-equip British industry to compete in the post-war world. Industrial production in the five years between 1946 and 1951 increased by one-third, while GDP grew at 3 per cent per annum over the last four years of the Labour government.[12] Until the outbreak of the Korean War and the partial switchback to the defence industries, British exports made a good recovery, rising by 67 per cent between 1947 and 1951.[13]

A more persuasive criticism is that, until the end of 1947 and Cripps's chancellorship, the government did not develop a coherent economic and financial strategy. Partly as a consequence, the government was nearly overwhelmed that year by a succession of crises from which it took time to recover. Then, after a successful eighteen months, the government was forced to devalue in 1949. It was not so much the act of devaluation (which led to an increase in exports and a sharp improvement in the balance of payments) but the delay in doing so which damaged Cripps's reputation. In 1950–51 the scale of British rearmament, following the outbreak of the Korean War, halted investment, reduced exports and left Britain with a larger defence burden than its continental competitors.

As a result of these setbacks, the government's economic competence was open to attack from its political opponents and, even more importantly, to growing public scepticism, to which sustained rationing contributed. However, economic historians have been more forgiving. Sir Alec Cairncross, in his authoritative analysis of the period, was critical of the government's shortcomings, especially of the scale of rearmament and its failure to change attitudes towards innovation and labour relations. Even so, he concluded that the Labour government 'pointed the economy in the right direction, rode out the various crises that the years of transition almost inevitably gave rise to, and, by 1951, had brought the economy near to eventual balance'.[14]

Linked to Labour's economic and financial shortcomings was the government's overestimation of British power. Like Winston Churchill, Labour's 'big five' were brought up in the imperial age. They had been members of the victorious wartime coalition. They still believed that Britain was and should remain a great power. With the exception of the Indian subcontinent, they were in favour of Britain remaining an empire, with far-flung territories. Sir Henry Tizard, chief scientific adviser to the Ministry of Defence, warned: 'We are not a great power and never will be again. We are a great nation, but if we continue to behave like a great power we shall soon cease to be a great nation.'[15] But Labour's leaders, Bevin, Morrison and Attlee as well, did not think it right to reduce substantially, let alone abandon, Britain's world-wide responsibilities, despite the changed circumstances. As a result, the British economy was seriously overstretched. It was in part because of their illusions about Britain's great power status that Labour's leaders rejected the opportunity to join the European Coal and Steel Community, a decision which, as Oliver Franks, UK ambassador to the United States, said, probably cost the country the leadership of Europe.

One of Labour's greatest failures was its inability to establish a political hegemony on the Swedish Social Democrat model. In 1945 Labour had won a landslide victory but by 1950 the Conservatives had recovered and Labour only scraped back into power. Despite getting more votes than the Tories, it was defeated in 1951, remaining out of office for the next thirteen years, thus missing out on the age of affluence.

It could be argued that, until 1979 and Thatcher's advent to power, the Tories accepted much of Labour's 1945–51 settlement, which, nationalisation apart, itself reflected a good deal of wartime coalition thinking. This may have been some consolation but the fact remains that by 1951 Labour had implemented its programme and had run out of steam. As Labour went into opposition, Attlee provided little or no leadership to a party deeply divided on what should happen next.

The 1945 government was a great reforming administration but its shadow was not as long as it could have been. It provided a golden moment rather than a sustained period of power. But it was, nevertheless, a wonderful golden moment which helped shape British society, and for that the tortoise and the hares together share the credit.

A note on sources

For major events and controversies from 1940 to 1951, I have consulted the Cabinet Papers at the National Archives/Public Record Office. The formal Cabinet conclusions sometimes gloss over disagreements; I have been able to draw on the confidential annexes of some Cabinet meetings (for example, the crucial decisions of May 1940). I have also benefited from the recent declassification of the longhand records of Cabinet discussions made by the Cabinet secretary, Sir Norman Brook (grouped under NA, PRO, CAB 195). The files from the Foreign Office, Treasury, Prime Minister's Office and the Cabinet Office reveal some of the high-level discussions between the tortoise and the hares.

The collection of Clement Attlee's papers at the Bodleian Library, Oxford, is worth looking at, especially the correspondence with his brother Tom. Attlee did not keep a diary and, except for the early years, his autobiography is astonishingly uninformative. Kenneth Harris's biography, based on interviews with the Labour leader and drawing on unpublished documents and correspondence, helps fill some of the gaps, though the lack of footnotes is a shortcoming. Other biographies about Attlee include Roy Jenkins's youthful work on Attlee's career up to 1945 and Francis Beckett's memoir volume, which is especially good on Attlee the man.

Herbert Morrison burnt twenty files of personal documents (the history of a lifetime according to his secretary) when he and his second wife moved house in 1960. His autobiography, though useful on his childhood, is otherwise hardly worth reading. Fortunately, Bernard Donoughue and G. W. Jones's excellent biography, based on a wide range of interviews, provides a comprehensive study of one of Labour's leading figures.

Any student of the life of Ernest Bevin is inevitably in the shadow of Alan Bullock's great three-volume biography, described by Attlee as 'a massive work about a massive man'. However, I also found that Francis Williams's attractive portrait of Bevin helped to bring him to life.

I have benefited from two recent biographies of Stafford Cripps. One, by my parliamentary colleague Chris Bryant, concentrates on Cripps's religious and economic ideas, while the other, by Peter Clarke, draws on his diaries and papers to highlight his relations with Churchill and Gandhi.

Hugh Dalton's corner is well protected: there are three lively volumes of autobiography and two volumes of diaries which put his side of the story, as well as Ben Pimlott's masterly biography.

There are two excellent biographies of Hugh Gaitskell, one by Philip Williams and the other by Brian Brivati. There are also Gaitskell's diaries, edited by Williams. The second volume of Michael Foot's work on Aneurin Bevan, as well as John Campbell's biography, are worth consulting.

For background to the 1945 Labour government, I have found four books essential reading: Paul Addison's *The Road to 1945*, Peter Hennessy's *Never Again*, Alec Cairncross's *Years of Recovery* and Kenneth O. Morgan's *Labour in Power 1945–1951*.

Other sources used are to be found in the notes.

Notes

Introduction

1. Peter Hennessy, *The Prime Minister: The Office and Its Holders since 1945* (London: Allen Lane, 2000), p. 530.
2. Ben Pimlott, *Independent on Sunday*, 16 March 1997.
3. Peter Riddell, 'Attlee's 1945 victory voted most decisive', *Times*, 30 November 2005.
4. Harold Wilson, interviewed for *Attlee: The Reasonable Revolutionary* (1983), a BBC programme by Jeremy Bennett and Roy Hattersley.
5. Hennessy, *Prime Minister*, p. 148.
6. Denis Healey, *The Time of My Life* (London: Michael Joseph, 1989), p. 153.
7. Harold Wilson, *A Prime Minister on Prime Ministers* (London: Weidenfeld & Nicolson/Michael Joseph, 1977), p. 297.

Prologue: A failed coup

1. Attlee to Dalton, 13 July 1945, Dalton papers, 1945.
2. Isaac Kramnick and Barry Sheerman, *Harold Laski: A Life on the Left* (London: Hamish Hamilton, 1993), pp. 480–81.
3. Morrison to Attlee, 24 July 1945, Attlee papers, Bodleian Library.
4. Francis Williams, *A Prime Minister Remembers: The War and Post-War Memoirs of the Rt. Hon. Earl Attlee Based on His Private Papers and on a Series of Recorded Conversations* (London: Heinemann, 1961), p. 4.
5. Chris Bryant, *Stafford Cripps: The First Modern Chancellor* (London: Hodder & Stoughton, 1997), pp. 355–7.
6. Alan Bullock, *The Life and Times of Ernest Bevin, vol. 2: Minister of Labour 1940–1945* (London: Heinemann, 1967), pp. 392–3.
7. Quoted in Bernard Donoughue and G. W. Jones, *Herbert Morrison* (London: Phoenix, 2001), p. 346.
8. Quoted ibid., p. 342.
9. Quoted in Hugh Dalton, *The Fateful Years: Memoirs 1931–1945* (London: Frederick Muller, 1957), p. 469.
10. Ibid., p. 468.

11. Bullock, *The Life and Times of Ernest Bevin*, p. 394.
12. Dalton, *Fateful Years*, p. 470.

Chapter 1: The tortoise

1. Niall Ferguson, *Empire: How Britain Made the Modern World* (London: Allen Lane, 2003), p. 240.
2. C. R. Attlee, *As It Happened* (London: Odhams Press, 1956), p. 9.
3. Ibid., p. 10.
4. Kenneth Harris, *Attlee* (London: Weidenfeld & Nicolson, 1982), p. 5.
5. Attlee, *As It Happened*, p. 12.
6. Roy Jenkins, *Mr Attlee: An Interim Biography* (London: William Heinemann, 1948), p. 12.
7. Quoted ibid., p. 15.
8. Quoted in Attlee, *As It Happened*, p. 21.
9. Harris, *Attlee*, p. 14.
10. Quoted ibid., p. 15.
11. Attlee, *As It Happened*, p. 24.
12. Harris, *Attlee*, p. 26.
13. Attlee, *As It Happened*, p. 26.
14. Quoted in Harris, *Attlee*, p. 18.
15. Attlee, *As It Happened*, p. 27.
16. Jenkins, *Mr Attlee*, p. 44.
17. Attlee, *As It Happened*, p. 30.
18. Harris, *Attlee*, p. 26.
19. Francis Beckett, *Clem Attlee* (London: Politico's, 2000), p. 28.
20. Quoted in Harris, *Attlee*, p. 27.
21. Jenkins, *Mr Attlee*, p. 54.
22. Attlee, *As It Happened*, p. 45.
23. Margaret Cole (ed.), *The Webbs and Their Work* (London: Frederick Muller, 1949), p. 138.
24. Quoted in Harris, *Attlee*, p. 29.
25. Quoted ibid., p. 32.
26. Quoted in Beckett, *Clem Attlee*, p. 41.
27. Attlee, *As It Happened*, p. 40.
28. Ibid., p. 45.
29. Quoted in Jenkins, *Mr Attlee*, p. 67.
30. John Keegan, *The First World War* (London: Pimlico, 1990), p. 268.
31. Attlee, *As It Happened*, p. 52.
32. Letter to Tom Attlee, 20 March 1918, quoted in Beckett, *Clem Attlee*, p. 52.
33. Quoted in Jenkins, *Mr Attlee*, p. 78.
34. Quoted ibid., p. 72.
35. Quoted ibid., p. 73.

36. Letter to Tom Attlee, 1917, quoted in Beckett, *Clem Attlee*, p. 53.
37. Quoted in Henry Pelling, *A Short History of the Labour Party*, 7th ed. (London: Macmillan, 1982), p. 42.

Chapter 2: The hares (1)

1. Quoted in Alan Bullock, *The Life and Times of Ernest Bevin, vol. 1: Trade Union Leader 1881–1940* (London: Heinemann, 1960), p. 2.
2. See Francis Williams, *Ernest Bevin: Portrait of a Great Englishman* (London: Hutchinson, 1952), p. 16.
3. Quoted ibid., p. 17.
4. Bullock, *The Life and Times of Ernest Bevin*, pp. 10–11.
5. See Williams, *Ernest Bevin*, p. 25; Bullock, *The Life and Times of Ernest Bevin*, pp. 19–21.
6. Bullock, *The Life and Times of Ernest Bevin*, p. 33.
7. Williams, *Ernest Bevin*, p. 41.
8. Bullock, *The Life and Times of Ernest Bevin*, pp. 44–5.
9. Quoted ibid., p. 70.
10. Lord Morrison of Lambeth, *Herbert Morrison: An Autobiography* (London: Odhams Press, 1960), p. 19.
11. Ibid., p. 17.
12. Bernard Donoughue and G. W. Jones, *Herbert Morrison* (London: Phoenix, 2001), p. 7.
13. Morrison, *Herbert Morrison*, p. 19.
14. Quoted in Donoughue and Jones, *Herbert Morrison*, pp. 7–8.
15. Quoted ibid., p. 12.
16. Morrison, *Herbert Morrison*, p. 24.
17. Ibid., pp. 50–51.
18. Ibid., p. 52.
19. Ibid., p. 53.
20. Ibid., p. 53.
21. Ibid., p. 49.
22. Quoted in Donoughue and Jones, *Herbert Morrison*, p. 28.
23. Morrison, *Herbert Morrison*, p. 71.

Chapter 3: The hares (2)

1. Margaret Cole (ed.), *Beatrice Webb's Diaries 1924–1932* (London: Longmans, Green, 1956), 27 July 1929.
2. Ben Pimlott, *Hugh Dalton* (London: Jonathan Cape, 1985), p. 5.
3. Hugh Dalton, *Call Back Yesterday: Memoirs 1887–1931* (London: Frederick Muller, 1953), p. 15.
4. Ibid., p. 16.

5. Ibid., p. 26.
6. Ibid., p. 26.
7. Ibid., p. 27.
8. Ibid., p. 34.
9. Quoted in Pimlott, *Hugh Dalton*, p. 33.
10. Dalton, *Call Back Yesterday*, p. 36.
11. Michael Holroyd, *Lytton Strachey: A Biography* (Harmondsworth: Penguin, 1971), p. 282.
12. Dalton, *Call Back Yesterday*, p. 38.
13. Pimlott, *Hugh Dalton*, p. 38.
14. Dalton, *Call Back Yesterday*, p. 44.
15. Quoted in Pimlott, *Hugh Dalton*, p. 42.
16. Beatrice Webb's diary, 15 September 1908, and Webb to Mary Playne, September 1908, both quoted in Pimlott, *Hugh Dalton*, p. 50.
17. See Dalton, *Call Back Yesterday*, p. 70.
18. Quoted ibid., p. 79.
19. Hugh Dalton, *Towards the Peace of Nations: A Study in International Politics* (London: George Routledge, 1928), p. 309.
20. Dalton, *Call Back Yesterday*, p. 91.
21. Ibid., p. 96.
22. Hugh Dalton, *With British Guns in Italy: A Tribute to Italian Achievement* (London: Methuen, 1919).
23. Peter Clarke, *The Cripps Version: The Life of Sir Stafford Cripps* (London: Allen Lane, 2002), p. 3.
24. Quoted ibid., p. 7.
25. Quoted in Chris Bryant, *Stafford Cripps: The First Modern Chancellor* (London: Hodder & Stoughton, 1997), p. 11.
26. Quoted in Clarke, *The Cripps Version*, p. 7.
27. Beatrice Webb's diary, 29 December 1894, quoted ibid., p. 9.
28. Quoted in Bryant, *Stafford Cripps*, p. 19.
29. Quoted ibid., pp. 28–9.
30. Quoted in Clarke, *The Cripps Version*, p. 19.
31. Quoted in Bryant, *Stafford Cripps*, p. 50.
32. Quoted in Clarke, *The Cripps Version*, p. 22.
33. Quoted ibid., p. 23.
34. Quoted ibid., p. 25.
35. Quoted ibid., p. 28.
36. Quoted ibid., p. 40.
37. Quoted ibid., p. 41.
38. Quoted ibid, p. 42.

Chapter 4: 1919–31

1. C. R. Attlee, *As It Happened* (London: Odhams Press, 1956), p. 63.
2. Lord Morrison of Lambeth, *Herbert Morrison: An Autobiography* (London: Odhams Press, 1960), p. 87.
3. Bernard Donoughue and G. W. Jones, *Herbert Morrison* (London: Phoenix, 2001), p. 92.
4. Francis Beckett, *Clem Attlee* (London: Politico's, 2000), p. 69.
5. Roy Jenkins, *Mr Attlee: An Interim Biography* (London: William Heinemann, 1948), pp. 99–100.
6. See Henry Pelling, *A Short History of the Labour Party*, 7th ed. (London: Macmillan, 1982), pp. 50–51.
7. Attlee, *As It Happened*, p. 72.
8. Kenneth Harris, *Attlee* (London: Weidenfeld & Nicolson, 1982), p. 60.
9. Attlee, *As It Happened*, p. 73.
10. Quoted in David Marquand, *Ramsay MacDonald* (London: Jonathan Cape, 1977), pp. 297–9.
11. Attlee, *As It Happened*, p. 75.
12. Quoted in Harris, *Attlee*, p. 64.
13. Morrison, *Herbert Morrison*, pp. 95–6.
14. Ibid., p. 109.
15. Hugh Dalton, *Call Back Yesterday: Memoirs 1887–1931* (London: Frederick Muller, 1953), p. 155.
16. See Ben Pimlott, *Hugh Dalton* (London: Jonathan Cape, 1985), p. 152.
17. Quoted in Alan Bullock, *The Life and Times of Ernest Bevin, vol. 1: Trade Union Leader 1881–1940* (London: Heinemann, 1960), p. 259.
18. Quoted in David Sinclair, *Two Georges: The Making of the Modern Monarchy* (London: Hodder & Stoughton, 1988), p. 105.
19. Quoted in Francis Williams, *Ernest Bevin: Portrait of a Great Englishman* (London: Hutchinson, 1952), p. 14.
20. Quoted in Harris, *Attlee*, p. 74.
21. Quoted ibid., p. 83.
22. Pimlott, *Hugh Dalton*, p. 169.
23. Quoted in Dalton, *Call Back Yesterday*, p. 202.
24. Quoted in Harris, *Attlee*, p. 81.
25. See Marquand, *Ramsay MacDonald*, pp. 533–9.
26. Attlee, *As It Happened*, p. 84.
27. Quoted in Hugh Dalton, *The Political Diary of Hugh Dalton 1918–40, 1945–60*, ed. Ben Pimlott (London: Jonathan Cape, 1986), 14 November 1930.
28. Quoted in Harris, *Attlee*, p. 88.
29. Quoted ibid., p. 89.
30. Pimlott, *Hugh Dalton*, pp. 188–9.
31. Quoted in Dalton, *The Political Diary of Hugh Dalton*, p. 135.
32. Quoted ibid., p. 124.

33. Margaret Cole (ed.), *Beatrice Webb's Diaries 1924–1932* (London: Longmans, Green, 1956), 23 January 1930.

34. Quoted ibid., 22 August 1931.

35. Quoted in Dalton, *Call Back Yesterday*, p. 273.

36. Quoted ibid., p. 274.

37. Quoted in Peter Clarke, *The Cripps Version: The Life of Sir Stafford Cripps* (London: Allen Lane, 2002), p. 44.

38. Quoted ibid., p. 50.

39. Quoted in Chris Bryant, *Stafford Cripps: The First Modern Chancellor* (London: Hodder & Stoughton, 1997), p. 84.

40. Morrison, *Herbert Morrison*, p. 127.

41. See Donoughue and Jones, *Herbert Morrison*, pp. 162–7.

Chapter 5: 1931–9

1. Henry Pelling, *A Short History of the Labour Party*, 7th ed. (London: Macmillan, 1982), pp. 71–87.

2. Hugh Dalton, *Call Back Yesterday: Memoirs 1887–1931* (London: Frederick Muller, 1953), p. 282.

3. Kenneth Harris, *Attlee* (London: Weidenfeld & Nicolson, 1982), p. 102.

4. C. R. Attlee, *As It Happened* (London: Odhams Press, 1956), p. 92.

5. Quoted in Chris Bryant, *Stafford Cripps: The First Modern Chancellor* (London: Hodder & Stoughton, 1997), p. 89.

6. Quoted in Harris, *Attlee*, p. 105.

7. Quoted in Hugh Dalton, *The Political Diary of Hugh Dalton: 1918–40, 1945–60*, ed. Ben Pimlott (London: Jonathan Cape, 1986), 8 October 1932.

8. Michael Foot, *Aneurin Bevan: A Biography, vol. 1 1897–1945* (London: MacGibbon & Kee, 1962), p. 155.

9. Quoted in the *Times*, 6 January 1934.

10. Dalton, *The Political Diary of Hugh Dalton*, pp. 181–2.

11. Hugh Dalton, *The Fateful Years: Memoirs 1931–1945* (London: Frederick Muller, 1957), p. 149.

12. Quoted in Harris, *Attlee*, p. 110.

13. Francis Williams, *Ernest Bevin: Portrait of a Great Englishman* (London: Hutchinson, 1952), p. 188.

14. Labour Party conference report, 1935.

15. Article in *Forward*, quoted in Bernard Donoughue and G. W. Jones, *Herbert Morrison* (London: Phoenix, 2001), p. 236.

16. Quoted in Donoughue and Jones, *Herbert Morrison*, p. 235.

17. See Harris, *Attlee*, p. 122.

18. Dalton, *The Fateful Years*, p. 82.

19. Ibid., p. 83.

20. Quoted in Alan Bullock, *The Life and Times of Ernest Bevin, vol. 1: Trade Union Leader 1881–1940* (London: Heinemann, 1960), p. 592.

21. Dalton, *The Fateful Years*, p. 142.
22. Quoted in Bryant, *Stafford Cripps*, p. 172.
23. See Roy Jenkins, *Mr Attlee: An Interim Biography* (London: William Heinemann, 1948), p. 204.
24. Quoted in Harris, *Attlee*, p. 159.
25. See Dalton, *The Fateful Years*, p. 223.
26. Dalton, *The Political Diary of Hugh Dalton*, 26 May to 2 June 1939.

Chapter 6: 1940–45

1. See Hugh Dalton, *The Political Diary of Hugh Dalton 1918–40, 1945–60*, ed. Ben Pimlott (London: Jonathan Cape, 1986), 6 September 1939.
2. Quoted in Kenneth Harris, *Attlee* (London: Weidenfeld & Nicolson, 1982), p. 168.
3. Quoted in C. R. Attlee, *As It Happened* (London: Odhams Press, 1956), pp. 125–9.
4. Winston S. Churchill, *The Second World War, vol. 1: The Gathering Storm* (London: Cassell, 1949), p. 526.
5. Hansard, HC Deb, 7 May 1940, vol. 360, col. 1092.
6. Ibid., col. 1093.
7. Ibid., col. 1094.
8. Ibid., col. 1150.
9. Lord Morrison of Lambeth, *Herbert Morrison: An Autobiography* (London: Odhams Press, 1960), p. 172.
10. Attlee, *As It Happened*, pp. 130–31.
11. Quoted in Paul Addison, *The Road to 1945: British Politics and the Second World War* (London: Quartet, 1977), pp. 95–6.
12. Harold Nicolson, *Diaries and Letters 1939–1945*, ed. Nigel Nicolson (London: Collins, 1967), p. 78.
13. Hansard, HC Deb, 8 May 1940, vol. 360, cols 1264–5.
14. Ibid., col. 1283.
15. Ibid., col. 1298.
16. Ibid., col. 1283.
17. Hugh Dalton, *The Fateful Years: Memoirs 1931–1945* (London: Frederick Muller, 1957), p. 306.
18. Duff Cooper, *Old Men Forget: The Autobiography of Duff Cooper* (London: Rupert Hart-Davis, 1953), p. 279.
19. Peter Hennessy, *Never Again: Britain 1945–1951* (London: Vintage, 1993), p. 22.
20. Francis Williams, *A Prime Minister Remembers: The War and Post-War Memoirs of the Rt. Hon. Earl Attlee Based on His Private Papers and on a Series of Recorded Conversations* (London: Heinemann, 1961), p. 33.
21. Dalton, *The Fateful Years*, p. 311.

22. War Cabinet no. 119 of 1940, 10 May.
23. Churchill, *The Gathering Storm*, p. 600. 'Mr Alexander' refers to A. V. Alexander (see page 106).
24. Quoted in Alan Bullock, *The Life and Times of Ernest Bevin, vol. 1: Trade Union Leader 1881–1940* (London: Heinemann, 1960), p. 652.
25. Quoted ibid.
26. Letter dated 13 May 1940 from Transport House, Churchill papers, 20/11, quoted in Martin Gilbert, *Finest Hour: Winston S. Churchill 1939–41* (London: Minerva, 1989), p. 331.
27. Quoted in Bernard Donoughue and G. W. Jones, *Herbert Morrison* (London: Phoenix, 2001), p. 274.
28. Quoted ibid., p. 276.
29. Attlee, *As It Happened*, p. 132.
30. Hugh Dalton, *The Second World War Diary of Hugh Dalton 1940–45*, ed. Ben Pimlott (London: Jonathan Cape, 1985), 18 May 1940.
31. Quoted in Dalton, *The Fateful Years*, p. 316.
32. *Report of the Annual Conference of the Labour Party*, 1940, pp. 123–4.
33. Hansard, HC Deb, 13 May 1940, vol. 360, col. 1502.
34. National Archives, Public Record Office [NA, PRO], CAB 65/13, Confidential Annexe to War Cabinet minutes, 26 May 1940, 9.00 a.m.
35. NA, PRO, CAB 65/13, Confidential Annexe to War Cabinet minutes, 26 May 1940, 2.00 p.m.
36. NA, PRO, CAB 65/13, Confidential Annexe to War Cabinet minutes, 27 May 1940, 4.30 p.m.
37. NA, PRO, CAB 65/13, Confidential Annexe to War Cabinet minutes, 28 May 1940, 4.00 p.m.
38. Ibid.
39. Quoted in Dalton, *The Fateful Years*, p. 336.
40. NA, PRO, CAB 65/13, Confidential Annexe to War Cabinet minutes, 28 May 1940, 7.00 p.m.
41. Angus Calder, *The People's War* (London: Panther, 1971), p. 168.
42. See Addison, *The Road to 1945*, Chapters IV and V.
43. TUC report of the special conference of trade union executives, 25 May 1940.
44. Quoted in Francis Williams, *Ernest Bevin: Portrait of a Great Englishman* (London: Hutchinson, 1952), p. 217.
45. See Alan Bullock, *The Life and Times of Ernest Bevin, vol. 2: Minister of Labour 1940–1945* (London: Heinemann, 1967), pp. 291–2.
46. See ibid., pp. 4–5.
47. Quoted in Dalton, *The Fateful Years*, p. 358.
48. Bullock, *The Life and Times of Ernest Bevin, vol. 2*, p. 107.
49. Quoted in Williams, *Ernest Bevin*, p. 232.
50. Quoted in Donoughue and Jones, *Herbert Morrison*, p. 288.

51. Quoted ibid., p. 306.
52. Quoted ibid., p. 312.
53. See Roy Jenkins, *Mr Attlee: An Interim Biography* (London: William Heinemann, 1948), p. 226.
54. Harris, *Attlee*, p. 179.
55. A London Diary, *New Statesman and Nation*, 4 August 1945, quoted in Jenkins, *Mr Attlee*, pp. 229–30.
56. Nicolson, *Diaries and Letters 1939–1945*, p. 276.
57. Ibid., pp. 295–6.
58. See Dalton, *The Second World War Diary of Hugh Dalton*, p. 501.
59. See Williams, *Ernest Bevin*, p. 231.
60. Quoted in Ben Pimlott, *Hugh Dalton* (London: Jonathan Cape, 1985), p. 297.
61. Quoted ibid., p. 348.
62. Winston Churchill, *The Second World War, vol. 4: The Hinge of Fate* (London: Cassell, 1951), p. 343.
63. Quoted in Peter Clarke, *The Cripps Version: The Life of Sir Stafford Cripps* (London: Allen Lane, 2002), p. 263.
64. Diary of R. M. Barrington-Ward, 19 February 1942.
65. Dalton, *The Second World War Diary of Hugh Dalton*, p. 373.
66. Martin Gilbert, *Road to Victory: Winston S. Churchill 1941–1945* (London: Heinemann, 1986), p. 254.
67. Quoted in Addison, *The Road to 1945*, p. 17.
68. Quoted in Harris, *Attlee*, pp. 220–21; for the official circulated record of the War Cabinet meetings of 12 and 15 February see NA, PRO, CAB 65/33, 28th and 29th conclusions; for the longhand record of the meetings contained in the Cabinet secretary's notebook see NA, PRO, CAB 195/2, pp. 76–81.
69. Quoted in Harris, *Attlee*, p. 222.
70. Quoted ibid., p. 224.

Chapter 7: 1945

1. Oliver Lyttelton, *The Memoirs of Lord Chandos* (London: Bodley Head, 1964), pp. 322–3.
2. National Archives, Public Record Office [NA, PRO], PREM 4/88/1 note by Churchill to Attlee, 20 November 1944.
3. Quoted in Kenneth Harris, *Attlee* (London: Weidenfeld & Nicolson, 1982), pp. 242–3.
4. Hansard, HC Deb, 31 October 1944, vol. 404, col. 667.
5. Winston Churchill, *The Second World War, vol. 6: Triumph and Tragedy* (London: Cassell, 1954), p. 512.
6. Hugh Dalton, *The Second World War Diary of Hugh Dalton 1940–45*, ed. Ben Pimlott (London: Jonathan Cape, 1985), 18 May 1945.

7.   Hugh Dalton, *The Fateful Years: Memoirs 1931–1945* (London: Frederick Muller, 1957), p. 459.

8.   Giles Radice (ed.), *What Needs to Change: New Visions for Britain* (London: HarperCollins, 1996), p. 250.

9.   Quoted in Bernard Donoughue and G. W. Jones, *Herbert Morrison* (London: Phoenix, 2001), p. 332.

10. Isaac Kramnick and Barry Sherman, *Harold Laski: A Life on the Left* (London: Hamish Hamilton, 1993), p. 481.

11. Quoted in Dalton, *The Second World War Diary of Hugh Dalton*, 28 May 1945.

12. Quoted in the *Listener*, 7 June 1945, p. 629.

13. Quoted in Paul Addison, *The Road to 1945: British Politics and the Second World War* (London: Quartet, 1977), p. 265.

14. Quoted in the *Listener*, 14 June 1945, p. 656.

15. Quoted in C. R. Attlee, *As It Happened* (London: Odhams Press, 1956), p. 165.

16. Roy Jenkins, *Churchill* (London: Macmillan, 2001), p. 794.

17. See Donoughue and Jones, *Herbert Morrison*, pp. 334–7.

18. Quoted in Harris, *Attlee*, p. 261.

19. R. B. McCallum and Alison Readman, *The British General Election of 1945* (London: Frank Cass, [1947] 1964), p. 175.

20. See Lord Morrison of Lambeth, *Herbert Morrison: An Autobiography* (London: Odhams Press, 1960), p. 236.

21. Roy Jenkins, *A Life at the Centre* (London: Macmillan, 1991), p. 25.

22. Quoted in Radice, *What Needs to Change*, p. 253.

23. McCallum and Readman, *The British General Election of 1945*, pp. 242–3.

24. Addison, *The Road to 1945*, p. 268.

25. Ibid.

26. Edmund Dell, *The Chancellors: A History of the Chancellors of the Exchequer 1945–90* (London: HarperCollins, 1996), p. 19.

27. Donoughue and Jones, *Herbert Morrison*, p. 248.

28. Quoted in Chris Bryant, *Stafford Cripps: The First Modern Chancellor* (London: Hodder & Stoughton, 1997), p. 345.

29. Brian Brivati, 'Aneurin Bevan', in Greg Rosen (ed.), *Dictionary of Labour Biography* (London: Politico's, 2001), p. 46.

30. Quoted in Michael Foot, *Aneurin Bevan: A Biography, vol. 1 1897–1945* (London: MacGibbon & Kee, 1962), p. 326.

31. Quoted ibid., p. 442.

32. Quoted ibid., p. 498.

33. Quoted in Harris, *Attlee*, p. 405.

34. Quoted in Foot, *Aneurin Bevan, vol. 1*, p. 510.

35. Dalton, *The Fateful Years*, p. 479.

36. Francis Williams, *A Prime Minister Remembers: The War and Post-War Memoirs of the Rt. Hon. Earl Attlee Based on His Private Papers and on a Series of Recorded Conversations* (London: Heinemann, 1961), p. 81.

37. Alan Bullock, *The Life and Times of Ernest Bevin, vol. 3: Foreign Secretary 1945–51* (London: Heinemann, 1983), p. 55.
38. Quoted in Harris, *Attlee*, p. 294.
39. Michael Foot, *Aneurin Bevan: A Biography, vol. 2 1945–1960* (London: Davis-Poynter, 1973), p. 32.
40. Douglas Jay, *Change and Fortune: A Political Record* (London: Hutchinson, 1980), pp. 135–6.
41. Williams, *A Prime Minister Remembers*, p. 150.
42. Kenneth O. Morgan, *Labour in Power 1945–1951* (Oxford: Clarendon Press, 1984), p. 7.
43. Dalton, *The Fateful Years*, p. 479.
44. Hansard, HC Deb, 16 August 1945, vol. 413, col. 73.
45. Hugh Gaitskell, *The Diary of Hugh Gaitskell 1945–1956*, ed. Philip M. Williams (London: Jonathan Cape, 1983), p. 19.
46. Hansard, HC Deb, 16 August 1945, vol. 413, col. 101.
47. Dalton, *The Fateful Years*, p. 482.
48. Winston S. Churchill, *The Second World War, vol. 2: Their Finest Hour* (London: Cassell, 1949), p. 503.
49. John Maynard Keynes, 'Our Overseas Financial Prospects', *The Collected Writings of John Maynard Keynes, vol. 24: Activities 1944–46 – The Transition to Peace*, ed. Donald Moggridge (London: Macmillan, 1979), pp. 398–411.
50. R. F. Harrod, *The Life of John Maynard Keynes* (London: Macmillan, 1951), p. 596.
51. Jay, *Change and Fortune*, p. 138.
52. Hugh Dalton, *High Tide and After: Memoirs 1945–1960* (London: Frederick Muller, 1962), p. 79.
53. NA, PRO, CAB 195/3, note by Sir Norman Brook, Cabinet secretary, National Archives, Public Record Office [NA, PRO], of Cabinet meeting, 6 November 1945, 4.30 p.m., p. 325.
54. Hansard, HL Deb, 18 December 1945, vol. 138, col. 783.
55. See Jay, *Change and Fortune*, pp. 139–40.
56. Peter Hennessy, *Never Again: Britain 1945–51* (London: Vintage, 1993), p. 268.
57. Bullock, *The Life and Times of Ernest Bevin*, p. 133.

Chapter 8: 1946

1. Hansard, HC Deb, 6 December 1945, vol. 416, cols 2534–5.
2. Roy Jenkins, *Churchill* (London: Macmillan, 2001), p. 807.
3. Hansard, HC Deb, 6 December 1945, vol. 416, col. 2565.
4. Quoted in Kenneth Harris, *Attlee* (London: Weidenfeld & Nicolson, 1982), p. 320.
5. Hansard HC Deb, 12 December 1945, vol. 417, col. 440.

6. See Edmund Dell, *The Chancellors: A History of the Chancellors of the Exchequer 1945–90* (London: HarperCollins, 1996), p. 61.

7. Bernard Donoughue and G. W. Jones, *Herbert Morrison* (London: Phoenix, 2001), p. 357.

8. Ibid., p. 376.

9. Donoughue and Jones, *Herbert Morrison*, p. 355.

10. Quoted ibid., p. 363.

11. Quoted ibid., p. 371.

12. Quoted in Michael Foot, *Aneurin Bevan: A Biography, vol. 2 1945–1960* (London: Davis-Poynter, 1973), p. 145.

13. Quoted ibid., p. 142.

14. Kenneth O. Morgan, *Labour in Power 1945–1951* (Oxford: Clarendon Press, 1984), p. 172.

15. Hugh Dalton, *High Tide and After: Memoirs 1945–1960* (London: Frederick Muller, 1962), p. 131.

16. Ibid., p. 5.

17. Foot, *Aneurin Bevan*, p. 35.

18. Diary of R. M. Barrington-Ward, 23 October 1945.

19. Dalton, *High Tide and After*, p. 109.

20. Ibid., p. 112.

21. See John Maynard Keynes, *The Collected Writings of John Maynard Keynes, vol. 24: Activities 1944–46 – The Transition to Peace*, ed. Donald Moggridge (London: Macmillan, 1979), p. 410.

22. Minute by Harvey, 11 March 1946, National Archives, Public Record Office [NA, PRO], FO 371, S7173, quoted in Alan Bullock, *The Life and Times of Ernest Bevin, vol. 3: Foreign Secretary 1945–51* (London: Heinemann, 1983), p. 235.

23. NA, PRO, CAB 128/6, 70th conclusions, 21 July 1946, 9.30 a.m.

Chapter 9: 1947

1. Quoted in Kenneth Harris, *Attlee* (London: Weidenfeld & Nicolson, 1982), p. 336.

2. Douglas Jay, *Change and Fortune: A Political Record* (London: Hutchinson, 1980), p. 143

3. Ibid., p. 147.

4. Ibid., p. 149.

5. National Archives, Public Record Office [NA, PRO], CAB 128/9, 3rd conclusions, 7 January 1947.

6. Hugh Dalton, *High Tide and After: Memoirs 1945–1960* (London: Frederick Muller, 1962), p. 205.

7. Ibid., p. 193.

8. See J. C. R. Dow, *The Management of the British Economy 1945–60* (Cambridge: Cambridge University Press, 1964), pp. 22–6.

9. Quoted in Dalton, *High Tide and After*, p. 193; CM7 (47) 16 January 1947.
10. Quoted ibid., pp. 194–8.
11. David Watt, 'Withdrawal from Greece', in Michael Sissons and Philip French (eds), *Age of Austerity* (London: Hodder & Stoughton, 1963), p. 105.
12. See Alan Bullock, *The Life and Times of Ernest Bevin, vol. 3: Foreign Secretary 1945–51* (London: Heinemann, 1983), p. 404.
13. Dalton, *High Tide and After*, p. 254.
14. Quoted in Ben Pimlott, *Hugh Dalton* (London: Jonathan Cape, 1985), p. 482.
15. Hansard, HC Deb, 8 July 1947, vol. 439, col. 2150.
16. Hugh Dalton, *The Political Diary of Hugh Dalton 1918–40, 1945–60*, ed. Ben Pimlott (London: Jonathan Cape, 1986), 30 July 1947.
17. For the circulated Cabinet record from this period see NA, PRO, CAB 128/10; and for the Cabinet secretaries' longhand notes see CAB 195/5.
18. Hansard, HC Deb, 6 August 1947, vol. 441, col. 1511.
19. Dalton, *The Political Diary of Hugh Dalton*, 8 August 1947.
20. Dalton, *High Tide and After*, p. 260.
21. Hansard, HC Deb, 7 August 1947, vol. 441, cols 1765–6.
22. NA, PRO, CAB 128/10, 71st conclusions, 17 August 1947.
23. Dalton, *High Tide and After*, p. 262.
24. Lord Morrison of Lambeth, *Herbert Morrison: An Autobiography* (London: Odhams Press, 1960), p. 260.
25. Pimlott, *Hugh Dalton*, p. 493.
26. Dalton, *High Tide and After*, p. 230.
27. Ibid., p. 230.
28. Dalton, *Political Diary of Hugh Dalton*, 25 July 1947.
29. Ibid., 26 July 1947.
30. From an account in the *Evening Standard*, 7 June 1961, quoted in Pimlott, *Hugh Dalton*, p. 507.
31. Quoted in Lord George-Brown, *In My Way: The Political Memoirs of Lord George-Brown* (London: Victor Gollancz, 1971), p. 51.
32. Dalton, *High Tide and After*, p. 240.
33. See ibid., p. 241.
34. Quoted ibid., p. 242.
35. Henry Pelling, *A Short History of the Labour Party* (London: Macmillan, 1961), p. 125.
36. See Dalton, *High Tide and After*, p. 245.
37. See Kenneth Harris, *Attlee*, p. 349.
38. Dalton, *High Tide and After*, p. 246.
39. Quoted in Harris, *Attlee*, p. 350.
40. Hugh Gaitskell, *The Diary of Hugh Gaitskell 1945–1956*, ed. Philip M. Williams (London: Jonathan Cape, 1983), p. 36.
41. Dow, *The Management of the British Economy*, p. 28.
42. See Dalton, *High Tide and After*, pp. 278–9.

43. See Kenneth Harris, *Attlee*, p. 353.
44. See Francis Beckett, *Clem Attlee* (London: Politico's, 2000), p. 239.
45. Quoted in Harris, *Attlee*, p. 373.
46. NA, PRO, FO 800/470, IND 47/2.
47. Quoted in Harris, *Attlee*, p. 382.
48. Hansard, HC Deb, 15 July 1947, vol. 440, col. 284.
49. Quoted in Peter Hennessy, *Never Again: Britain 1945–51* (London: Vintage, 1993), p. 237.
50. Francis Williams, *A Prime Minister Remembers: The War and Post-War Memoirs of the Rt. Hon. Earl Attlee Based on His Private Papers and on a Series of Recorded Conversations* (London: Heinemann, 1961), p. 211.
51. Quoted in Lawrence James, *Raj: The Making and Unmaking of British India* (London: Little, Brown, 1997), p. 612.
52. Harris, *Attlee*, p. 385.

Chapter 10: 1948–9

1. Quoted in Alan Bullock, *The Life and Times of Ernest Bevin, vol. 3: Foreign Secretary 1945–51* (London: Heinemann, 1983), p. 549.
2. Nicholas Davenport, *Memoirs of a City Radical* (London: Weidenfeld & Nicolson, 1974), p. 173; interview with Olga Davenport.
3. Ben Pimlott, *Hugh Dalton* (London: Jonathan Cape, 1985), p. 550.
4. Ibid., p. 551.
5. Quoted in Bernard Donoughue and G. W. Jones, *Herbert Morrison* (London: Phoenix, 2001), p. 425.
6. Hugh Gaitskell, *The Diary of Hugh Gaitskell 1945–1956*, ed. Philip M. Williams (London: Jonathan Cape, 1983), pp. 55–6.
7. Robert Hall, *The Robert Hall Diaries 1947–1953*, ed. Alec Cairncross (London: Unwin Hyman, 1989), p. 222.
8. See Peter Clarke, *The Cripps Version: The Life of Sir Stafford Cripps* (London: Allen Lane, 2002), p. 492.
9. Quoted in Douglas Jay, *Change and Fortune: A Political Record* (London: Hutchinson, 1980), p. 177.
10. Ibid., p. 173.
11. Gaitskell, *The Diary of Hugh Gaitskell*, p. 61.
12. Quoted in Jay, *Change and Fortune*, p. 179.
13. Gaitskell, *The Diary of Hugh Gaitskell*, p. 62.
14. See Peter Hennessy, *Never Again: Britain 1945–51* (London: Vintage, 1993), pp. 330–31.
15. Quoted in J. C. R. Dow, *The Management of the British Economy 1945–60* (Cambridge: Cambridge University Press, 1964), pp. 34–5.
16. See Edwin Plowden, *An Industrialist in the Treasury: The Post-War Years* (London: Andre Deutsch, 1989), pp. 20–21; Chris Bryant, *Stafford Cripps: The First Modern Chancellor* (London: Hodder & Stoughton, 1997), pp. 408–38.

17. Hansard, HC Deb, 6 April 1948, vol. 449, col. 37.
18. See Alec Cairncross, *Years of Recovery: British Economic Policy 1945–51* (London: Methuen, 1985), p. 421, Table 15.2.
19. Hansard, HC Deb, 6 April 1948, vol. 449, col. 71.
20. Hall, *The Robert Hall Diaries*, p. 22.
21. See ibid., p. 508.
22. Quoted in Clarke, *The Cripps Version*, p. 509.
23. Quoted ibid., p. 510.
24. See Hansard, HC Deb, 6 April 1949, vol. 463, cols 2090–91.
25. Hansard, HC Deb, 7 February 1946, vol. 418, cols 1900–01.
26. Hall, *The Robert Hall Diaries*, 6 April 1949.
27. See Kenneth O. Morgan, *Labour in Power 1945–1951* (Oxford: Clarendon Press, 1984), p. 369.
28. Quoted in Clarke, *The Cripps Version*, p. 505.
29. Morgan, *Labour in Power*, p. 275.
30. Hansard, 22 January 1948, vol. 446, cols 383–409.
31. 'Western union', *Times*, 23 January 1948.
32. CP (48) 71, 3 March, quoted in Bullock, *Ernest Bevin*, p. 526.
33. Quoted in Bullock, *Ernest Bevin*, p. 526.
34. Marshall to British ambassador, 12 March 1948, *Foreign Relations of the United States*.
35. Bullock, *Ernest Bevin*, p. 672.
36. Roderick Barclay, *Ernest Bevin and the Foreign Office 1932–1969* (Latimer: Roderick Barclay, 1975), pp. 81–2, quoted in Bullock, *Ernest Bevin*, p. 98.
37. Quoted in Bullock, *Ernest Bevin*, p. 99.
38. Lord George-Brown, *In My Way: The Political Memoirs of Lord George-Brown* (London: Victor Gollancz, 1971), p. 235.
39. Quoted in Barclay, *Ernest Bevin and the Foreign Office*, p. 44.
40. Quoted ibid., p. 45.
41. Quoted in Kenneth Harris, *Attlee* (London: Weidenfeld & Nicolson, 1982), p. 427.
42. See ibid., pp. 424–5.

Chapter 11: 1949–50

1. See Hugh Dalton, *The Political Diary of Hugh Dalton 1918–40, 1945–60*, ed. Ben Pimlott (London: Jonathan Cape, 1986), 15 September 1948.
2. Ibid., 11 September 1948.
3. Quoted in Peter Clarke, *The Cripps Version: The Life of Sir Stafford Cripps* (London: Allen Lane, 2002), p. 513.
4. See J. C. R. Dow, *The Management of the British Economy 1945–60* (Cambridge: Cambridge University Press, 1964), p. 41.
5. Quoted ibid., p. 41.

6. See Alec Cairncross, *Years of Recovery: British Economic Policy 1945–51* (London: Methuen, 1985), p. 197.
7. Hansard, HC Deb, 7 July 1949, vol. 466, col. 2160.
8. National Archives, Public Record Office [NA, PRO], CAB 134/200, minutes of Cabinet Economic Policy Committee, 17 June 1949.
9. Quoted in Cairncross, *Years of Recovery*, pp. 173–4; Dalton, *Political Diary of Hugh Dalton*, 17 June 1949.
10. NA, PRO, CAB 134/200, Minutes of Cabinet Economic Policy Committee, 1 July 1949.
11. Hugh Gaitskell, *The Diary of Hugh Gaitskell 1945–1956*, ed. Philip M. Williams (London: Jonathan Cape, 1983), p. 126.
12. See Hansard, HC Deb, 18 July 1949, vol. 467, cols 972–3.
13. Gaitskell, *The Diary of Hugh Gaitskell*, p. 131.
14. Douglas Jay, *Change and Fortune: A Political Record* (London: Hutchinson, 1980), p. 187.
15. Quoted ibid., p. 188.
16. Quoted in Gaitskell, *The Diary of Hugh Gaitskell*, pp. 136–7.
17. Quoted ibid., p. 137.
18. NA, PRO, CAB 128/16, 54th conclusions, 29 August 1949.
19. See Edwin Plowden, *An Industrialist in the Treasury: The Post-War Years* (London: Andre Deutsch, 1989), pp. 61–2.
20. Quoted ibid., p. 64.
21. Quoted ibid., p. 65.
22. See Clarke, *The Cripps Version*, p. 518.
23. Quoted in Jay, *Change and Fortune*, p. 191.
24. Quoted ibid., p. 193.
25. See Kenneth O. Morgan, *Labour in Power 1945–1951* (Oxford: Clarendon Press, 1984), p. 404.
26. Quoted in H. G. Nicholas, *The British General Election of 1950* (London: Macmillan, 1951); see Chapter 5 for a discussion of the campaign.
27. Gaitskell, *The Diary of Hugh Gaitskell*, p. 166.
28. Bernard Donoughue and G. W. Jones, *Herbert Morrison* (London: Phoenix, 2001), p. 451.
29. Quoted ibid., p. 452.
30. Quoted in Clarke, *The Cripps Version*, p. 522.

Chapter 12: 1950–51

1. Peter Hennessy, *Never Again: Britain 1945–51* (London: Vintage, 1993), p. 385.
2. National Archives, Public Record Office [NA, PRO], CAB 128/17, 5th conclusions, 25 February 1950.
3. Hugh Gaitskell, *The Diary of Hugh Gaitskell 1945–1956*, ed. Philip M. Williams (London: Jonathan Cape, 1983), 26 May 1950.

4. NA, PRO, T 171/400, Attlee to Cripps, 11 March 1950, quoted in Peter Clarke, *The Cripps Version: The Life of Sir Stafford Cripps* (London: Allen Lane, 2002), p. 501.
5. Hansard, HC Deb, 18 April 1950, vol. 474, cols 59–60.
6. NA, PRO, CAB 128/17, 17th & 18th conclusions, 3–4 April 1950.
7. Quoted in Michael Foot, *Aneurin Bevan: A Biography, vol. 2 1945–1960* (London: Davis-Poynter, 1973), p. 296.
8. Gaitskell, *The Diary of Hugh Gaitskell*, p. 193.
9. See Giles Radice, *Southern Discomfort* (London: Fabian Society, 1992).
10. Memorandum for 19–21 May meeting, quoted in Bernard Donoughue and G. W. Jones, *Herbert Morrison* (London: Phoenix, 2001), p. 456.
11. Nicholas Davenport, *Memoirs of a City Radical* (London: Weidenfeld & Nicolson, 1974), p. 171.
12. Quoted in Ben Pimlott, *Hugh Dalton* (London: Jonathan Cape, 1985), p. 589.
13. Quoted ibid., p. 585.
14. Quoted in Kenneth Harris, *Attlee* (London: Weidenfeld & Nicolson, 1982), p. 453.
15. See Francis Beckett, *Clem Attlee* (London: Politico's, 2000), pp. 274–6.
16. Quoted in Harris, *Attlee*, p. 404.
17. Quoted ibid., p. 411.
18. Quoted in Harris, *Attlee*, p. 446.
19. Quoted ibid., p. 403.
20. Quoted in Peter Hennessy, *The Prime Minister: The Office and Its Holders since 1945* (London: Allen Lane, 2000), p. 149.
21. Edwin Plowden, *An Industrialist in the Treasury: The Post-War Years* (London: Andre Deutsch, 1989), p. 72.
22. Quoted in Alan Bullock, *The Life and Times of Ernest Bevin, vol. 3: Foreign Secretary 1945–51* (London: Heinemann, 1983), p. 520.
23. Quoted ibid., p. 659.
24. Quoted in Plowden, *An Industrialist in the Treasury*, p. 95.
25. Hansard, HC Deb, 11 May 1950, vol. 475, col. 587.
26. Jean Monnet, *Memoirs*, tr. Richard Mayne (London: Collins, 1976), p. 308.
27. *Documents on British Policy Overseas*, series II, vol. 2, p. 24.
28. Ibid.
29. See Edmund Dell, *The Schuman Plan and the British Abdication of Leadership in Europe* (Oxford: Oxford University Press, 1995), pp. 138–70.
30. Dean Acheson, *Present at the Creation: My Years in the State Department* (London: Hamish Hamilton, 1970), p. 384.
31. Kenneth Younger, *In the Midst of Events: The Foreign Office Diaries and Papers of Kenneth Younger February 1950–October 1951*, ed. Geoffrey Warner (London: Routledge, 2005), 14 May 1950.
32. Quoted in Plowden, *An Industrialist in the Treasury*, p. 91.
33. Quoted in the *Manchester Guardian*, 10 June 1950.

34.   These words were used in a minute by Kenneth Younger earlier that day. *Documents on British Policy Overseas*, p. 82.

35.   Quoted in Leslie Hunter, *The Road to Brighton Pier* (London: Arthur Barker, 1959), p. 13.

36.   *Documents on British Policy Overseas*, p. 76.

37.   Cmd 7970/13.

38.   Younger, *In the Midst of Events*, 6 July 1950.

39.   *European Unity: A Statement by the National Executive Committee of the British Labour Party* (London: Labour Party, 1950), p. 4.

40.   Hansard, HC Deb, 26 June 1950, vol. 476, col. 1907.

41.   Letter to Tom Attlee, 30 June 1950, Attlee papers.

42.   Acheson, *Present at the Creation*, p. 387.

43.   Oliver Franks, *Britain and the Tide of World Affairs: The BBC Reith Lectures 1954* (London: Oxford University Press, 1955), p. 75.

44.   Plowden, *An Industrialist in the Treasury*, p. 93.

45.   NA, PRO, CAB 129/48, 'United Europe: note by the Prime Minister and Minister of Defence', C (51) 32, 29 November 1951.

46.   Quoted in Plowden, *An Industrialist in the Treasury*, p. 85.

47.   Hugh Dalton, *The Political Diary of Hugh Dalton 1918–40, 1945–60*, ed. Ben Pimlott (London: Jonathan Cape, 1986), 27 June 1950; NA, PRO, CAB 128/17 39th conclusions, 27 June 1950.

48.   NA, PRO, PREM 8/1405, Franks to Attlee, 15 July 1950.

49.   NA, PRO, CAB 128/18, 50th conclusions, 25 July 1950.

50.   Acheson, *Present at the Creation*, p. 478.

51.   Kenneth O. Morgan, *Labour in Power 1945–1951* (Oxford: Clarendon Press, 1984), p. 441.

52.   Quoted in Plowden, *An Industrialist in the Treasury*, p. 105.

53.   See Harris, *Attlee*, p. 460.

54.   Foot, *Aneurin Bevan*, p. 299.

55.   See Morgan, *Labour in Power*, p. 441.

56.   Quoted in Foot, *Aneurin Bevan*, p. 295.

57.   Douglas Jay, *Change and Fortune: A Political Record* (London: Hutchinson, 1980), p. 202.

58.   Quoted in Foot, *Aneurin Bevan*, p. 300.

59.   Gaitskell, *The Diary of Hugh Gaitskell*, p. 174.

60.   See Foot, *Aneurin Bevan*, p. 311.

61.   Quoted in Bullock, *The Life and Times of Ernest Bevin*, p. 833.

62.   Quoted in Harris, *Attlee*, p. 472.

63.   Interview with Lord Shawcross, quoted in Donoughue and Jones, *Herbert Morrison*, p. 468.

64.   See Hugh Dalton, *High Tide and After: Memoirs 1945–1960* (London: Frederick Muller, 1962), p. 359.

65.   Quoted in Harris, *Attlee*, p. 472.

66. Quoted in Morgan, *Labour in Power*, p. 443.
67. Quoted in Bullock, *The Life and Times of Ernest Bevin*, p. 843.
68. Francis Williams, *A Prime Minister Remembers: The War and Post-War Memoirs of the Rt. Hon. Earl Attlee Based on His Private Papers and on a Series of Recorded Conversations* (London: Heinemann, 1961), p. 246.
69. J. C. R. Dow, *The Management of the British Economy 1945–60* (Cambridge: Cambridge University Press, 1964), pp. 56–7.
70. NA, PRO, CAB 128/19, 22 conclusions, 22 March 1951; Morgan, *Labour in Power*, pp. 447–8.
71. Williams, *A Prime Minister Remembers*, p. 246.
72. See Jay, *Change and Fortune*, pp. 204–5.
73. Quoted in Foot, *Aneurin Bevan*, p. 320.
74. Gaitskell, *The Diary of Hugh Gaitskell*, pp. 244–5.
75. Ibid., p. 246.
76. Quoted ibid., p. 252.
77. Dalton, *High Tide and After*, p. 365.
78. Gaitskell, *The Diary of Hugh Gaitskell*, 4 May 1951.
79. Quoted in Philip M. Williams, *Hugh Gaitskell: A Political Biography* (London: Jonathan Cape, 1979), p. 266.
80. See Donoughue and Jones, *Herbert Morrison*, p. 490.
81. Morgan, *Labour in Power*, p. 462.
82. See Donoughue and Jones, *Herbert Morrison*, p. 510.
83. Quoted ibid., p. 505.
84. Quoted in Williams, *Hugh Gaitskell*, p. 283.
85. Quoted in Harris, *Attlee*, p. 491.
86. David Butler, *The British General Election of 1951* (London: Macmillan, 1952), p. 72.

Chapter 13: 1952–5

1. Hugh Dalton, *The Political Diary of Hugh Dalton 1918–40, 1945–60*, ed. Ben Pimlott (London: Jonathan Cape, 1986), p. 567.
2. Ibid., p. 569.
3. Lord Morrison of Lambeth, *Herbert Morrison: An Autobiography* (London: Odhams Press, 1960), pp. 293–4.
4. Quoted in Kenneth Harris, *Attlee* (London: Weidenfeld & Nicolson, 1982), p. 450.
5. Quoted in R. H. S. Crossman, *The Backbench Diaries of Richard Crossman*, ed. Janet Morgan (London: Hamish Hamilton/Jonathan Cape, 1981), 24 March 1955, p. 410.
6. Michael Foot, *Aneurin Bevan: A Biography, vol. 2 1945–1960* (London: Davis-Poynter, 1973), p. 367.
7. David Marquand, *The Progressive Dilemma: From Lloyd George to Kinnock*

(London: Heinemann, 1981), p. 118; Aneurin Bevan, *In Place of Fear*, new ed. (Wakefield: EP, 1976), p. 201.

8. Philip M. Williams, *Hugh Gaitskell: A Political Biography* (London: Jonathan Cape, 1979), p. 300.
9. Foot, *Aneurin Bevan*, p. 379.
10. Dalton, *The Political Diary of Hugh Dalton*, p. 599.
11. Quoted in Bernard Donoughue and G. W. Jones, *Herbert Morrison* (London: Phoenix, 2001), p. 520.
12. Quoted in Harris, *Attlee*, p. 505.
13. Crossman, *The Backbench Diaries of Richard Crossman*, 30 September 1952.
14. See Donoughue and Jones, *Herbert Morrison*, p. 521.
15. Brian Brivati, *Hugh Gaitskell* (London: Richard Cohen, 1996), p. 176.
16. Foot, *Aneurin Bevan*, p. 383.
17. Francis Beckett, *Clem Attlee* (London: Politico's, 2000), p. 298.
18. Crossman, *The Backbench Diaries of Richard Crossman*, p. 186.
19. Quoted in Williams, *Hugh Gaitskell*, p. 371.
20. Foot, *Aneurin Bevan*, p. 429.
21. Quoted ibid., p. 431.
22. Hansard, 2 March 1955, vol. 537, col. 2176.
23. Harris, *Attlee*, pp. 531–2.
24. Dalton, *The Political Diary of Hugh Dalton*, 9 June 1955.
25. Quoted in Leslie Hunter, *The Road to Brighton Pier* (London: Arthur Barker, 1959), p. 134.
26. Hansard, HC Deb, 27 October 1955, vol. 545, col. 408.
27. Quoted in Williams, *Hugh Gaitskell*, p. 363.

Chapter 14: The end of the race

1. Quoted in Ben Pimlott, *Hugh Dalton* (London: Jonathan Cape, 1985), pp. 626–7.
2. R. H. S. Crossman, *The Backbench Diaries of Richard Crossman*, ed. Janet Morgan (London: Hamish Hamilton/Jonathan Cape, 1981), 23 June 1959.
3. Quoted in Pimlott, *Hugh Dalton*, p. 635.
4. Quoted in Bernard Donoughue and G. W. Jones, *Herbert Morrison* (London: Phoenix, 2001), p. 543.
5. See ibid., p. 549.
6. Ibid., p. 560.
7. Quoted in Kenneth Harris, *Attlee* (London: Weidenfeld & Nicolson, 1982), pp. 544–62.
8. See Denis Healey, *The Time of My Life* (London: Michael Joseph, 1989), p. 156.

Conclusion

1. In questions after an LSE lecture in the 1950s – information provided by G. W. Jones.
2. Quoted in Bernard Donoughue and G. W. Jones, *Herbert Morrison* (London: Phoenix, 2001), p. 552.
3. Quoted in Kenneth Harris, *Attlee* (London: Weidenfeld & Nicolson, 1982), p. 545.
4. Kenneth O. Morgan, *Labour in Power 1945–1951* (Oxford: Clarendon Press, 1984), p. 503.
5. Quoted in Peter Hennessy, *Never Again: Britain 1945–51* (London: Vintage, 1993), p. 423.
6. See ibid., p. 450.
7. See Alec Cairncross, *Years of Recovery: British Economic Policy 1945–51* (London: Methuen, 1985), p. 500.
8. Robert Hall, *The Robert Hall Diaries 1947–1953*, ed. Alec Cairncross (London: Unwin Hyman, 1989), p. 161.
9. Quoted in Hennessy, *Never Again*, pp. 424–5.
10. See ibid., p. 182.
11. Office for National Statistics.
12. See Cairncross, *Years of Recovery*, p. 18.
13. See Douglas Jay, *Change and Fortune: A Political Record* (London: Hutchinson, 1980), p. 211.
14. Cairncross, *Years of Recovery*, p. 509.
15. Quoted in Hennessy, *Never Again*, p. 431.

Appendix: Election results, 1918–55

1918, 14 December

Party	Total votes	MPs elected	% share of total vote
Coalition	5,121,359	478	47.6
Labour	2,385,472	63	22.2
Liberal	1,298,808	28	12.1

1922, 15 November

Party	Total votes	MPs elected	% share of total vote
Conservative	5,500,382	345	38.2
Labour	4,241,383	142	29.5
Liberal	2,516,287	54	17.5

1923, 6 December

Party	Total votes	MPs elected	% share of total vote
Conservative	5,538,824	258	38.1
Labour	4,438,508	191	30.5
Liberal	4,311,147	159	29.6

Labour formed minority government

1924, 29 October

Party	Total votes	MPs elected	% share of total vote
Conservative	8,039,598	419	48.3
Labour	5,489,077	151	33.0
Liberal	2,928,747	40	17.6

1929, 30 May

Party	Total votes	MPs elected	% Share of total vote
Conservative	8,656,473	260	38.2
Labour	8,389,512	288	37.1
Liberal	5,308,510	59	23.4

Labour formed minority government

1931, 27 October

Party	Total votes	MPs elected	% Share of total vote
National	14,532,519	554	67.0
Labour	6,649,630	52	30.6
Ind. Liberal	106,106	4	0.5

1935, 14 November

Party	Total votes	MPs elected	% Share of total vote
Conservative	11,810,158	432	53.7
Labour	8,325,491	154	37.9
Liberal	1,422,116	20	6.4

1945, 5 July

Party	Total votes	MPs elected	% Share of total vote
Conservative	9,988,306	213	39.8
Labour	11,995,152	393	47.8
Liberal	2,248,226	12	9.0

1950, 23 February

Party	Total votes	MPs elected	% Share of total vote
Conservative	12,502,567	298	43.5
Labour	13,266,592	315	46.1
Liberal	2,621,548	9	9.1

1951, 25 October

Party	Total votes	MPs elected	% Share of total vote
Conservative	13,717,538	321	48.0
Labour	13,948,605	295	48.8
Liberal	730,556	6	2.5

1955, 26 May

Party	Total votes	MPs elected	% Share of total vote
Conservative	13,286,569	344	49.7
Labour	12,404,970	277	46.4
Liberal	722,405	6	2.7

Index